Sacred

Sexual

Healing

The SHAMAN Method of Sex Magic

**Baba Dez Nichols &
Kamala Devi**

ZENDOW PRESS

Published by Zendow Press

Library of Congress Cataloging-in-Publication Data

Nichols, Baba Dez & Devi, Kamala
Sacred Sexual Healing / Baba Dez Nichols & Kamala Devi

"Summoning of the Muse" cover painting reproduced with permission of
Andrew Gonzales, www.Sublimatrix.com.

Rumi Quatrain #158 translated by Coleman Barks; reproduced
with permission by Shambhala Publications.

Cuddle Party® rules reproduced with permission of Atlas Spooned.
Cuddle Party® is a registered trademark of Atlas Spooned.

"A Gift from Aphrodite" reproduced with permission of
Anyaa McAndrew, www.GoddessOnTheLoose.com.

"Love's Journey" printed with permission by Goddess Maya,
www.TheGoddessMaya.com.

ISBN: 978-0-9896485-0-9

First Edition: copyright © 2008 Baba Dez Nichols & Kamala Devi
Second Edition: copyright © 2013 Baba Dez Nichols & Kamala Devi

Praise
for Sacred Sexual Healing

"Many Tantra books are either full of technical details about sex or incomprehensibly esoteric. I loved this book because it offers modern practical advice on living a juicier, more integrated life."
— **Deborah Taj Anapol, Author of** *The Seven Natural Laws of Love*

"As a Shakti Ma of the modern Tantra movement in the West, I applaud these two for further defining the indefinable. What a fun, juicy, mix of erotic teachings and spiritual concepts."
— **Caroline Muir, Founder Co-author of** *Tantra: The Art of Conscious Loving*

"If you only have time to read one book in the field of sexuality this year, then you had better read this one! A very open, frank, yet gentle exploration of sexual healing and awakening. A must read!"
— **Lawrence Lanoff, Author of** *A Course In Freedom: The Drunken Monkey Speaks*

"In my twenty years of Wicca, Shamanism, and Tantra I have practiced sex magic often, but never with such powerful results in my body and in my pocketbook as I experienced with the SHAMAN Method of Sex Magic offered in this book."
— **Kypris Aster Drake, Author of** *Journey to Sexual Wholeness: The Six Gateways to Sacred Sexuality*

"This book reads very much like a novel. It is intelligent yet sensuous - instructive and sexy. I find the sometimes conflicting views expressed by Kamala and Baba Dez refreshing and courageous! You will discover both erotic entertainment and enlightenment in the pages of Sacred Sexual Healing."
— **Veronica Monet, Author of** *Sex Secrets of Escorts—Tips from a Pro*

"This book is hot. Not only does it address the most important issues at the cutting edge of humanity, it is a totally refreshing plunge into the deeper waters of expanded awareness in freedom based relationships. Kamala Devi and Baba Dez's integrated experience is profoundly expressed thru this super sexy soul-journ into the heart of love, mysticism and sexuality."
— **Kelly Bryson, Author of** *Don't be Nice, Be Real: Balancing Passion for Self with Compassion for Others*

"Bold. Intimate. Real. I highly recommend *Sacred Sexual Healing* to anyone who feels the burning desire to go beyond our culture's limiting views of sexuality. Journey through these pages, and enter a beautiful world where spirit and flesh merge, and conscious sexuality shines as a divine expression of our humanity."
— **Cain Carroll, Author of** *Partner Yoga: Making Contact for Physical, Emotional, and Spiritual Growth*

"With language and concepts that are accessible to everyone, this book will be of great value to you, your lovers, your students, and your friends no matter where they may be in their journey."
— **Reid Mihalko, Creator of Cuddle Party**℠

"Full of exceptional sacred sex practices and exercises for solo-sex or to do with a partner; truly a bold re-visioning toward a more 'healthy male/healthy female' sexual consciousness and practice."
— **Dr. Beth Hedva, Author of *Betrayal, Trust, and Forgiveness: A Guide to Emotional Healing and Self-Renewal***

"It's a must-read for anyone curious about the connection between sexuality and spirituality. The book is engaging and lively even when it addresses complex spiritual theories. Anyone interested in reaching deeper connections and personal awakening through sexual experience will find this book thoroughly gratifying."
— **Vicki Vantoch, Author of *The Threesome Handbook: A Practical Guide to Sleeping with Three***

"*Sacred Sexual Healing* is a comprehensive study of all things Tantric. We enjoyed the simple, seductive, erotic, playfulness of it. Caution: Read this book slowly, that way when your life changes it will be easier to swallow."
— **Kip Moore and Lexi Fisher, Creators of DVD *Tantra 101 Love Lessons***

"*Sacred Sexual Healing* is beautifully written, honest, and a great guide to the often misunderstood world of Tantra, and the section on Methods of sexual magic is a must read for anyone aspiring to be a great lover."
— **Nick Karras, Author of *Petals***

"What a gift for the rest of us that these two masterful teachers came together to create this awesome contribution to the field. May it bring sexual health and erotic freedom to everyone that reads it."
— **Leela Sullivan, Dakini**

"Dez and Kamala demystify this very important esoteric territory with sweetness, practicality and personal depth. Sacred sexuality is best transmitted by those who live it…these two embody it!"
— **Anyaa McAndrew, Priestess, Psychotherapist, Sacred Sexual Healer**

"Down to earth Tantra books are rare, yet Kamala and Dez sew up the Yin/Yang of it with warmth, clarity and compassion."
— **Charla Hathaway, Author of *Erotic Massage***

Dedications

Table of Consciousness

INTRODUCTION: Welcome to the Journey **9**
Genesis, Make Love Not War, Four Kinds of Sex, Road Map, How This
Book was Channeled, How to Read This Book

White

1. What is Tantra, Anyway? 19
Types of Tantra, Colors of Tantra, Sex Magic, Neo-Tantra, What is
Shamanism?, Non-Duality in a Nutshell, Moving Meditation, Mindfulness

2. Basic Tools for the Body Temple 29
Breath Work, Boundaries, Chakra System

3. The Shamanic Approach 43
What is Sacred Sexual Healing? Symptoms, Sources, Solutions, Mind is
Masculine, Body Seeks Pleasure, The Belly/Womb is Feminine, The Heart
Loves

4. Re-scripting Your Reality 67
Cultural Conditioning, Archetypes, Sex Education, Early Sexual
Experiences, Re-Framing Past Pain, Re-Parent Your Inner Child,
Forgiveness, Cutting Cords, Gravitational Pull, Affirmations

Pink

5. The God-Goddess Within 91
Yin-Yang, Shiva-Shakti, Anima-Animus, Right-Brain, Left-Brain and the
Crossover, A Shamanic Perspective, Healthy Male and Female, Etheric
Lingam and Yoni, A Gift from Aphrodite

6. Masturbation Meditation 111
But You'll Go Blind!, Self-Love, Masturbation Meditation, Sacred Self
Healing, Running Sexual Energy, Inner Union, Manifesting the Ideal Mate,
Spice it Up, The Great Debate, A Word on Addiction

7. The Tantric Orgasm...... 125

To Cum or not to Cum?, Ejaculatory Choice, The Upward Draw, Breathing it Down to Mother Earth, Exploring the Edge, EC in Sacred Union, Multiple Orgasms for Men, Multiple Orgasms for Women, Whole Body Orgasms, Female Ejaculation or Amrita

8. Modern Dakas & Dakinis...... 143

Seeking a Pro, Who Are We?, But What Exactly Do You Do?, Our Services, Shopping for Transformation, On Becoming a Sexual Healer, Ethics—A Touch Subject, Sacred union

9. The SHAMAN Method of Sex Magic...... 165

Does it Really Work?, The First Ingredient is Intention, The SHAMAN Method of Sex Magic, Sacred Ritual, Holding Space, Activate the Kundalini, Merging, Affirming, Next Step, Variations, Why Isn't it Working?, Conscious Conception

10. The Sacred Spot Ritual...... 187

G is for Goddess Spot, Body Armoring, Presence, Presence, Presence, Preparing the Body Temple, Sacred Yoni Healing, Yoni Mapping, Sacred Spot Massage for Women, Closing the Ritual, Divination, Keeping the Container, The "He" Spot massage, Before the Ritual Begins, Sacred Spot Massage for Men, Taboo

11. The Sacred Path of Poly...... 209

What is Polyamory?, But isn't that Swinging?, Poly-Tantra, An Initiation, Why Poly?, Poly Jargon, But Don't You Get Jealous?, Having Needs is Not Needy, Top Ten Poly Concerns, Negotiating Agreements, Kamala Devi's Poly Profile, Baba Dez's Relational Profile

EPILOGUE: Blossoming Into Wholeness...... 231
ABOUT THE AUTHORS...... 233
AFTERWORD...... 245
APPENDIX of Exercises...... 251
GLOSSARY of Tantric Terms...... 265
RECOMMENDED READINGS...... 283

LIST OF EXERCISES:

1: Sensate Focusing. Chapter 1 and Appendix
2: Natural Breath. Chapter 2 and Appendix
3: Complete Breath. Chapter 2 and Appendix
4: Alternate Nostril Breathing. Chapter 2 and Appendix
5: Boundary Setting. Chapter 2 and Appendix
6: Rainbow Relaxation. Chapter 2 and Appendix
7: Shakti Shake. Chapter 3
8: Feeding the Demons. Chapter 3
9: Shamanic Journey. Chapter 3
10: Examine Your Sexual Conditioning. Chapter 4
11: Re-Parenting. Chapter 4
12: Forgiveness List. Chapter 4
13: Cord Cutting Ceremony. Chapter 4
14: Chakra Affirmations. Chapter 4 and Appendix
15: Inner Marriage. Chapter 5
16: Exploring the Edge. Chapter 7

Disclaimer:

This book is not specifically intended for the survivors of sexual abuse, incest or sexual addiction. Even so, much of the philosophy and practices herein can be enlightening and transformative to people working on these issues. If you are in a sexual healing crisis we encourage you to reach out for help immediately. There are many compassionate sacred sexual healers, counselors, therapists and hot-line operators who are looking forward to supporting your sexual wholeness.

This book is not intended to offer legal or professional advice. We ask that you take full responsibility for your choice to participate with this material. The author and publisher are not responsible for any affects this book may have on your life. We intend that these teachings and transmissions be used in highest good of all.

Introduction
Welcome to the Journey

> *God created the magnificent rainforests, waterfalls, beaches and sunsets. And when creation was complete, God looked at the gorgeous canvas and wondered what to do with the paint and paintbrushes. God knew that these creative tools were so tremendous that they would be dangerous in the hands of mere mortals.*
>
> *"I could hide them at the top of the highest mountain," thought God, "but man would surely learn to climb and if he obtained these gifts, all of mankind would war over them."*
>
> *"I could hide them at the bottom of the deepest valley on the ocean floor," God thought, "but eventually man would learn to dive to great depths to retrieve these gifts and I wouldn't want them to destroy each other fighting over them."*
>
> *So God decided to hide the paintbrush inside every man and the magical paints deep within every woman. That way only the most worthy seekers would discover their power and they would have to cooperate in order to create.*
>
> *— Genesis as told by a Peruvian Shaman*

We're going to let you in on a little secret. OK, maybe it's not so little. The contents of this book reveal sexual practices that have been coveted for centuries. Similar teachings have been passed on from Shaman to apprentice, from priestess to coven, from courtesan to sexual initiate throughout history. These practices are considered taboo and are regarded as too powerful for the mainstream. People trained in the sexual arts have been labeled witches, whores, perverts and outcasts. The consequence of practicing this work has been persecution, excommunication, exile and death.

That's why we present this work with caution. Think twice before disclosing these practices to your doctor, police force, local congressman and especially your church.

Although these officials may desperately need sexual healing, we wouldn't want their collective guilt, shame, and fear to interfere with your sexual awakening.

There are many wonderful books that outline the history of sacred sex, ancient Tantric scriptures and sexual Shamanic practices, but this is not one of them. Traditional Tantra teachings may have worked well in feudalistic Tibet, but they have little relevance to our lives today. This book offers down-to-earth practice techniques to help modern seekers realize the profound spiritual potential of their sexuality.

The motivation for writing this book is to communicate the process and procedures for becoming sexually and spiritually whole, so that we can reclaim our power, expand our container and experience more pleasure. Once the sensual and the sacred are integrated, every sexual act can be infused with prayer, which, when done with conscious intention, brings heaven to earth.

MAKE LOVE NOT WAR

What does sacred sex have to do with changing the world? Everything. Sex is how we all got here. It is the most powerful creative force on the planet. But few people ever learn to harness its potential.

The countries with the highest degree of violence correlate with the most negative attitudes toward sex. Consider liberal countries such as Sweden, Norway and the Netherlands, which have high standards of sexual education and women's liberation, and low levels of homicide, assault and abuse. Then contrast these countries with the warring nature of fundamental Islamic states where women are covered head-to-toe with burkas and walk several paces behind their men. It seems that greater sexual liberation reduces human conflict.

The ancient Tantric and Hindu texts discuss time on Earth as being divided into four main periods. The original period, when time began, is called the Satya Yuga, or Golden Age, where humanity was still connected to its God-like innocence. In the second stage, called Treta Yuga, or Silver

Age, spiritual awareness spiraled downward about a fourth. Next came the Dvapara Yuga, or Copper Age, where there were equal portions of darkness and ignorance as there were light. We are now in the final era called the Kali Yuga, or Iron Age, which is said to be the darkest time, intended to test the spirit of humankind. It has been prophesized that Tantric practices will resurge and thrive during this time because people are finally grounded enough to embrace their shadow and sensual nature. The world is ripe for a sexual healing revolution.

If enough people learn to imbue their orgasmic energy with prayer, we can manifest more peace. This is not just a New Age, hippie concept. It has been written in ancient texts and recently became the subject of study for quantum theorists.

Admittedly, awakening the planet is no easy task, and is perhaps a little utopic, but we don't need the entire world to awaken, just a small but powerful percentage. Ever hear of the hundredth monkey theory, or morphic resonance? It simply states that the evolution of the collective undergoes a spontaneous leap when a new awareness or behavior hits critical mass. The four-minute mile is a perfect example of something that was once thought to be impossible, but is now a cultural standard. If enough people practice sacred sex and sex magic, we'll contribute a loving and nonviolent current to help people around the world overcome the illusion of separation and conflict.

Consider the possibility that our individual body temple is a microcosm of the collective consciousness. As we heal our own shallow breathing patterns, we'll stop polluting the air. As we heal our unhealthy eating habits, we'll stop consuming and wasting nonrenewable resources on the planet. As we heal our emotional wounding, the world's waters will run clear again. As we heal our sexual wounds, all beings may be happy and all beings may be free.

FOUR KINDS OF SEX

True liberation does not occur simply because people are enjoying sex. There are specific sexual practices and sacred rituals that, when learned, can raise the vibration of the collective consciousness. In essence, there are four categories of sexual activity:

1. Reproductive.
2. Recreational.
3. Restorative.
4. Transformational.

Reproductive sex is driven by the primal urge to procreate and perpetuate offspring. Its purpose is to further the species. Reproductive sex is instinctual. It's built into our DNA; it's part of our animal coding. It manifests as urgent, natural, primitive, and is connected to the first chakra.

Recreational sex is about physical enjoyment. It is driven by our desire to experience pleasure in the body. It is characterized by sensual indulgence. Recreational sex often involves intoxicating substances such as drugs, alcohol, food, music, and visual stimulation such as costumes or pornography. It is often done simultaneously with some form of birth control. It is stimulated by second and third chakras.

Restorative sex is used for overall healing of the body/ mind complex. Most Taoist practices exemplify restorative sex in that they teach various methods to bring awareness to various systems within the body. Restorative sex builds personal power and is practiced to cultivate health, longevity, vitality and immortality. Restorative sex tends to balance all the chakras but especially focuses on the heart.

Transformational sex is where the body is used for conscious evolution and manifestation. In transformational sex, we become divine conduits transmuting passion into devotion, which results in expanding consciousness, awakening and magic. Consequently it transforms everything we see and touch. Transformational sexual practices allow us to experience the vibration of creation. This type of sex simultaneously opens the crown and the root, drawing heaven downward into the body and Mother Earth upward into the cosmos.

ROAD MAP

This book deals primarily with the last two types of sex. In order to excel at the transformative experience of sexuality, one must have a strong foundation in restorative and healing practices. This book is divided into three parts: White, Pink and Red, named after the three primary classifications of Tantric paths.

Generally speaking, White Tantra refers to the more philosophical, spiritual and heart-centered aspects of the practice. Thus, our journey begins by helping the seeker cultivate awareness and power. We lay a foundation with basic tools, then move into Shamanic and Tantric principles and practices. We learn to engage our entire being, work through past and present wounds, and then practice new paradigms to upgrade our experience of reality.

Pink Tantra is the full path, a blend of white and red practices that embraces both the esoteric and the sexual teachings. In the Pink section, we cultivate sensual energy between the God and Goddess within. We re-pattern our relationship to orgasm, and when we're ready to take our healing to the next level, we explore the services and styles of sacred sexual healers who do this work.

Red Tantra focuses on the hot sensual aspects of sacred sexuality. Once we've overcome our sexual guilt, fear and shame, we begin to access the deep creative force within and learn to direct that power toward a higher intention. This is where we introduce the SHAMAN Method of Sex Magic, we elaborate on the intricate details of the sacred spot ritual and explore liberating new relationship paradigms and practices.

HOW THIS BOOK WAS CHANNELED

Traditionally, Tantra is an oral tradition. It is believed that when teachings are passed from spirit to teacher to student, the spoken word transmits a subtle power that awakens the dormant wisdom within the student. Thus, many sacred sexual lessons have never been put into print. To honor the energetic transmission of these teachings, the entire book was created during a ninety-day window wherein we transcribed live talks from our interviews, lectures and playshops. We collaborated across the span of Sedona, San Diego, Hawaii, Mexico and through telepathic channels. We simply distilled our most significant lessons and arranged them in a logical progression. The words, as fashioned, are intended to strike an energetic cord within your body. Stay present to the effects they may have on your own nervous system.

We found that writing about ourselves in third person increased our witness consciousness and enabled us to share our truth with less ego. Both Baba Dez and Kamala Devi have strong personalities, and distinct public speaking styles. Kamala tends to be straightforward and down to earth, whereas Dez is a poetic visionary. If you find yourself touched to tears over a profound human insight, it's most likely Dez, whereas if you're laughing out loud at some irreverent story, that is probably Kamala. We maintain that the content of this book is not original. It did not originate in us, but came through us. We hope through this transmission you're able to make it your own.

HOW TO READ THIS BOOK

Because these teachings run counter to the current of mainstream thinking, you may be called to question some of your own assumptions or even ethics. We are not trying to convert or recruit. We simply invite you to open your mind and your heart to new possibilities.

You are welcome to skim this book, but without doing the exercises, your sacred healing journey will be like a quick trip to Honolulu, where all you have to do is pack your swim trunks and expect everyone to speak your language and serve you Mai Tais. At best, you are likely to get a luxurious escape.

If you are committed to experiencing your sexual potential, you must be willing to engage deeply with the teachings. This is unknown, exotic territory where the cultural norms are bound to make you feel a little uncomfortable at first. You might even find yourself picking up a new language (which is why we've included a glossary) and additional guides and teachers might show up to help you along your path.

Approach this work as you would a new language: immerse yourself, be patient, give yourself permission to make mistakes and practice, practice, practice!

Scheduling a specific time and place to practice these rituals is essential for your success. Treat it like a sacred contract with your soul and notice how resistant the ego becomes when you are asked to do the work. Your mind will very convincingly tell you things like:

- ❋ I'm too busy to do these practices.
- ❋ I'll just do them later.
- ❋ Oh, I'm not really sexually wounded.
- ❋ I've done all these practices before.
- ❋ I don't want to do them if I'm not doing them right.
- ❋ I'll wait until I have the right teacher or a partner.
- ❋ I can read about it, visualize the exercises and get all the benefits.

Resistance is a natural part of the spiritual process, but don't kid yourself. Unless you actually schedule the time and space to do these exercises, you're likely to miss out on the full value of this book.

We want to prepare you for the likelihood that throughout the process emotional bubbles will arise, some like little hiccups and others like full-blown breakdowns.

Throughout the journey we invite you to dialog with your own intuition, your inner guru. Ask yourself what is real, what is relevant, and what resonates. You may or may not agree with all of our opinions and perspectives (we often disagree with each other!), but ultimately it's your job to take what works for you and leave behind whatever does not.

Let's take a moment, now, to set an intention. If this book were a magic lamp that could help you in any area of your spiritual or sexual practice, what would you ask for? Deepen your breath as you read these words. Inhale fully, expand your belly and then let it collapse. Now wiggle your toes. Bring more awareness to your body as you resume your natural rhythm of breath. You may intend:

❀ to rekindle the passion with your spouse.
❀ to attract a soul mate.
❀ to make love at least once a month, week or day.
❀ to be able to make love for as long as you'd like.
❀ to overcome sexual guilt, shame and fear.
❀ to experience deeper, more powerful multiple orgasms.
❀ to heal a specific sexual wound.
❀ to experience sex as a vehicle to know God.
❀ to be able to talk about sex with greater confidence.
❀ to know how to create a ritual for lovemaking.
❀ to manifest more ease, health and abundance in your life.

What does full sexual expression look like for you? Be honest, be specific, and if you read this book with a sincere heart, your intention is sure to manifest.

Ultimately, we hope you receive as much pleasure from reading this book as we had writing it.

White

One

What is Tantra, Anyway?

Ever hear the famous Zen koan, "What is the sound of one hand clapping?" Monks have meditated on this riddle for years, only to result in an empty mind. The logical head bangs itself against a concrete wall trying to answer the unanswerable. When sincere seekers ask, "What is Tantra?" we might say, "Tantra does not exist outside of you," and invite them to meditate on their embodiment. But many modern students are stubborn and insist on a mental answer, even if it's a partial answer, which leads to the common assumption that Tantra is some kind of sexual yoga. (Isn't it?)

Like Zen, the Tao and Buddhism, Tantra is a path to enlightenment. But understanding the spontaneous nature of this non-linear path will challenge the mind. Our favorite textbook definition of Tantra points to its Sanskrit roots. The prefix "Tan" implies expansion and "tra" means liberation. Thus, Tantra can be interpreted to mean liberation through expansion. Sure, it's poetic, but it's altogether too intellectual. Tantra doesn't occur between the ears. Nor does it occur between the legs.

If you were to ask Baba Dez what Tantra is, he might outstretch his arms as if he were offering a big embrace and reply, "Tantra encompasses every aspect of living. Tantra is about how we live, how we breathe, eat, sleep, work, play and love. It's about everything. And the practice of Tantra is a practice of living life in a way that creates power and magic and divinity. It is any practice that supports us in embodying our divinity."

The intention of this chapter is to paint a big picture in broad strokes of the scope of modern Western Tantra, laying the foundation for some deeper practices to come.

TYPES OF TANTRA

Our combined explorations in Tantra have led us through a vast continuum of practices that range from Goddess worship to shadow work; from mind-altering meditations to transcendental lovemaking; from erotic massage to chanting in cemeteries; from Sex Magic to self-inquiry.

Tantra is like a wise old tree with a vast and deep root system. Some of its more developed branches include:

❋ Tibetan Tantric Buddhism or Vajrayana Tantra
❋ Hindu Tantra (Shakta) or village Goddess worship
❋ Kashmiri Shiviaism or Kaula as taught by Abhinavagupta, or more recently, Daniel Odier
❋ Taoist healing arts as taught by master Mantak Chia
❋ Kundalini Tantra as popularized by Sikh Yogi Bhajan
❋ Left-Handed Tantra as practiced by followers of Osho
❋ Ipsalu Tantra as taught by Bodhi Avinashina, based on Avatar Baba Ji's teachings
❋ Quodoshka practiced by Native Americans, Mayan, Toltec and Cherokee
❋ Shamanic sexual healing as practiced by aborigines across the planet
❋ Sex Magic as practiced by Celtic Pagan Covens and Aleister Crowley Cults
❋ Modern Tantra as popularized by Charles Muir through the Source School of Tantra and Carolyn Muir through the Divine Feminine Institute
❋ Other types of Tantra, such as Bonpo, Animism, Jain and the sacred path of no-path that comes with direct download, Shakti-pat and spontaneous awakening

This list is in no way exhaustive or complete, but we can conclusively say that Tantra, like yoga, is not a religion. We've encountered Buddhists, Christians, Muslims, Jews and Hindus alike on the Tantric path. There is even a resurgence of teachings that Jesus practiced Tantra with Mary Magdalene. And this lineage sources back to the Egyptian Goddess cult of Isis.

Tantra does not exclude any portion of the human experience—it includes the full spectrum of humanity. It embraces not only the light but the shadow. Tantrikas give permission for every experience, especially the shadowy aspects of self that are not usually accepted. Embracing the shadow is embracing our humanity. When we shine the light of acceptance on our darkness it always transforms. Instead of judging or preaching, Tantra meets people wherever they are and offers tools for them to expand. The different types of Tantra appeal to different types of people who have different needs.

COLORS OF TANTRA

Tantra is further subdivided in terms of color: White, Pink and Red.

White Tantra orients around the subtle practices and philosophies. Physical touch and sexual practices are not necessary in order to advance on this path. Tibetan Tantric Buddhist monks, for example, can engage in profound lovemaking rites with deities through meditation and visualization.

Vajrayana Tantra involves many powerful concentration exercises that bring universal awareness down from the crown chakra into the heart, without activating the lower chakras. Yogi Bhajan's Kundalini Yoga also offers partnered exercises that include eye gazing, and breathing and sounding exercises that circulate and build sensual energy without sexual contact. Similar practices are commonly referred to as Solo Practice, Right-Handed Tantra or the path of the Dakhsini Marga or Bramachari.

Pink Tantra embraces both the spiritual and the sexual aspects of the practice. This is the path where the heart is opened and lovemaking is practiced with honor and reverence. It is a merging of embodied souls, for both pleasure and enlightenment. This path can also encompass transcendental lovemaking, Taoist sexual healing arts and the sweet, sensual exercises in modern Tantra pujas. This path is sometimes referred to as violet, the middle Tantra or the full path.

Red Tantra consists of many passionate sexual practices. Traditionally the color red connotes femininity, potency, passion and sex. This path can be liberating for the sexually repressed and may also hold interest for the sexually obsessed. The fiery Kundalini practices of Red Tantra use taste and touch to experience the primal sexual impulse that can create intense purifications and awakenings. Practitioners of Red Tantra see the sacred in the profane and instead of bringing the Kundalini energy up to the crown, they draw spiritual energy down into the root, sex and power chakras. These Tantrikas are also known as Vama Marga, Left-Handed Path and sometimes negatively called California Tantra or the Cult of Ecstasy.

There is also the lesser talked about branch of Tantra known as Black Tantra. This is an aboriginal Shamanic practice, like black magic, which transforms physical energy with or without the consent of all parties involved. During Kamala Devi's first pilgrimage to India, she was astounded to discover that most Indian villagers feared and revered Tantra and thought of it as witchcraft. The Aghori are an example of an extremely secretive Hindu sect of Black Tantra practitioners. Aghori is a Sanskrit word that means non-terrifying. The practitioners have been known to cover themselves with ash from graveyards and use human bones in their rituals.

After years of advanced Tantric practice, many yogis begin to experience siddhis or supernatural powers. These powers can be used for personal gain or for service. Throughout India today, people seek Tantrikas for hire, like wizards or witch doctors. They are paid to cast spells, end legal battles, even burn down someone's farm. Of course, powerful karmic consequences can result from using sexual energy to manipulate others. Many people who begin to play with these superpowers often get lost on their path. Instead of advancing towards enlightenment, Black Tantra may lead people further away from enlightenment.

SEX MAGIC

There's a huge distinction to be made between Black Tantra and Sex Magic. Out of fear or ignorance, many people confuse the two. Sex Magic is controversial not only in our puritanical Western society, but also in Hindu, Tibetan Buddhist and other Tantric belief systems. Most maintain that sexual energy is to be preserved for spiritual advancement not material gain.

Throughout this book, we assert a non-dualistic philosophy that does not judge material or sensual pleasures. We teach practices that cultivate sexual life force energy for healing, pleasure and God realization.

In Chapter 9, we proudly introduce a powerful, practical and accessible system called the SHAMAN Method of Sex Magic. We offer this method with pure intent and maintain that the practices within this book are safe and heart-centered. Eventually your body's inner guidance system will tell you what is in your highest good. If you feel yourself expand in love then you are sincere in your practice. If you feel yourself contract in fear, guilt, shame, anger, jealousy or competition, then you may want to stop, breathe and come back to the practice when you've raised your vibration. Sending negative energy into the universe may beget negative manifestations, but more likely it won't manifest anything because lower vibrations drain our personal power, which is necessary in order to manifest.

NEO-TANTRA

Tantra may have deep roots in India and Tibet, but new seeds were planted in the West during the sexual revolution of the 1960s and '70s, and have been growing like wildflowers ever since! The modern resurgence of the message that sexual liberation can lead to spiritual liberation is often referred to as Neo-Tantra. Various gurus, travelers and teachers have been spreading the word by way of weekend workshops and evening pujas. Some teach techniques for better, longer, more satisfying sex, while others seek enlightenment, liberation and God-realization. The more practical Tantric practices adopted by Western Tantra include balancing chakras, raising the Kundalini, Goddess worship and expanding orgasmic energy.

Traditionalists criticize Neo-Tantra and warn that these New Age practices are incomplete without the use of gurus, mantras, yantras, tapas and other disciplines. Many feel that swingers and sex clubs from the '70s and '80s are usurping the name Tantra for their sexual practices to justify, validate and mask sexual addiction. Regardless of its many manifestations, Tantra is an embodied spiritual path that continues to evolve and spontaneously inspire practitioners at whatever level they are ready.

WHAT IS SHAMANISM?

Shamanism is believed to have originated in Siberia. The word Shaman means "to know" and is the earliest known spirituality sourcing back to prehistoric time beyond measure. Archaeological evidence of Shamanism has been found from 40,000 years ago, and Shamanic practices have existed in every culture throughout history. Shamans have been known to:

❀ heal human suffering,
❀ interpret dreams,
❀ reveal prophecy,
❀ reverse disease,
❀ control the weather,
❀ project their spirits out of their bodies,
❀ exorcise spirits from other bodies,
❀ channel animal guides and spiritual entities,
❀ shape shift,
❀ and time travel.

Michael Harner, who has dedicated his life to studying and preserving Shamanic teachings through the Foundation for Shamanic Studies, says, "A Shaman is a type of medicine man or woman especially distinguished by the use of journeys to hidden worlds otherwise mainly known through myth, dream and near-death experiences." Shamans are widely known as intermediaries who use trance and spirit guides to travel between realms. Trance is induced through singing, dancing, drumming, meditating, breath control, fasting or ingesting natural psychoactive drugs.

Both Tantra and Shamanism use specific principles and practices for sexual healing and enlightenment. Some of the basic tools include breath, sound, movement, prayer, chanting, lovemaking and ritual. Tantra is also about cutting through the illusion, veils, dreams and maya so we can break free of the nightmare of the collective unconscious.

Scholar of Tibetan Shamanism, Terence McKenna, makes the correlation between Shamanism and Tantra apparent in his book ***The Archaic Revival***. He states that Shamans "use archaic techniques of ecstasy that were developed independent of any religious philosophy." He further defines ecstasy as "the contemplation of wholeness."

NON-DUALITY IN A NUTSHELL

Have you ever had that mystical sense that we are all one? Do you remember the last time you felt totally connected? That's the essence of Advaita, or non-dual Tantric philosophy. Advaita is a Sanskrit word meaning "not two." It maintains that all matter, regardless of its distinctly different properties, may appear to be separate but is still connected to the whole of existence. In other words, non-duality is the philosophical perspective that separation is an illusion.

There is a classical metaphor of a clay pot used to answer the oft-asked question, "If it is all one thing why don't I experience it that way?" The clay exists before the potter forms it into an individual pot. The pot is then used to carry water, and though it has a specific function, it is not separate from the clay. Even after the pot is broken, the clay remains. Advaita points out that the clay exists in the past, present and future. Though it may change shape and function, the individual pot is always made of clay. Similarly, everything in the world, from mineral to man, may have a different appearance and function, but ultimately it's all made of source energy.

Another Tantric approach to the non-dual nature of reality is the practice of self-inquiry. In order to transcend the ego and experience union with the absolute, the guru Ramana Maharish advocates that we ask ourselves, Who am I? Through a devoted pursuit to know oneself, seekers discover that they are not separate from the one who is sought.

Take a deep breath now, and notice the words you are seeing on this page. If you are looking at these words, where does the looking stop and the looker begin? Can you pinpoint where your eyes are reading? Where does your comprehension stop and YOU begin? Who are you? Consider the possibility that the words being seen, the seeing and the seer are all one. In the sincere contemplation of self, the ego ultimately dissolves into oneness. We challenge you to continue this contemplation throughout every action of the day. (Beginners be warned! You may get enlightened, but you may also get a headache.)

Osho implores you to contemplate opposites if you want to experience enlightenment. In Tantra, we explore the polarities of male/female, giving/receiving, active/passive, self/other, mind/body, naughty/nice, even dualism/non-dualism to lead us to greater levels of truth. Tantra is a non-dual spiritual practice that embraces and transcends the illusion of separation. Instead of seeing the body as the opposite of spirit, the body is accepted as a spiritual vessel. Rumi illuminates this teaching in his poetry:

> *Of wrong-doing and right-doing, there is a field. I'll meet you there. When the soul lies down in that grass, the world is too full to talk about. Ideas, language, even the phrase, each other doesn't make any sense.*
> *— Translated by John Moyne and Coleman Barks*

Sexual excitement carries within it the impulse for two to become one. One does not have to practice Tantra to experience the urge to merge, but a true Tantrika understands that this primal impulse to copulate is also the desire to commune with God. Wanting to connect with the beloved comes from wanting to acquaint ourselves with the divine. We embrace the illusion that we are separate because without it, we couldn't share the juicy experience of reconnecting with the beautiful light from which we originally separated. It is a cosmic game of hide and seek, a divine play. We separate into many forms and creations not only to merge again, but also to explore the vast kaleidoscope of possible experience.

From the perspective of non-dual realization, one can easily see that all physical matter is a manifestation of divine energy. Some manifestations are more subtle and some more dense, but they are all equal expressions of the divine. God exists in both the sacred and the profane. God's grace can be felt equally from the highest bell tower as from the darkest storage basement. Divinity is acknowledged not only in the beautiful food one eats, but also in what our bodies later excrete. Prayer can be equally powerful through worship at a sacred altar or through anal sex with a conscious lover. Full Tantric non-dual philosophy recognizes that we are half human, half animal and all divine.

MOVING MEDITATION

In Tantra and Shamanism, meditation does not have to be still and silent. We invite our whole body and all of our senses into whatever we're doing whether walking, eating, or making love. In every meditation there is the component of listening to God, which means we are listening to the minute and magnificent details of the moment and tuning in to the great creation within and around us.

During a walking meditation we may notice the sounds of the birds and whatever other creatures cross our paths. Signs of infinite intelligence abound. In eating, we savor the fullness of each flavor. In making love, we are listening to the body, breath, and smile of the beloved. We notice how God animates the beloved, thereby making love to the divine. Magic happens when people feel listened to with such reverence and attention that they open, to unfurl and glow. Their God self shines through.

MINDFULNESS

Where is your awareness right now? Are you thinking about a past lovemaking experience or something you have to do? Perhaps your body is aching and crying out for some attention. What's happening right now... right now... and right now? All three "right nows" are separate moments, and when we pay attention to the subtlety of every moment, we can connect with the abundance of creativity and love that is available right here and now.

In Buddhist theory, this concept is referred to as mindfulness. Today it's a popular spiritual teaching that is incorporated into modern stress management programs. It is generally accepted that if we practice mindfulness in everything we do, we experience the richness that life has to offer.

Sex therapists, educators and surrogates are constantly helping people learn to slow down. Anxiety, stress and tension are the primary causes of most sexual dysfunction. To help couples and individuals increase sexual mindfulness and decrease sexual anxiety, Masters and Johnson introduced a series of sexual exercises called "Sensate Focusing." These exercises are widely used in the therapeutic community and in Tantra 101 classes and detailed in the Appendix as Exercise #1. These simple techniques can be practiced at home or in conjunction with a comprehensive psychotherapy program. Sensate focusing can be used for restorative healing of sexual dysfunction or to bring more presence, conscious awareness and competency to the Tantra seeker.

Tantra is experiential. Now that we have introduced some basic theory, we can commence the practice. In the next chapter we present the three most basic tools for creating a sacred sexual healing practice: breath, boundaries and chakras. Read on to discover how treating your body like a sacred temple will expand your healing, pleasure and ability to manifest magic.

Two
Basic Tools for the Body Temple

> *Do you not know that your body is a temple of the Holy Spirit, who is in you, whom you have received from God? ... Therefore worship God with your body.*
> — *Corinthians 6:19-20*

A temple usually refers to a structure used for religious or spiritual prayers, rites or sacrifices. In Tantra, our body temple is not just the place we go to pray and meditate—it is the very dwelling place for the divine. Our physical form is a vessel for the God self. The anatomy of the human body is every bit as magnificent as that of the ancient cathedrals of the Roman Empire.

The human body displays an exquisite design. Unlike most animal forms, it stands erect, tall and vertical. Our spine is a living channel between Father Sky and Mother Earth. Microscopic cells work together to make up the heart, toenails, eyeballs and belly button. It's a miracle that everything works together so that we can see, hear, taste and dance.

The body is built for pleasure. We are wired with sensory nerves: big ones like the sciatic nerve that goes through the gluteus and thigh, and little ones like the estimated 8,000 nerve endings packed into the head of the clitoris. This intricate superhighway of nerves sends and receives sensual signals between the body and brain. This is how we come to experience hot breath on the back of our neck, or the smell of stale coffee on someone's breath. Our body interprets immense amounts of information about our safety, our state of arousal, and our more subtle energetic impulses that we call the sixth sense.

This chapter outlines three basic tools that help us experience the sacredness of our body temple: breath, boundaries, and chakras. These primary practices are prerequisites on the path of embodied enlightenment. When practiced on a consistent basis, the tools and teachings offered here build a solid foundation on which to base your sacred sexual practice.

BREATH WORK

Breath is like sex. Without it none of us would be here. We owe our lives to sex and breath. Even before we are born our diaphragm starts practicing; that's why babies get hiccups while still in their mothers' bellies.

From our first inhale when the umbilical cord is cut, until we exhale our last breath and die, breath is our constant companion. Yet most people take it for granted. Without breath we would last only a few minutes. How much time do you spend consciously breathing each day?

One of the great secrets of breath is that it creates a bridge between the conscious and the unconscious. It connects the sympathetic and parasympathetic nervous systems. Like blinking, we can breathe involuntarily or with deliberate intention. Breathing practices bring intention to the functions of the body over which we do not usually have voluntary control.

The rhythmic process of expansion and contraction mirrors the natural rhythms of nature, such as night and day, wake and sleep, birth and death. Breath is the microcosm of all existence. Pranayama is the umbrella term for all breathing practices. Prana, the Sanskrit word for breath, also means life force. Yama means control or to expand. Thus, Pranayama literally means the control of life energy. Breathing techniques are used to change subtle energies within the body for health, vitality and sexual wholeness.

In the Appendix we offer three foundational breathing practices which we invite you to learn and begin practicing right away. Exercise #2 is Natural Breath, Exercise #3 is Complete Breath and Exercise #4 is Alternate Nostril

Breathing. If you are an experienced practitioner, we of..
variations to take your current practice to the next level.

BASIC GUIDELINES FOR PRANAYAMA

❀ Before engaging in any Pranayama exercises, blow
your nose to clear out as much mucus and debris as
possible. At the entrance to Osho's Pyramid Temple in
Pune, there is a long granite counter with Kleenex and
wastebaskets for devotees to blow their noses before
beginning their daily practice.

❀ Breath work is best practiced in the presence of
ample fresh air. Do not practice Pranayama in traffic
where you may be exposed to carbon monoxide, or
behind closed doors where there is exposure to smoke,
chemicals or other toxins.

❀ Room temperature (68 degrees Fahrenheit) is the best
temperature for breath work. Environments that are too
cold or too hot challenge the immune system.

❀ If you ever feel faint, dizzy, light-headed or start to see
spots, please stop the breathing practice and allow your
breath to find its natural rhythm.

❀ If you have a heart condition, asthma, bronchitis,
high or low blood pressure, or if you are pregnant or
nursing, feel free to modify the breathing practice for
optimal ease and comfort. If you have other concerns or
conditions, consult a professional.

❀ It is recommended that you not practice Pranayama or
energy work in a cemetery or during a lightning storm,
unless under the supervision of a guru or trained master.

BOUNDARIES

The body temple functions best when it is protected by
healthy boundaries. On the global level, boundaries are lines
between countries that give the nations autonomy. Boundaries
individuate and create identity. Within one nation there are also
boundaries between states. Within states there are cities that are
further divided into neighborhoods. In some neighborhoods,

houses are surrounded by white picket fences. Other houses may use barbed wire to ward off unwelcome guests. Inside most houses, there are walls and doors between rooms. Some doors have locks and bolts; others are always open.

Humans also have boundaries, acting as energetic doors that let other people approach to the desired degree. Essentially, boundaries create the container that provides safety for the body, emotions, and heart.

Unlike walls, barriers, and blocks, human boundaries are not static—they are permeable. Boundaries can be used as checkpoints: a place to stop, breathe, and choose to move forward or not. They are important because they allow us to pause and make sure we're safe.

There is a preliminary discussion of boundaries in most Tantric circles and workshops. It's commonly taught that if someone touches you in a way you don't want to be touched, you say STOP. Of course, this assumes that we already know what our boundaries are and that we're comfortable speaking up when they're crossed.

Unfortunately, this rule means that in order to learn what someone's boundaries are, we first might have to cross them. Once we've learned our boundaries, of course, we can implement more empowered communication.

Relationship coaches Reid Mihalko and Marcia Baczynski are the creators of the Cuddle Party® and are masters at boundary setting. Though these workshops are non-sexual, we can learn a lot by implementing the following rules. (cuddleparty.com)

❀ You must ask permission and receive a verbal YES before you touch anyone. (Be as specific in your request as you can.)
❀ You don't have to cuddle anyone at a Cuddle Party, ever.
❀ If you're a yes, say YES.
❀ If you're a no, say NO.
❀ If you're a maybe, say NO.
❀ You are encouraged to change your mind.

❀ Respect your relationship agreements and communicate with your partner.

❀ Tears and laughter are both welcome.

❀ Respect people's privacy when sharing about the Cuddle Party.

❀ Keep the Cuddle space tidy.

When we ask before touching someone, we empower them by acknowledging that they are always at choice. And by giving people permission to change their mind, we are encouraging everyone to stay connected to how they feel in the moment and not engage in touch or connection out of a sense of obligation. This creates the safety for people to stay connected to their bodies, bellies, and hearts.

Since all of life is not as conscious as a Cuddle Party, and people aren't always in the habit of asking for permission before touching, it's important for you to know exactly how far you're willing to go, and what to say if your boundaries are crossed. In order to develop clear healthy boundaries we offer instructions on how to compose a comprehensive list of your personal limits. Exercise #5 is called Boundary Setting and can be found in the Appendix.

Once you have clarified your boundaries, you may fail to uphold them, which can leave you feeling betrayed and abandoned. Be patient with yourself. Enforcing your boundaries takes diligence and practice.

Ten Tips for Communicating Clear Boundaries

1. Instead of seeing a boundary as a limit or an imaginary wall that you have to protect with a sword, consider it a rule that allows you to feel safe and be more fully expressed.

2. People don't know your boundaries until you inform them.

3. When possible, inform people what your boundaries are before they are ever breached. Example: "I've been doing boundary work lately and I've recognized a few basic rules that, when observed, allow me to be at my best. Would you like to hear my boundaries? Do you have any boundaries that you'd like me to honor?"

4. Let people know how you like to be treated without blaming, shaming, or making them wrong.

5. True friends are happy to hear how you like to be treated.

6. When a boundary is breached, it's best to have a cleanup conversation as soon as possible after the breach. Example: "There's something I'd like to clean up with you…is this a good time?"

7. You always have a choice. If someone crosses your boundaries and does not respond positively to you informing them how you like to be treated, you can simply leave, or ask that person to leave, in either case without creating a scene. If someone repeatedly breaches your boundaries, it is your choice to spend time with that person or not.

8. Boundary setting becomes easier and more graceful each time you practice. Eventually it will feel natural and automatic.

9. Appreciate and validate your friends when they have appropriately observed your boundaries.

10. Boundaries evolve as we evolve.

Sometimes boundaries have to be revised. Listen to your body, heart, and belly. Feel. Find out where you stand by bringing awareness to the truth of where you are in your evolution. Because we are all growing, expanding, and evolving beings, our boundaries are constantly changing. As we build power we feel safer, and we create more comfortable boundaries. For example, Dez had a client who didn't get naked with people because she was abused when she was naked. That boundary kept her safe but it also kept her from sexual intimacy and healing. As she evolved she began to build safety and power. She was eventually able to take off her clothes and trust that she could say no if she didn't want to be sexual.

Many of the exercises in this book are designed for two players, who can be a couple, friends, teacher and student, or healer and seeker. We suggest you initiate a boundary discussion with whomever you chose to practice. That conversation might sound like this:

"Thank you for agreeing to join me in this exercise. I'm working on really listening to my body and honoring new boundaries as they arise. There are things that I already know I definitely don't want to do such as _____. There are things that I definitely do want to try such as _____. And there are things that I want to breathe into and see how it feels and flows, such as _____.

"I'll try to be clear with you in my process, so I want permission to stop, if necessary, so I can really listen to my body in the moment. If some emotion comes up for me, I may ask you to stop so that I can breathe and feel into what's going on inside and then I'll let you know whether I want to proceed or to stop altogether.

"Of course, I want to respect your boundaries and your comfort, as well, so please don't say yes unless you really mean yes. If you're a maybe or you're not sure, we'd better not do it. Are there specific things you want to avoid? Are there specific things you want to see happen?"

CHAKRA SYSTEM

We have seven days in each week that are named after the seven Roman Gods. We have seven major planets. The moon takes on a new phase every seventh day. God created the world in seven days.

At a traditional Jewish wedding, the woman circles her man seven times, and no Hindu marriage is considered complete unless the bride and groom walk together around the sacred fire seven times.

Catholics celebrate the seven sacraments and seven virtues and preach about the seven deadly sins. The Arabs have seven Holy Temples. Persian occult seekers had to pass through seven spacious caverns. Are you seeing a theme here?

The Pyramids at Giza are one of the seven Wonders of the World. The sacred geometry of pyramids points to the magic number seven (four corners of the square base plus three sides of the structure equal seven). This is why Pythagoras called seven the perfect number.

The musical scale is composed of seven notes. When sunlight passes through a crystal prism it produces seven distinct colors of the spectrum. This is all leading up to the fact that the human body temple has seven major chakras.

In Sanskrit, chakra means wheel or circle and refers to seven major energy centers which run up the spine. Learning and working with the chakra system not only dramatically increases the awareness within our bodies but connects us to the infinite intelligence of the collective consciousness beyond our bodies. There are worlds inside and outside of us, and the more acquainted we become with the chakras, the more gracefully we dance between these worlds.

The body is a very subtle and complex system. At the most dense level is the skeletal structure, which then becomes the softer, more agile muscular system. Modern scientists know that the nervous system operates with electrical impulses and that the respiratory system somehow converts invisible air into vital energy. Though modern science has not been able to quantify the chakra system, it has been mapped out by mystics in various ancient cultures and it is intimately associated with the endocrine system.

There is evidence that the chakra system originated in India more than four thousand years ago. The first written mentions were in the Yoga Upanishads in 600 A.D. In the West, our understanding of the chakras comes primarily from Arthur Avalon, an Englishman who translated Tantric texts, including **The Serpent Power**, in the 1920s.

If you have never been formally initiated into how to use this system, we highly recommend you schedule a session with a Daka or Dakini or Kundalini yoga teacher who has embodied experience with this work. At minimum we suggest you practice chakra meditations with friends or lovers because chakras communicate, resonate and vibrate in ways that you can't experience by reading words on a page or practicing alone. If you have already attained some level of mastery in the chakras, then you'll appreciate reviewing the foundation we have laid here, and we hope you enjoy the advanced variations offered after each exercise.

The central energy channel in the body (which runs along the spinal column) is called the shushumna. If you think of your body as a big tree, the trunk or the central axis would be the shushumna. Your tailbone would be the base of the tree, which branches down towards the center of the earth. The crown of your head would be where the branches expand out into the sky. The tailbone is your root chakra, which connects you to the earth, and your crown is your crown chakra, which connects you to the heavens. Between the root and the crown, there are five energy centers along the spine that are associated with different colors, qualities, and aspects of life.

Chakras act like psychic organs to produce, contain, and distribute energies throughout your being. People who are unaware or in denial of subtle energy may not be able to feel their energy centers because they are not active. A trained intuitive can feel someone's chakras even when they are closed or shut down. A sacred sexual healer can see, feel or sense chakras in themselves, their lovers and other seekers. Chakras can be visualized as colorful circles, lotus blossoms or spheres of energy that open, close, darken, brighten, morph and spin.

Following is a list of the seven major chakras and their color, location, properties, sacred geometry and corresponding mantra or sound.

1. MULADHARA ~ Earth ~ RED

The first chakra is also referred to as the root chakra. This energy center resides between the anus and the genitals, in the region around the pubococcygeal (PC) muscles. When the Kundalini energy is dormant, she rests like a snake, coiled three and a quarter times at the base of the spine. The root chakra connects us to Mother Earth and forms our foundation. It corresponds with primal drives and animal instincts such as the desires to procreate, be secure and survive. When the root chakra is out of balance we become fearful or destructive. If you are having trouble with money or general health, try walking barefoot, gardening, spending time in nature or sitting directly on the earth. When healthy, the root chakra anchors us and brings us roundedness, abundance and non-dominating power. Symbolized by a lotus with four petals. The mantra is LAM.

2. SVADHISTHANA ~ Water ~ ORANGE

The second chakra is sometimes called the sacral, sexual or spleen chakra. It is located in the sexual organs, groin and abdomen. It corresponds to the testicles or the ovaries that produce various sex hormones and mood swings. This chakra connects us to our sexuality, creativity, sensuality and emotions. It controls feelings, desires and sense of taste. If you are feeling attached or creatively blocked, work on this chakra through dance, Kegel exercises or pelvic rocking. When balanced, the second chakra brings us depth of feeling, sexual fulfillment and the ability to accept change. Symbolized by a lotus with six petals. The mantra is VAM.

3. MANIPURA ~ Fire ~ YELLOW

The third chakra is called the solar plexus, stomach or power chakra. It is located in the upper stomach area just below the rib cage. It rules our personal power and gut feeling. This center is the source for body wisdom, will power and individuality. It is the foundation of the personality. It also corresponds to our digestion, governing our ability to turn food matter into energy for the body, as well as to digest emotional issues and process feelings. This is the home of our emotional bodies or feminine aspect. When the third chakra is out of balance we feel insecure, needy and depressed. Rubbing your belly, deep diaphragmatic breathing and eating healthfully can realign the power center. When healthy, the third chakra brings us energy, effectiveness, organization, discipline, enthusiasm and laughter. Symbolized by a lotus with ten petals. The mantra is RAM.

4. ANAHATA ~ Air ~ GREEN

The fourth chakra is known as the heart chakra and is the middle chakra in the system of seven. The Sufis considered the heart chakra the seat of the soul. It is located in the chest and affects the thymus, lungs and heart. Imbalances in the heart chakra manifest as loneliness, isolation, sensitivity to touch and abandonment. Hugging, massage, affirmations and service can open and strengthen the heart center. This is the home of our heart's desire. A healthy fourth chakra allows us to connect with others, feel compassion, fall in love and have a deep sense of peace and purpose. Symbolized by a lotus with twelve petals. The mantra is AH or YAM.

5. VISHUDDA ~ Sound ~ BLUE

The fifth chakra is the throat chakra or expression center. It surrounds and emanates from the vocal cords and thyroid. It relates to growth, communication, speech, eloquence and hearing. An unhealthy throat chakra can make it hard to speak the truth and result in argument, miscommunication and sore throats. Work on the throat by chanting, singing, humming and practicing Pranayama. The healthy manifestation of the throat chakra is full creative expression. Symbolized by a lotus with sixteen petals. The mantra is HAM.

6. ANJA ~ Light ~ INDIGO

The sixth chakra is called the third eye, bindu or brow point. It is located on the forehead, just slightly above and between the eyebrows. This is a doorway to the middle of the mind and is related to intuition, insight, vision and precognition. It is linked to the pineal gland and is associated with clear mental processes. When the third eye is out of balance, we are clouded by ignorance and lack of foresight. Guided meditation and visualization strengthen the third eye center. This is the home of our masculine aspect. It also governs our ability to manifest our dreams. When healthy, the sixth chakra allows us to create safety, hold space, witness without judgment, see clearly and experience increased concentration and focus. Symbolized by a lotus with two petals. The mantra is KSHAM or ONG.

7. SAHASRARA ~ Thought ~ VIOLET

The seventh chakra is known as the crown chakra or the thousand-petaled lotus. The crown point is located at the very top of the head, or at a short distance above the head. It governs the aura around the entire body. This is the center for higher consciousness and is a gateway to ascended masters, Christ consciousness and the higher self. It is our connection to the spirit world. Meditation, puja and energy work help open the crown. A healthy crown leads us to divine wisdom, inspiration, union and bliss. Symbolized by a lotus with nine hundred and seventy-two petals. The mantra is HAMSA or AUM.

It's easy enough to read about chakras. You can study the qualities and even buy a pretty laminated cheat-sheet at any spiritual shop, but that doesn't necessarily further you on the Tantric path. The trick is to stay present to the direct experience within your own body. So regardless of what all the chakras supposedly look like and represent, the more vital question is what's going on inside of you? One of the best methods to awaken these energy centers is by practicing Exercise #6: Rainbow Relaxation, which is found in the Appendix.

Instead of learning this system as an abstract and esoteric concept, we invite you to keep it simple. Simply do the practices and accept only what proves to be true. Your understanding of these energy organs will evolve in time and practice. Working with the chakras creates opportunities for us to start feeling our power or lack of it. We ask ourselves:

1. How grounded are we?
2. How connected are we to our passion?
3. What's our relationship to our power?
4. Are we in touch with our love?
5. Are we able to speak and live the truth?
6. Are we connected to our seeing and knowing?
7. How is our ability to create communion and connect with the divine?

As we become more proficient in these energy centers, we are able to breathe divine inspiration into every aspect of our lives until our divinity is actually grounded, rooted and manifested on earth. In effect, we become divine conduits.

Embodied enlightenment is a direct experience beyond the processes of the mind. In the next chapter we'll illumine how to overcome our habit of thinking and how to tap into the profound wisdom and guidance of our bodies, hearts and bellies. We'll also help identify symptoms, sources and solutions to your sexual wound(s) by using the Shamanic approach for healing.

Three

The Shamanic Approach

Have you ever had a bladder infection? Frankly, it feels like your urethra is on fire and you're peeing lighter fluid. Kamala Devi got her first bladder infection when she was sixteen and her parents were away on a business trip. Frantic, she called her sweet, wise aunt who informed her that it was a common side effect of having too much sex, also known as "honeymooner's disease." She and her high school sweetheart often had "too much" sex when her parents weren't home. Because Kamala was young, in pain, and feeling guilty, it was easy for her to imagine that God was punishing her for lascivious ways.

Kamala's God wasn't so punitive when it came to lesbians. Kamala never worried about bladder infections during the seven years she was primarily loving women. And then, in her last semester at college, she decided to switch teams. As soon as she slept with her new boy toy, she got branded with a UTI (urinary tract infection). She came to know that acronym well, because as long as she was heterosexually active, a UTI was a monthly visitor. The Western medical approach is to zap it with antibiotics, which, of course, not only kill the bad bacteria but also kill all the harmonious yeast culture that kept Kamala's yoni smelling fresh. As long as she was playing with a penis, she was stuck on a treadmill of sex, UTI, antibiotic, yeast infection, Monistat 7; and the cycle would repeat every time she was sexually active.

Through the years she experimented with a variety of different healing modalities and natural remedies. She tried gallons of unsweetened cranberry juice, young coconut milk, boiled corn silk, marshmallow tincture, a variety of non-latex contraceptives, talk therapy, hypnosis, reflexology and acupuncture, all to no avail. In the most extreme episode, Kamala was in the audience of a live stage performance when she fell off the riser and went into convulsions. She drifted in and out of consciousness during her ambulance ride to the hospital, where she was diagnosed with an acute kidney infection.

When a Western doctor insisted that Kamala schedule a surgery to stretch her urethra, Kamala finally sought out a Shamanic healer. This turned out to be the solution to her suffering. Jess has a gentle, holistic and intuitive nature. Ironically, she handled Kamala's case with a shotgun. The healing was a battery of methods ranging from dream work, coaching, cranial-sacral massage, acupuncture and suggested sexual positions. Jess used every emotional, physical, mental and spiritual remedy in her bag with no attachment to which one would work. After only four dizzying sessions, Kamala won a ten-year battle with chronic bladder infections!

Typically, a bladder infection is not considered a sexual wound. Yet, this issue had a major impact on Kamala's sex life and sexual self-esteem. In fact, it was the primary wound that started Kamala on her sexual healing journey. She since has met hundreds of people who've healed commonly-overlooked sexual wounds and totally transformed their sex lives. This story illustrates that every sexual healing case is unique and there are no definitive solutions that work for everybody. Sacred sexual healing is not a science; it is an art that requires great willingness, intuition and desire to heal oneself.

The intention of this chapter is to take you on a Shamanic journey through the mind, body, belly and heart; to bring conscious awareness to your sexual wound; and to initiate you into a nonlinear path of transformation. These are the core teachings of Dez's life's work. He has initiated thousands of people into the Shamanic approach in workshops and private sessions.

If you find yourself "glazing over" or "checking out" while reading the next few pages, that is natural. This chapter contains deep personal growth work and sacred sexual healing is not easy. If you are not ready to work through the following exercises it's perfectly OK to move on to another chapter. You can also call in help from a partner or a professional practitioner.

Now, we invite you to engage in this chapter as if you were participating in an afternoon discussion on deep sexual healing. We've interwoven exercises and questions to help you interact deeply with the material. Breathe, contemplate, and journal. Ask questions. You can even argue with the teachings if you like, as long as you stay connected to your intuition. We may not know what your sexual healing will look like— sometimes we don't even know what the sexual block or challenge is—but we trust that if you're sincere in your desire for healing and if you are willing to use your power on behalf of the greatest good of all, then sexual wholeness is yours.

Since most sacred sexual healing begins with a meditation, spiritual invocation or prayer, this is the perfect opportunity for you to ask your guides, gurus or higher power for guidance and support throughout the upcoming journey.

"Divine spirit, guides, gurus and ascendant masters, we invite you to join us on a journey through the shadow of the head, body, belly and heart. May all the super-conscious information that needs to come in, come in. May all feelings that we need to feel be felt. May all the limiting beliefs and obstacles that need to be shifted, shift. We welcome our full sexual expression and a total realignment with the divine!"
Aho!

WHAT IS SACRED SEXUAL HEALING?

Sacred sexual healing is a holistic approach to embodied enlightenment. We work with men, women or couples through a variety of modalities to feel what's going on in their minds, bodies, bellies and heart. Then we do whatever it takes to support their next step towards total health and greater integration in their life. Sexual issues not only affect our sex lives and our sexual expression—they reach into relationships, careers, finance, health and all other aspects of our lives.

There is a big difference between conventional methods of sexual healing and sacred sexual healing. Mainstream medical methods diagnose the problem, view it as physiological or psychological, and treat it with medication, therapy or both.

Sacred sexual healers have a broader, more inclusive, more intimate and more integrated approach to sexual healing. Sexual wounds are defined as anything that negatively affects our healthy sex life. The wound can be an experience, a belief, an attitude, a physical condition, a virus, a bacterial infection, a mental disease or a subtle energetic misalignment. Sexual issues can be chronic or newly acquired, and they can occur every time during sex or only in certain circumstances.

Instead of treating the wound directly, sacred sexual healers consciously circulate sexual energy through the body. This can not only heal sexual wounds, but all kinds of physical ailments including headaches, allergies, acne, depression and even myopia. Sacred sexual healers see sexual energy as divine energy that is cultivated and integrated into physical form. Most of what we share is energetic, and the goal is to empower people to tap into their own emotional guidance system.

SYMPTOMS

A vague sense of discomfort in one's body, a sense that there is something more to sex or a longing to meet God while making love is enough to start many people on this eye-opening path. Still, most people seek sacred sexual healing because their body is crying out for it.

The following is a partial list of conditions that may drive someone to seek a sacred sexual healer. The conditions listed here are not necessarily sexual wounds or problems unless they interfere with our ability to have healthy sexual relations. Read through this list and notice if you have experienced any of these manifestations in your own body, now or in the past.

❈ AIDS
❈ Bladder infections
❈ Breast cancer
❈ Blocked milk duct
❈ Blue balls
❈ Chlamydia
❈ Crabs
❈ Cramps
❈ Enlarged prostate
❈ Erectile dysfunction
❈ Frigidity
❈ Gender identity disorder
❈ HPV and Genital wards
❈ Herpes
❈ Hemorrhoids
❈ HIV
❈ Inorgasmia
❈ Low sex drive
❈ Molluscum Contagiosum
❈ Paraphilia
❈ Pain during intercourse
❈ Penis envy
❈ Performance anxiety
❈ Premature ejaculation
❈ Prostate cancer
❈ PMS
❈ Sacred spot stagnation
❈ Scabies
❈ Syphilis
❈ Inferiority complex in bed
❈ Yeast infections
❈ Vaginal contractions

Following is a list of secondary symptoms and disorders that can manifest as a result of sexual trauma. Please note that if you have experienced any of these, it does not necessarily mean that you were sexually abused or wounded.

❀ Anxiety
❀ Anger management issues
❀ Alcoholism
❀ Blocking out childhood memories
❀ Body image issues
❀ Bondage and discipline
❀ Depression
❀ Disassociation from the body
❀ Dysfunctional relationships
❀ Eating disorders
❀ Fear of intimacy
❀ Fetishes
❀ Guilt, shame and fear
❀ Kinks
❀ Low self-esteem
❀ Distrust in God
❀ Nightmares
❀ Numbness
❀ Paranoia
❀ Insomnia
❀ Sadomasochism
❀ Self-mutilation
❀ Sexual addiction
❀ Substance abuse
❀ Trust issues
❀ Violence

How many of these primary or secondary symptoms have you experienced? Perhaps you've already done a fair amount of work on your wounds and the accompanying social stigma. Take a few deep breaths and acknowledge the healing that you've already done to get where you are.

Now ask yourself honestly, "What is my current sexual wounding? Which wounds are active in my sex life now? What are the obstacles to my full sexual expression?"

SOURCES

Approximately one in four children worldwide has been sexually abused before adulthood. Even the most conservative studies estimate that one in three American women has been raped. Sadly, there's no way to estimate the far-reaching effects of emotional and psychological sexual abuse. Physical sexual abuse is a global problem that manifests as an unhealthy attitude toward sex worldwide. The abused perpetuate the abuse cycle, if not physically then emotionally.

Sexual wounding has a complex continuum of underlying causes. Let's brainstorm now about some of these sources. Scan this list with an authentic and vulnerable consideration of which issues you may have been affected by. Notice how you feel in your body as you read these words. Pay particular attention if you blush, tighten, shake your head or clench your jaw.

❀ Abandonment
❀ Cesarean
❀ Caught masturbating
❀ Cult indoctrination
❀ Date rape
❀ Humiliation
❀ Incest
❀ Ignorance
❀ Inappropriate touch
❀ Insensitive lovers
❀ Malpractice
❀ Mixed messages
❀ Molestation
❀ Neglect
❀ Punitive partners
❀ Physical abuse
❀ Public humiliation
❀ Rape
❀ Religious damage
❀ Rejection

❋ Sexual abuse
❋ Shaming
❋ Surgery on sexual organs
❋ Social stigma
❋ Soul loss
❋ Unprotected sex
❋ Unconscious sex
❋ Verbal abuse

How many of the above experiences do you consciously recall? Are they issues from childhood or are they more recent occurrences? Which memories are the most charged? How did these events have an impact on your sex life?

If you are a sensitive or psychic individual, you don't have to experience the trauma yourself. Perhaps someone you know went through abuse or trauma. Perhaps it's the collective unconscious and no one in particular you know. In *The Power of Now*, Eckhart Tolle suggests that the reason most women get menstrual cramps is because they are empathetic toward the pain of the collective wounding of women throughout history.

As we move into our healing, it's important for us to feel our cramps, our shallow breathing, our clenched jaw or whatever other information our bodies want to reveal. These are our doorways to wholeness. It's time to start feeling the pain in our collective womb, the love in our communal heart and the pleasure of our shared bodies. Most importantly, we must stop letting our thinking dominate our entire experience of life.

SOLUTIONS

So we've looked at the Symptoms and brainstormed about Sources. It's time to move onto the third "S". Let's talk about Solutions. Sacred Sexual Solutions!

Problems cannot be solved by the same level of thinking that created them.
— *Albert Einstein*

The mind tells us that it wants to solve this sexual problem. Our mind insists it's tried everything, but nothing works. According to our mind, there is no hope. It tells us that our sexual wound is permanent and impossible. That's what our mind does. It tells us a lot of things that aren't true.

Dwelling on past experiences and projecting onto future experiences, the mind exists in linear time. When we're in thought, we're making judgments based on past or future fears. It's like a monkey jumping around and gathering evidence about why we can't do this and can't do that.

The mind not only tells us what we should think, but what we should say, what we should do, how we should feel, what emotions are appropriate, and worst of all, our mind tries to tell us how to love. What a bummer, because love doesn't happen in the mind.

The solution to our sexual wounding can be found in the integration between the mind, body, belly and heart. In essence, the Shamanic approach to sacred sexual healing is the practice of allowing the mind to honor and hold space for the body, belly and heart.

So take a deep breath and make whatever adjustments you need to feel more comfortable in your body temple. The body's wisdom is deep. When we manage to get our minds out of the way, the body can share its wisdom on how to generate health, well-being and pleasure. The body knows what feels good. It's not interested in the separation, pain and discomfort that result from our unconscious and conscious mental choices.

Next our mind can hold space for us to feel what's in our belly. The belly is the home of our emotional body or divine feminine. She is our womb. She wants to feel everything deeply. In doing so, she can shower us with amazing gifts. Our belly is our power. The wisdom in the belly is timeless. She lives in the absolutely here and now. All of creation and creativity comes from our womb. How long have we walked around with a tight knot in our belly, cutting off our cosmic wisdom, cutting off the divine feminine? When we are out of touch with the emotion in our belly, we are embodying the dysfunctional masculine, which doesn't know how to hold space for the divine feminine. It's time to step back and allow ourselves to feel.

Next we can breathe into our heart and see what it wants. The heart's agenda is communion, connection and love. It wants everything and everyone to get along with ease and grace. When we start coming from our heart, we start creating more community and joy in our lives.

The Shamanic path to sacred sexual healing requires practice, presence and an acute awareness of total integration. When we only listen to the body, we might become too hedonistic or create drama. Similarly, if we act only in accordance with the belly, we might get swept under and swallowed by our emotions. If we only listen to the heart, we may deny the intuitive warning signals from the belly. When we live in total integration, honor all of our aspects, and don't sacrifice any part of our being, we become walking instruments of divine love.

Many disciplines speak of attaining balance, which implies that when something goes up, something else goes down. This dualistic concept of trying to achieve balance can perpetuate struggle and stress. When we have intention for integration rather than balance, we can simply add to our life experience without holding the belief that something will be sacrificed.

Becoming fully integrated with our body, belly and heart automatically aligns us with God-Goddess or the divine. This is when the divine feminine starts to vibrate. Practicing congruence helps us reclaim our personal power so we can move in the direction of our true desires. This work of integration and alignment will empower us in sex magic.

Before we can manifest everything we want, there's a lot of deep emotional work to do. The belly and the heart have been neglected, emaciated and ignored for too long. This culture is lopsided toward the mind and away from the body. At an early age we learn that we are rewarded for what we memorize in school and we are prized for logic skills. We're also revered for developing our body. We become popular if we are pretty enough or thin enough or are star athletes.

How many times are we told, "Don't cry!" or "It's not nice to be angry." How often have we pushed away or stuffed our feelings, until the flow of information has been conditioned to go downward from the mind to the body to the belly. Our minds have become bullies. Instead of asking our body, belly and heart how they feel, our minds rob us of their wisdom. So there's a tremendous backlog of feelings and wisdom that hasn't been accessed, thus we are disconnected from our power.

In order to recognize how deeply we feel and how much we love, we need to re-evaluate what it takes to be successful in this culture and on this planet. We must begin unlearning. In order to restore power, safety and wholeness, we must move ruthlessly into truth with our whole selves to ensure that our minds aren't bullying us. It is a radical paradigm shift. Once we begin to walk this path in presence, it may challenge our current living structure, jobs, relationships and everything that we have in terms of security.

Since the mind is a powerful entity, this is not an easy process. The mind will spin stories and explanations in order to run the show. It takes a lot of discipline and support to reclaim the emotional body. It sometimes takes professional help. Ultimately, the greatest ingredient towards sexual healing is desire. If you have a burning desire and dedication to break through your sexual wound, you will eventually attract sexual wholeness.

Given all the possible solutions, let's brainstorm a little. Read through the following list and see which solutions speak to you. In future chapters we will offer more in-depth descriptions of many of these tools.

❀ Attend a Tantra workshop
❀ Bodywork
❀ Boundary work
❀ Breath work

❀ Call a friend for support
❀ Confession
❀ Communication exercises
❀ Consult a Daka or Dakini
❀ Detox
❀ Discussion group
❀ Erotic role playing
❀ Energy work on the chakras
❀ Exercise
❀ Hands-on healing
❀ Journaling
❀ Laughter yoga
❀ Masturbation meditation
❀ Puja
❀ Relationship Coaching
❀ Re-birthing
❀ Re-scripting limiting beliefs
❀ Re-parenting your inner child
❀ See a Shaman
❀ Self pleasuring
❀ Support group
❀ Sound healing
❀ Tantric lovemaking
❀ Talk therapy
❀ Trance dance
❀ Writing a letter to someone who hurt you
❀ Yoga

Which would you be willing to try?

Let's proceed by checking in with the mind, body, belly and heart to see what wisdom our integrated being has to share. All the information we need to create alignment and magic is right here within our beings—this belief is core to the Shamanic approach to sacred sexual healing.

MIND IS MASCULINE

Usually the mind wants to analyze, discuss and process. What is sexual health anyway? At this point in our playshop, we would facilitate a wisdom circle where the participants can pass around a talking stick and define sexual wholeness for themselves.

Here is a working definition of sexual health to chew on. The World Health Organization defines sexual health as, "A state of physical, emotional, mental and social well-being related to sexuality; not merely the absence of disease, dysfunction or infirmity. Sexual health requires a positive and respectful approach to sexuality and sexual relationships, as well as the possibility of having pleasurable and safe sexual experiences, free of coercion, discrimination and violence. For sexual health to be attained and maintained, the sexual rights of all persons must be protected, respected and fulfilled." The International Association of Sexual Educators, Counselors & Therapists has adopted this comprehensive definition.

The Shamanic approach to sexual health would add that sex is a spiritual practice beyond the performance-driven, orgasm-focused deed. Sacred sexual healing involves deep consensual connection that enriches the lives of all parties and the society at large.

Now, what's your personal definition of sexual health?

And what does my mind think I need in order to be fully sexually expressed?

Thank you, mind. Namaste.

Once the mind has been expressed, we can call out our healthy masculine aspect and ask for our inner God-Goddess to witness without judgment, to create safety and to hold space so that we can consider the other aspects of our integrated being.

BODY SEEKS PLEASURE

What does my body feel I need in order to be in full sexual health? There's a good chance that after all this thinking and reading your body wants to wake up, stretch and move. This is the point during our playshop when we begin some bioenergetic or somatic movement.

Peter A. Levine is the author of **Sexual Healing: Transforming the Sacred Wound.** Levine refers to sexual wounds as somatic symptoms and asserts that the "experience of trauma plays out in the theater of the body." He studied animals and their natural behavior patterns and found that while their survival is constantly being threatened, they don't hold onto trauma the way humans do. Animals have a natural mechanism in their nervous system that guides them to find a safe place to shake off the fear. This prevents them from becoming neurotic and allows them to stay present. They simply shake off fear the way a dog shakes off water after a bath.

Humans have lost this natural capacity because it is not socially acceptable to go into convulsions or we're afraid of all the emotions that come up. We worry that we'll go crazy, but the objective of this exercise is literally to go out of your mind.

Osho developed a profound somatic meditation that he prescribed to his students every morning at sunrise. It's called Dynamic Meditation. The intention is to become more fully alive, which means that we are not only physically present but able to feel all of our emotions.

The Shakti Shake, a similar exercise, is a favorite warm-up in Tantric playshops. It discharges the stress and tension of daily routine and raises spiritual vibration before people begin to interact with each other.

Exercise #7: Shakti Shake

BENEFITS: This simple but powerful solo practice offers the deep somatic healing benefits of discharging trauma. It stimulates blood and lymph circulation, awakens the senses, reduces stress and generally feels good.

PREPARATION: Wear loose-fitting or no clothing. Put on active music.

METHOD: Stand up and shake. Shake your body. Don't worry about looking silly, just pretend your whole body is a pond and there are ripples moving through it. Shake. Shake. Shake! Put all your weight on one foot and shake the other foot and leg. Switch. Shake your calves. Shake your knees. Shake your thighs, hamstrings, hips. Really shake your hips. Shake your hips some more. Shake your entire pelvis, shake your buttocks, shake your yoni/lingam and shake your reproductive system. Breathe lots of juicy energy into your sex center. Shake here as long as you can. Now shake your belly, twist your torso, shake your chest, shake your shoulders, lift your arms into the air and shake your armpits, biceps, elbows, forearms, wrists, hands and fingertips. Shake your arms like crazy! Let your arms down and shake your head. Shake your jaw, lips, tongue, nose, eyes, cheeks, ears, forehead and hair. Shake your entire body. Shake the space around your body. Now FREEZE! Stop. Close your eyes and breathe. Notice the energy moving through your entire system. Where do you feel open? Where do you feel closed? Where is your body still? Where is it still moving? Notice the subtle energy moving and then quietly sit down for a meditation.

Now ask your body, what does it need to be sexually whole?

_____

_____

_____

_____

_____

Thank you, body. Namaste.

THE BELLY/WOMB IS FEMININE

Dez teaches the Shamanic approach out of his devotion to the divine feminine and his commitment to increasing awareness of the emotional body. He sees many Tantra seekers who think sexual healing is about integrating the pelvis and the heart and they completely overlook the belly! Unfortunately, many sacred sex teachers also override the emotions and try to open hearts without a foundation in safety. Their students suffer.

The mind tries to convince us this is what you should do, this is what it means to be an adult or a Tantrika; but if the belly is not ready, the sexual work only compounds the separation, guilt, shame and fear. For years, Dez has seen the emotional body so denied and dishonored that she has become wounded. When the wounded feminine is not safe there's a lot of resentment, anger and manipulation.

The womb is the core of our power. The feminine holds the power; the masculine witnesses it. How present are you to witness your power? How much do you desire to call your power fully back?

In our playshops, we support the mind to step away and then we activate the emotional body. We touch it and it vibrates and we create spaciousness for it to vibrate more. When we start to do this work, drama disappears and is replaced by ease and abundance.

We're going to lead you through a Tibetan Shamanic ritual to help you stay present to your emotional reality. This is a non-logical process. Allow yourself to play in the realm of dream and fantasy. Give yourself permission to scream, yell or cry out loud. Do not judge or try to make sense of the symbolic gifts that come from your sub- and super-consciousness. Notice without judgment what is happening within your body.

Exercise #8: Feeding the Demons

PREPARATION: Pick a private space. Bring tissues and at least two pillows.

METHOD: Sit on a pillow in comfortable cross-legged position. Set a pillow before you. Set a clear intention for safety and healing. Intend that emotional energy can move in a way that will not bring harm to you, anyone or anything. Get clear in your mind which wound or sexual block you would like to work on. Perhaps even give it a label, so you have a clear sense of what you're dealing with. Relax the body and visualize a clear, compassionate presence of your higher self or a familiar deity standing behind you.

Where in your physical body do you feel the wound or block? What does it feel like? Imagine your higher self performing a Shamanic surgery to pull the wound out. Watch it take form on the pillow. Notice what shape it takes. What does it look like?

Notice that it begins to grow eyes. Imagine it is looking at you. Then notice something about it that you didn't notice before.

Stay relaxed and calm and compassionate. Ask the wound, out loud, "What do you want?" Get up and switch positions so that you are now sitting on the pillow where you placed your wound. Let your body take the shape of the wound. How does your wound sit? How does your wound breathe? What does its body feel like?

Now imagine that you are the wound, looking across at your physical body, and you have just been asked what you want. Get a sense of what it is that the wound wants from your body, its host. Get a clear answer in your mind and say it out loud. I want_____.

Switch sides again. Sit normally in your own body and look across at your imagined wound. Can you feel the presence of your higher self behind you? This higher entity has the infinite capacity to give this wound (or demon) whatever it wants.

Relax with your eyes closed and observe as the being behind you feeds the demon. From an infinite source, it gives the demon what it wants and the demon begins to transform in front of your eyes. Allow this process to take as long as it needs. When the wound becomes full and its needs are satiated, it changes shape. Notice the new shape it is taking. Notice something you didn't notice before.

The being behind you is still strong and light and compassionate and touches your body at the very point where it pulled the wound out to make sure you are complete and whole. When you feel complete, nod goodbye to your higher self and watch as they bow Namaste. Now take a few deep breaths and come back into your body and into the room.

Notice how your belly expands as you inhale and collapses as you exhale. Exhale and let it all go. Relax your mind, your body and your heart so that you're fully present to hear what your belly has to say. Breathe into your divine feminine. Breathe into your etheric womb. Breathe into the storehouse of your power and your emotions.

Now ask your belly, what do I need to do or feel to be sexually whole?

Namaste, belly.

THE HEART LOVES

Now we invite you into the healing of the heart…the deep heart. In Sufi mysticism, this is the seat of the soul. The heart chakra is known as the center of our energetic body; it is the integration point for all the chakras and governs our relationship with self and others. In its natural, healthy state it emanates love, compassion and connection with all that is. Once forged, it is hard to break these connections, which is why people suffer so much from betrayal, rejection, separation, divorce or death of a loved one.

The Shaman enters the realm of the heart to practice soul retrieval and to maintain healthy bonding relationships. Kamala was first introduced to Shamanism by her life partner, Michael. He had been studying Shamanism for more than a decade. He was the one who originally downloaded the Shamanic sexual healing journey that we are about to introduce.

Shamanic work doesn't happen on the linear plane of cause and effect. We have practiced Shamanic journeys with hundreds of seekers who will say, "I didn't feel anything," or "I don't know if I was doing it right." Then several days after the session, they'll call or write to tell us how the journey completely transformed their lives! We don't understand how it happens, but something always happens.

Next, we invite you to embark on a very powerful, very sacred Shamanic journey and though we don't know how, why or what is going to happen, we trust if you do this practice with a sincere heart, you'll be amazed by the results.

Exercise #9: Shamanic Journey

PREPARATION: Many people fast or cleanse their bodies with steam or sage before they journey. When we practice this process at our playshops, we often burn sage and play drums and/or rattles to induce trance and journey into the underworld. For purposes of this book, I recommend playing a Shamanic drumming CD by Michael Harner or Mickey Hart.

Also, a lover friend or healer can read the following script to you while you relax and visualize the healing. Alternatively, you could read the script into a recording device, using your own voice as a guide. Or, purchase a copy of this recording from KamalaDevi.com.

METHOD: Lay your body in a comfortable prone position.

Relax your toes, feet and ankles. Your feet are completely relaxed.

Relax your calves, shins, knees, thighs and hamstrings. Your legs are completely relaxed.

Relax your buttocks, pelvis, hips and genitals. Your pelvic region is completely relaxed.

Relax your low back, belly, mid-back, ribs, shoulder blades and chest. Your torso is completely relaxed.

Relax your shoulders, biceps, triceps, elbows, forearms, wrists, hands and fingers. Your arms and hands are completely relaxed.

Relax your neck, throat, jaw, ears, mouth, tongue, cheeks, nose, eyes, eyebrows, forehead and scalp. Your head and neck are completely relaxed.

Now imagine yourself lying in a beautiful garden. Your body is relaxed against the earth. You're watching the wind blow through the grass. Your head is at the trunk of a big beautiful tree. It's a familiar tree, perhaps from your childhood or your neighborhood, but it's in a totally new location: a beautiful healing garden. In the distance there is a running river. You can hear the water babbling over the rocks. There is a bridge that crosses over and out of sight. Notice the garden around your tree. What is the grass like? Notice the individual blades of grass as they sway in the warm wind. It's as if you become the grass. Then notice how the leaves and branches also sway in the breeze. It's as if you become the tree. And then notice the solid trunk of the tree. What does the bark look like? Imagine feeling the texture with your hands.

Follow the trunk all the way down to where the trunk roots down into the soil. It's as if you slip right into the earth with the roots. You feel yourself going deeper and deeper through the earth's crust and into the underworld. You are safe here. You are not alone. Though it is dark, you sense there is a pair of eyes watching you. This is your animal spirit. Turn your body to look at your animal guide. And quickly look away and do a double take. Is your animal spirit still there? Notice what kind of animal it is. Perhaps you move a bit and turn back a third time to see if it's still the same animal. Notice something about your animal guide that you didn't notice at first. And then allow the animal to guide you deeper into the underworld.

It's as if you're moving through a long dark tunnel until you reach the doors of a sacred temple. Notice what those doors look like. Your animal spirit indicates for you to enter. And when those doors open you see a warm bright room with a bed where your higher self is sitting. Notice what it looks like. Notice what it is wearing. Notice what it is holding in its hands. Your higher self indicates for you to come in and lay down. You feel so safe and relaxed that you are happy to oblige. You lay your head in the lap of your higher self and stretch your body out on the bed and relax even deeper.

Your higher self calls your animal spirit over to your feet. Your animal spirit knows exactly what to do to heal you. It senses your energy first, slowly accessing your entire body, then goes directly to the part of your body that needs healing. You relax even deeper as your animal spirit works its magic. Notice how the animal spirit seems to be extracting the wound from your body. It's like psychic surgery; your wound is being removed. Your animal spirit uses its paws or claws or mouth to take the wound across the room where you can see it. Your higher self places its hands on your body where the wound has been removed, but you feel no pain. Notice how the wound seems to change as it is carried away and out of the temple by your animal spirit. Breathe deeply into your body, feeling the warm, healing presence of your higher self.

Allow your mind to drift off and for the healing to come in. Breathe and notice if any memories, thoughts or ideas arise. Don't judge; just notice what happens. When your healing is complete for today, thank your higher self and say goodbye with a Namaste or an embrace.

You find your body resting in the garden beneath the tree where you started your journey. Notice the leaves of the tree swaying in the wind, notice the grass beneath you and then look toward the river. You see your animal spirit at the river washing away the last of your wound. Notice how the last of the wound is pushed downstream and gets smaller as it floats away. Your animal spirit watches it until it floats completely out of sight and then returns to your side. Your animal spirit is still a little wet and has droplets of healing water on its fur or feathers and touches you with this holy water. Your body immediately feels whole and complete and healthier than ever. Take a moment now to thank your animal guide and say goodbye in whatever way feels appropriate. Your animal spirit may choose to go off into the garden, or it may choose to return to the underworld from where it came, but you know you can always come to this garden and call on your animal spirit whenever you want.

Breathe deeply now into your feet and toes and become aware of where your body is in the room. Come back into present time by wiggling your fingers and wiggling your toes, stretching your arms up over your head. Draw your knees up to your chest and give yourself a little squeeze. Draw your chin toward your chest and curl up into a ball, then roll over to your left side and take a few breaths before gently transitioning to sitting.

ADDITIONAL NOTES:

At this point in our playshop, we might take a few minutes to decompress and share our experiences. If you are alone, this is a good time to journal about your experience. Or if you have a friend or a lover who is joining you on this journey, ask each other the following questions. There is tremendous value in remembering your trance because it helps you integrate the subconscious with the conscious. It also creates space for more healing to come in.

What did your tree look like?

Who was your animal spirit?

What did you notice about your higher self?

Where was your wound in your body?

What did your wound look like?

Are there any other significant details you can remember from your journey?

Now take a few deep breaths. This is the work of the deep heart. Say to yourself: Am I present? Am I holding space? Am I creating safety? Heart, what do you desire?

Now, what do I need to be fully sexually whole?

Once your heart has spoken, acknowledge your heart with a Namaste.

Take a moment to acknowledge all the wisdom that your body, belly and heart have offered. Even if they have conflicting desires, this is your embodied wisdom. The mind must practice holding space, witnessing without judgment and creating safety on an ongoing basis in order to stay current with the truth. With practice, we're able to move through emotional backlog and create space for new information, experience and feelings to come in. With time the process becomes easier. It will take just a breath or two to drop into the body, belly and heart. The wisdom will keep flowing. So we can remain present, ready to receive the next moment.

Now that we've called back our power, we're able to take greater responsibility for our lives. In the next chapter we use the law of attraction to rewrite any negative sexual scripting from the past in order to make room for an empowering new reality. You'll see how easy it is to become the writer, director and performer of your own adventure!

Four

Re-scripting Your Reality

The sacred sex practitioners at the Daka-Dakini Conference in Chicago 2007 had a running joke: We endearingly called non-sacred sex practitioners "muggles." Before we would break for lunch or dinner, Baba Dez would remind us to lower our voices when talking about sacred sex, to limit our public display of affection and not to accidentally flash any muggles as we passed through the hotel lobby. The term actually refers to the non-magical beings in the Harry Potter series.

The analogy between sacred sexual healing arts and Harry Potter is fitting because many practitioners see themselves as wizards, witches and warlocks who are aware of their innate power to create a magical reality. We are not victims hopelessly living out a life story that someone else scripted—we are authors of our own reality.

The law of attraction actually has its roots in ancient Tantric texts. The **Mahanirvana Tantra** scriptures, for example, contemplate that the origin of form emerges from infinite consciousness. In essence, the law of attraction states that our most frequent and powerful thoughts, beliefs, feelings, words and actions actually manifest our material reality. Tantrikas cultivate desire and develop the capacity of their third eye so that they can magnetically attract people, things and circumstances that match their vibration.

Consciously creating our lives can feel like casting an enchanting spell. In this chapter, we take a trip down memory lane to call out our inner child, the one who still believes in magic. We'll look at the effects of our early sexual conditioning, work on forgiving past hurts, learn to re-parent ourselves and ultimately re-script a sexually-empowered future.

CULTURAL CONDITIONING

Sugar and spice and everything nice,
that's what little girls are made of.
Snips and snails and puppy dog tails,
that's what little boys are made of.
— Mother Goose Nursery Rhymes

What cultural or mythological messages did you receive about sex or gender during your childhood? This simple nursery rhyme suggests that boys are supposed to be coarse troublemakers, while girls are sweet and obedient. Before our conscious memory begins, gender roles and expectations are already outlined for us. Through infancy, adolescence, puberty and early adulthood, we are bombarded with messages about how we should be, feel, think and act.

There is a huge discrepancy between the sexual conditioning of women and men in Western culture. The cliché, of course, is that a man who sleeps around is considered a stud, whereas the same behavior would seal a woman's reputation as a whore. Actually, this cultural double standard affects and controls both women and men.

Women are often taught not to have sex before marriage, or they are not supposed to have sex unless it's with someone they really, really love. As a result, when a young woman feels a natural attraction to someone, she automatically starts to fantasize about love and marriage. Some women who decide to hold off on sex until they're married spend a good portion of their adult life secretly mourning never having had time for exploration, adventure and premarital sex. Other women follow their natural urges and take on the guilt, shame and low self-esteem that come with the socially-prescribed label of slut.

The sexual conditioning of young men is equally insidious. Boys are unconsciously indoctrinated into the idea that in order to be a man you have to go out and conquer. Young men are applauded for their blatant sexuality and their conquests. Love stories are labeled "chick flicks" and romance is for "pussies." Virginity is a social stigma. Real men don't fall in love with the first woman they make love to, so sexual experience is gained at the expense of some girl's feelings.

If we're going to truly experience our full sexual potential we have to be willing to listen to who we really are, not who society expects us to be. In order to do that, there's a whole lot of cultural conditioning we're going to have to untangle.

ARCHETYPES

Let's start by looking at archetypes, which are collective role models or stereotypes. They represent ideals for how we "should" be, what we "should" look like. As soon as we start "shoulding" we imprison ourselves and others. Take the archetype of the good housewife, for example. If she happens to love sex and prefers to be in the bedroom rather than vacuuming the living room, she might suffer guilt and shame around not fulfilling society's expectations. There are subtle messages that make her wrong for wanting to go out to a dance club instead of staying home for a quiet night. Any cultural messages that disallow us to listen to what is truly in our hearts can be confining, unhealthy and even damaging.

Perhaps the most common cultural archetypes for women are the Madonna and the whore, terms popularized by the psychological community when Freud introduced the Madonna-whore complex. Originally this condition referred to a man whose wife is fulfilling the role of his mother. He is so immature and in need of the mother figure that he is not able to conceive of her as his wife, and therefore has trouble making love to her.

More commonly, the term is used to describe a man's desire to have his woman exhibit two mutually exclusive traits: the pure and nurturing mother and the sexy vixen. The complex becomes acute when men feel they cannot love women who can satisfy their sexual fantasy, yet are unable to be sexually stimulated by the type of women they do love. The term is used even more broadly to describe society's pressure on women to become both a virginal Madonna in society and a sexy whore in the bedroom.

There are also conflicting archetypal roles for men. For example, the rugged Marlboro man or the unshaven stud in the leather jacket contrasts greatly with the Sensitive New Age Male (SNAG). The paradox is that women long for the sensitive poetic type and then run off with the bad boy on the Harley-Davidson. Women are often dissatisfied with their men's inability to communicate, but men fear that too much communication will end up in women wanting to be "just friends." According to Barbara DeAngelis, what a woman really wants is a man of velvet and a man of steel. We want men who can protect and defend us, yet are not afraid to cry when they are afraid.

Other important archetypes to consider for men and women are from the Tarot. These visual images are symbolic of the collective consciousness. Here are some archetypes from the Major Arcana. Which archetypes resonate with you?

TAROT	ARCHETYPE
The Fool	The Student
The Magician	The Inventor
The High Priestess	The Witch
The Empress	The Mother
The Emperor	The Providing Father
The Hierophant	The Priest
The Lover	The Romantic
The Chariot	The Warrior
The Hermit	The Yogi
The Hanged Man	The Martyr

SEX EDUCATION

Our first sexual impressions leave a formative imprint on our self-concept as adults. Prepubescent children would have a whole different experience in life if their parents taught them, gently, that sex is beautiful and natural. Too often young people are fed shameful stories of all the horrible things that can happen if they have sex before marriage. What's worse, some kids have no formal training; their only sex education is overhearing older boys in the locker room bragging about how they scored over the weekend. Do you remember school kids talking about baseball as a metaphor for sex? Kissing is first base, petting is second base, oral sex is third base, and of course, going all the way is a home run!

The debate over sex education in the schools is almost as heated as the abortion controversy. In the United States and other countries, church, state and concerned parents battle over issues of condom use, premarital sex, teenage pregnancy and sexually transmitted infections. While conservative groups support and advocate abstinence-only education, liberal parties advocate more comprehensive sex education programs. There are U.S. bills that offer millions of dollars in incentives to public schools to narrow the focus of sex education to teach that sex outside of marriage has harmful psychological and physical effects. These abstinence-only programs often rely on "fear-based tactics combined with withholding information about contraception, abortion, gay issues and masturbation," according to Janice Irvine in **Talk About Sex: The Battles Over Sex Education in the United States**. Irvine points to the irony that countries with the most conservative sex-ed programs (including the U.S. and the U.K.) have a higher incidence of STIs and teenage pregnancy.

Kamala Devi remembers her first formal sex education class at her conservative Orange County elementary school. The boys were taken out to the blacktop to play handball while the girls were shown an outdated slide show with a clinical explanation of menstruation. There was no discussion of sex or contraception. The lecture was followed by a Q & A session where students wrote questions on index cards because they were too embarrassed to raise their hands.

Baba Dez went to a Catholic high school. He was fifteen when he attended sex education classes and had already figured out that God wasn't going to strike him down for masturbating. Like most sex educators of that era, the teacher lacked all understanding of what it means to be a sacred sexual being. In the world we envision, curious kids will have healthy, sexually-realized role models presenting the concept of sacred sexuality.

If you haven't already, it's high time to question your sexual conditioning. Your answers to the following questions may reveal some of your most fundamental beliefs. Unexamined attitudes and thoughts may be looping unconsciously through your head like a broken record. Time to give the old jukebox a swift kick and consider actually listening to a song of your choice.

Exercise #10: Examine Your Sexual Conditioning

Get out your journal and write your answers to these questions as quickly as you can without premeditation. White-hot writing reveals your true subconscious thoughts.

1. What did my parents teach me about my vagina/penis?
2. What did they teach me about sex?
3. What actions or attitudes did they model about sex?
4. What did my classmates feel/think/say about sex?
5. What did I learn in formal sex-ed?
6. What did my doctor and health providers teach me?
7. What did my church or temple teach me?
8. What is the earliest negative message about sex that I remember?
9. What is the earliest positive message about sex that I remember?
10. What did I learn about the relationship between sex and spirit?

Now, look at what you've written. Are you surprised by your own responses? Do you see any themes? What subtle messages have you adopted? Is there still hurt, pain, guilt or shame behind any of these teachings? Do these thoughts and ideas still serve you?

EARLY SEXUAL EXPERIENCES

Directly remembering childhood experiences can override our conditioning. Let's shine a light on the most formative of all sexual experiences: the first orgasm. What were the circumstances surrounding your first O? For many people, though not all, there are powerful stimuli and anchors around that memorable experience.

It's well documented that fetishes and kinks are developed because of the circumstances surrounding a first orgasm. A classic example is the boy whose mother used to spank him with a hair brush and since this stimulated his first orgasm, he needs his wife to spank him every time he wants to ejaculate. But the kinks illustrate the extreme.

If someone's first orgasm happened while masturbating in the bathroom, and an older brother yelled to hurry, that person may have decided that sex has to be done quickly behind closed doors.

A woman whose first orgasm is on her back may find that this is the only position in which she can consistently orgasm. First associations can also be healthy and natural.

Kamala Devi's first orgasm occurred when she was lying on a cool wet towel against a concrete poolside. Her boyfriend's parents were out of town, so they were alone in his backyard during a warm summer afternoon. He was wading in the shallow end, leaning over the edge of the pool, giving her oral sex. She was lying on her back wearing only a bikini top, her thighs wrapped around his neck. He used his whole face to drive her to an awe-inspiring climax. After several minutes of feeling her whole body vibrate, she opened her eyes and saw the sun shimmering off the pool water onto the branches of the oak tree overhead. Kamala has since anchored her orgasmic experience to Mother Nature. To this day she finds herself aroused by a warm summer breeze.

Take the time to recall your first orgasmic experience and see if you've created any lasting emotional or mental associations from that experience. What are your beliefs now as an adult?

Even if you personally can't recall any memorable negative teachings, mainstream attitudes toward sex have a way of leaking into your psyche long after your early sexual conditioning. What are the attitudes of the people who surround you? What do your friends, co-workers, acquaintances and family members believe? And how might this affect your own position?

To identify your current feelings, thoughts, concepts and beliefs around sex, complete the following sentences, writing as quickly as possible:

1. Often, after I orgasm I...
2. When I think about sex I...
3. When I talk about sex I feel...
4. I'm afraid to admit this but...
5. My favorite thing about having sex is...
6. My least favorite thing about having sex is...
7. I would have more sex if...
8. I feel foreplay is...
9. Women who have multiple partners are...
10. Men who have multiple partners are...
11. My most exciting sexual fantasy is...
12. Sometimes when I masturbate I feel...
13. When it comes to masturbation I...
14. I would masturbate more but...
15. The thing about sex is...
16. When it comes to sex I am afraid to...
17. When it comes to sex I am ashamed about...
18. When it comes to sex I feel guilty about...
19. When it comes to sex I am excited to...
20. Sacred sex seems...

RE-FRAMING PAST PAIN

Now look over your answers. Do your ideas, beliefs and concepts about sex serve you? Do your attitudes about sex bring more freedom, happiness and life satisfaction? If the answer is no, then it's time to start re-scripting, re-working, re-framing and re-creating your reality.

With awareness, our pain can be turned into opportunity. Past hurts are not only learning lessons, they are genuine gifts. When the intensity of our negative conditioning is brought into the emotional body, and we are allowed to feel the pain of our past, we can consciously choose to end the suffering. We can say, "I'm done with this path, these beliefs, this negativity and I'm committed to creating a new reality."

Think of sex like art. It can be featured or degraded based on the frame you put around it. A good frame takes into consideration the lighting, the size, the color and the space around the experience. If the frame is old, too tight or placed in a dim light, the sex is going to look and feel terrible. Whereas, if you take mediocre art and put it in a beautiful frame it's likely to shine.

Our friend, Nick Karras, is a sexologist and a gifted photographer. He is the author of ***Petals***, a beautiful black and white book of yoni photography. He frames sex positively when he says that even if the actual act of sex isn't the most mind-blowing experience, or if the woman doesn't look like a runway model, he always feels honored that she would share the miracle of her body with him.

You are a conscious creator. You create your own reality with your thoughts, words and actions. Do your thoughts match up with the reality you want to live in? Do you want to continue to entertain sex-negative thoughts? If you want to be fully sexually expressed, then chances are you have to embrace a whole, sex-positive outlook on life, which might take some serious re-scripting.

RE-PARENT YOUR INNER CHILD

A full sexual awakening doesn't just affect how you see the possibilities in the future—it affects how you regard your past. We can achieve liberation and power with a tool therapists call re-parenting, a process that forms a strong, healthy bond between the adult you are today and the inner child who lives inside.

Re-parenting allows you to give your wounded inner child whatever nurturing, affection, attention, recognition, guidance, direction and self-discipline you didn't get from your own parents. In the process you may also let go of any guilt, shame, fear or other self-defeating feelings that you've been carrying around since childhood, so that you can look back without lingering pain and regret. By re-scripting your past, you create the possibility of a new empowered future where you take responsibility for your own life.

Re-parenting is about asking yourself, "What are the pieces and fragments of myself that were pushed away and disowned?" Are you willing to pull them back in?

What happens for many of us as we go back and re-parent ourselves is that we're able to consciously recreate events, feelings and circumstances that we could have had in the womb, in our birth, as a baby, in our childhood and during our formative teenage years. We go back and look at where we were met, and where we were not. Each soul has its own specific journey and in our work with hundreds of people, including ourselves, we always find that reclaiming our history and her-story is an amazing gift.

The simple key to this process of remembering is presence. Presence is the natural antidote to what we've been told and what we've believed. It is also potentially the answer to everything we have longed for. With presence, all experience can unfold naturally. No matter how intense the memory is, all you have to do is feel your feet, wiggle your toes, breathe and take it all in. If you are fully in this moment while witnessing the pain of your past, everything will change. As we start asking to reclaim all of the traumatic situations and circumstances of our lives, while simultaneously aligning with this moment, the magic can come in. This is how we reclaim our power.

Exercise #11: Re-Parenting

BENEFITS: Re-parenting can help you overcome chronic depression, negativity and low self-esteem. It can help you stop nitpicking, faultfinding and blaming. It dramatically increases self-love and self-esteem. It helps develop emotional maturity and helps you establish healthy boundaries in future relationships.

PREPARATION: Make sure you are fed and rested before beginning this journey. Disconnect the telephones. Prepare a soft space to lie down, relax and visualize. Optionally you can select soft music without words, like a lullaby, to support your visualization. Have a journal and a pen handy.

METHOD: Start by closing your eyes. Get in touch with the part of you that has been neglected and needy. Look for the small, ignored and wounded aspect of yourself.

Remember a time when you were mistreated by one or both of your parents. Try to find a specific incident. Where were you? What were you doing? What does your inner child look like? What is the expression on your parent's face? Can you remember what your parents did or said to you? Hold that picture in your mind and simultaneously come back into the moment by wiggling your toes and deepening your breath.

Return to the present. Focus for a moment on the strengths, abilities and competencies that you possess today. Gather up your self-acceptance, self-confidence, self-worth and self-love.

Now, as an integrated adult, go back into that scene from your childhood. What does your inner child really want in that moment? Imagine giving your inner child exactly what she needs. If he wants to be held, hold him. If she wants to play, then play with her. If he wants to be praised, then praise him. If she wants to cry or scream, let her. Don't assume you know what your inner child wants until you ask.

After that immediate need has been fulfilled, you can invite your inner child to some special time together. Ask your inner child, "Where would you like to go?" Is there a special place that would make your inner child feel totally safe and loved and special? Imagine that you are stepping into another scene with your inner child. Perhaps it's a garden or the backyard or a sandbox. See your higher self taking care of your inner child in that secure place. What does your higher self say to your inner child? What does your inner child say to your higher self?

Now that this important relationship has been established, you can continue to maintain it on a daily basis. Say good-bye to your inner child for now, and slowly come back into the moment. Open your journal and record the details of what you experienced.

Another practice for healing the negative conditioning and misinformation we received as children is to look back in time and visualize your ideal sexual history. Use the following questions to re-inform and empower your inner child to have a healthier sexual environment.

What would it look like if you grew up in a household that honored sex? What if your curiosity was encouraged and your sexual exploration celebrated? What if during puberty all of your questions were answered in a responsible and age-appropriate manner? Would your first sexual experience from virginity have happened in the same way? Would you have made the same choices about when, with whom and how to share sex? Would you have treated your lovers the same as how you have treated them since? What if touch was considered healthy and natural and no one was starved for touch, love and affection? What if we were generous with our intimacy and opened our heart to friends and ex-lovers, and all of our communication was conscious and mature? What difference would this make in your confidence and your service in other areas of your life? How would it affect your creativity, relationships, career and your life purpose?

VARIATIONS:

1. Have a conversation with your inner child by placing your inner child on a pillow before you. Allow full

emotional expression.

2. Write a letter to your inner child.

3. Use a full-length mirror, sit face-to-face with yourself and practice positive affirmations. This option is especially powerful if you are working on accepting your body image and want to increase your attractiveness, self-worth and physical beauty.

4. Work with a professional sacred sexual healer using hypnosis, Gestalt, EMDR, re-birthing or any other modalities. These options are especially powerful for people who experienced neglect, rape, sexual abuse and emotional abuse as children.

FORGIVENESS

God forgives us in every moment. God gives us this moment and if we're not fully in love and present, we get this moment, and the next moment. And if we don't get it right, we get another moment to try again! That's what true forgiveness is: letting go of the past and creating a possibility for whole new ways of being in every moment.

What benefit is there to holding on to past pains? We tell ourselves that we remember that hurt so it won't happen again, but we underestimate ourselves. We are capable of letting go of the hurt and resentment and then making agreements and choices not to have those issues come up again.

Kamala Devi has been working through this lesson with her mother for years. When Kamala was sixteen, her mother found out that she had contracted an STD. Her mother called her a whore and said, "You're the reason people are afraid to sit on public toilets. They don't want to get infections from people like you."

For years Kamala harbored hurt and shame. But when she was thirty and her mother was sixty, she saw that her pain was not serving anyone. Kamala went back and re-parented her inner teenager. She found that instead of being blamed, her inner child wanted to be reassured that she was still lovable. As an adult, Kamala was able to give her inner child that comfort.

The healing was not complete, however, until Kamala forgave her mother. After the re-parenting, she conjured the scene with her mother again and empathetically felt how afraid her mother was for her daughter's safety and how she felt like she had failed as a mother. Kamala could see how her mother had no intention to scar her daughter; she simply didn't have the impulse control to handle the situation. In essence, her mother was doing the best she could at the time. Today, Kamala and her mother have a sweet friendship.

Forgiveness does not mean we let people continue to abuse us. If Kamala's mother flies into a fit of rage and yells cruel things at her, she will simply leave. Kamala has a clear boundary that if someone's voice rises in anger, she will leave or hang up the phone and wait for things to cool down. These boundaries sometimes feel impossible to uphold around family, but without them, some people might not be safe to forgive and love.

There are times when we have to practice forgiveness with people who are no longer part of our life. When we look back at our past and realize that the greatest hurts came from people we no longer know or who have passed, it is still important to do the forgiveness work because it sets us free. So this work looks like a conversation with a substitute or a proxy. You can use your lover, friend, partner, therapist, full-length mirror or teddy bear. Have this person listen to you as you go through your forgiveness process. Or you can write a letter.

Simply thinking about forgiveness does not have the same effect as being witnessed. Emotion is energy in motion. Thinking does not move energy; it only activates it. The only way to release energy is to move it, so talk out loud to a mirror or to a friend.

When you relax and do the work, it moves through you without resistance. When you are emotionally charged and all worked up, you risk getting reactivated. Sometimes it's a good idea to start with a meditation, a prayer or even a nap.

Exercise #12: Forgiveness List

PREPARATION: Get your journal and a pen. Number 1–25 vertically down the page.

METHOD: Make a list of 25 people in your past who have hurt you. Ask yourself, "How have I been hurt, emotionally or sexually?" Write one sentence for each person, starting with your mother and your father, your siblings, your ex-lovers. Write quickly and don't dwell. Notice what's coming up but don't get caught up in your story.

You may be surprised at what you're still holding onto. You may have a hard time coming up with 25 people. Or perhaps this number doesn't make a dent in the list of all the people who have hurt you. That's OK, just do it. Notice whatever comes up for you.

Look over your list and ask yourself, "Am I taking responsibility for the hurt in this situation? What do I need to do to forgive this person? What do I need to do to forgive myself?"

Now lie down. Breathe deeply and progressively relax your whole body. Call to mind the face of the individual who hurt you most. Send that person love and forgiveness. If you cannot access the forgiveness, pray to a higher power to help you forgive and love. Ask that person to forgive and love you, as well.

VARIATION: Journal as much or as little as you need on these issues. Journaling is therapeutic. Trust your intuition to know when you're complete.

CUTTING CORDS

If you love someone set them free.
— Sting

We come into the world with a cord connecting us to our mother for life-giving support. The physical umbilical cord is cut after the baby is born, but the energetic apron strings may not be cut for years. Once the energetic bond is removed, the child can form a healthy primary relationship with a more appropriate mate.

The attachments we form with others are often unhealthy, inappropriate and tangled. When we undergo a painful breakup, we often maintain unconscious cords that continue to drain emotion. In fact, we leak energy and power whenever we are out of alignment in relationship, whether with family, competitors, ex-lovers, or business partners.

Attachments are also called chakra cords, karmic connections or emotional ties. Many psychic seers actually perceive these bonds as transparent filaments, like tendrils of a jellyfish that receive or transmit energy. Inappropriate attachments are said to have hooks or barbs at the ends of them.

Releasing these cords can help to break up old ways of interacting. This does not mean we are cutting these people out of our lives; it simply means we are letting go of old ways of relating that no longer serve us. Cutting and/or releasing the cords between former lovers can allow people to develop a healthy friendship after the breakup. Cutting the cords between parent and child can allow the child to have a mature relationship with the parent. Between business partners, this ritual can open space for clean career choices. Healers may also want to cut cords with seekers, or parents with their children.

Exercise #13: Cord-Cutting Ceremony

BENEFITS: This Shamanic reclamation ritual helps you regain autonomy and power.

PREPARATION: Make sure you have eaten and are rested. Turn off your phone. Have music cued up and incense or essential oils ready for later. It is natural to feel a full spectrum of emotions during this process, so make sure that you are in a safe space and can be as loud as you need.

METHOD: Begin in silence with a deep breath. Begin breathing into your primary connection to Mother Earth. Breathe long, full breaths without retention throughout the practice. Release on the exhalation and imagine freedom on the inhalation.

Once you feel grounded, open your upper chakras by speaking an invocation and asking for the guidance and protection of your higher self, guides and gurus. If it's appropriate to your belief system, you may call on Archangel Michael, who is particularly powerful in assisting this process with his magical sword. Feel the power and presence of your allies as they gather around you.

When you are ready, visualize the face of the individual you wish to release. See yourself standing, sitting or lying at a healthy distance from that person's body.

Now use your intuition to locate the cords you wish to sever. When you have a clear picture of these cords, imagine retrieving your own cords on the inhalation; imagine giving back the other's cords on the exhalation. Some of the lighter filaments may naturally float back into place. Some of the stronger cords may be like rubber bands that painlessly snap back. Some of the cords may be thick, like cables, and need to be cut with Archangel Michael's sword. Romantic cords may be more concentrated around the heart, the navel or sex center depending on whether this energetic connection was about sex, power or love. Spiritual and mental relationships tend to bundle around the top three chakras. Ultimately, some cords may refuse to be severed because they are still serving a purpose.

After all cords have been released or cut, if you feel your auric field has been left with scars or holes, then visualize healing light. This healing light may be violet, amber, God's light or sunlight. It fills the room where you have done this work and guides your future relationships. Complete the ritual with a visualization of yourself as whole, strong and free from this other person.

Afterward, simply rest. You can turn on relaxing music, slip off to sleep, or smudge your area with incense or sage. Even though the ceremony is complete, the energetic ripples are still in motion. Relationship attachments take time to dissolve and heal.

VARIATIONS: Some practices include speaking the following incantation, "I now cut and release the cords of my relationship with_____. I release and let you go. Good-bye."

Also, you may move your arms around your body as if you are physically cutting cords with a sword. Don't forget to cut above your head and below your feet, as well.

If you have a friendship and good communication with the person you are releasing, you can co-create a ritual to lovingly withdraw cords from each other.

ADDITIONAL NOTES: This practice should always come from a loving and nurturing intention as opposed to a place of hurt or revenge. Essential oils and natural supplements can support us in keeping a high vibration during this process.

Cutting cords can be like pulling weeds, where you have to get the root out or the cord will grow back. Repeat this exercise as needed until you are free and clear from emotional enmeshment. Some teachers practice this ritual on a daily basis, while others don't recommend doing the ceremony more than once a month because they feel time is needed to assimilate the work that has been done.

GRAVITATIONAL PULL

Relationship is the great teacher. Relationships offer the greatest reflections for us to see ourselves. In fact, we tend to attract others who can reflect that which we most need to learn about ourselves.

We use the metaphor of the solar system to conceptualize the creation and maintenance of our many relationships. You are at the center of the system. Your power and the brightness depend on how strong your connection is to your self and/or the divine. The deeper the core relationship, the stronger the gravitational pull you have on all relationships that radiate outward. Love is like gravity. The more self-love you have, the more attractive you are to others.

Moving out from the first ring with the self are the

more intimate relationships with your beloveds, your children, your family, your tribe and to everyone you know. These rings continue to radiate outward to acquaintances and to people you've never met. In each ring, there are all these different beings and they are all moving in and out of relationship with you and with one another. Someone might be in the place of beloved, then move out to close friend or tribe, and then come back in again.

There is a natural flow or orbit for each relationship. It's healthy for you to allow natural shifts. Notice your feelings as someone moves in or out. See where you try to lock particular people into particular orbits in order to feel secure.

And then there are other celestial bodies such as asteroids, which have totally different orbits. These are the people who seem to show up from nowhere, get really close, maybe as close as a beloved or family, and then they accelerate back out to the outer rings or even out of sight. This cycle might even repeat every few years, like Halley's comet. It's sweet when it comes in close, it's brief, and perhaps it's hard to say good-bye.

Again, when we're really in the flow, we don't hold onto relationships. Better to work on our core relationship and trust that everything else is a result of that since all relationships start with self.

AFFIRMATIONS

One of the most powerful ways to improve self-concept and self-esteem is by saying or writing affirmations. People avoid affirmations because they are embarrassed or feel goofy saying them. It's like that character on *Saturday Night Live* sitting in the bathtub chanting "…gosh darn, people like me!" Once you get over the initial silliness of talking to yourself, you'll start witnessing the magic that you create all around you.

With all the negative programming that has been going into our sexual selves for so many years, it's time we start counteracting those messages with positive programming. Now that we've mined some of our own limiting beliefs and negative thoughts about sex, we can re-script with positive affirmations that empower us.

The human system can be compared to a supercomputer with hours of tapes of negative sexual experiences. In order to override old programming, we can simply run positive programs instead. When done correctly, this is one of the most powerful tools to upgrade our lives. In our work as Dakas and Dakinis, we have seen affirmations heal broken hearts, recover lost sex lives and give people the courage to follow their dreams.

Unfortunately, affirmations are often misused. People are taught to repeat affirmations over and over like a parrot. Unless affirmations are combined with genuine feelings, they are a waste of time. Further, people are told to do them in the morning when they wake up, which is better than not using them at all, but it's only a fraction as powerful as practicing during the deep relaxation that comes minutes before drifting off to sleep, or during the heightened consciousness of orgasm. These are potent windows when affirmations drive directly into the sub- and super-consciousness memory of your supercomputer.

AFFIRMATION GUIDELINES

The most effective affirmations are the ones that you create for yourself because they resonate more deeply with your own value system. Exercise #14 in the Appendix provides ten powerful sacred sexual affirmations for each of the seven chakras. You are welcome to use them directly, or as examples of how to write your own affirmations. Following are a few tips on how to formulate your own empowering affirmations and some creative ideas of how to supercharge your super-consciousness in order to get the best results:

❀ Use only positive words. The subconscious doesn't acknowledge words such as "not" or "don't." So, instead of saying "I am not poor" (the subconscious will only hear "I am poor"), say "I have enough money to meet all my needs."

❀ Create your affirmation in present tense. Place yourself in the situation you want. If you talk about yourself in future tense, you may always find yourself waiting for it to happen, some day in the future.

❀ Keep your affirmation short and specific. Focus on one key element at a time, without the clutter of many desires all at once.

❀ Notice any thoughts or feelings that may arise that are in conflict with your affirmation. Expressing and releasing these thoughts and feelings is like dissolving the glue that holds sabotaging beliefs in place.

❀ Work a single affirmation a maximum of two weeks. This isn't too long for staleness to set in, but long enough for the message to sink into every corner of your self-perception.

❀ Indulge yourself in the moment as your affirmation sinks in. Then, let it go. By not dwelling on how the change might show up, you let the subconscious work her magic naturally.

❀ Write the affirmation out longhand 108 times, imprinting it into your subconscious mind. Repetition of your affirmation means your desire can sink into every fiber of your being, settling naturally into your way of life.

❀ Write your affirmations in a love letter to yourself and send it in a self-addressed envelope by post.

❀ Record your affirmations into an audio machine and listen to them as you drift off to sleep.

❀ Put them on a sticky note on your computer.

❀ Write them in lipstick on your bathroom mirror.

❀ Write them out longhand before going to bed each night.

❀ Read through them each morning.

❀ Pick one to repeat to yourself throughout the day.

❀ Say your affirmations to your lover before and after making love.

❀ Write them out and put them on your altar.
❀ Say them out loud to yourself in the mirror.
❀ Decorate your favorite affirmations on poster board.
❀ Write them on your body with eyeliner.
❀ Write them on your lover's body with
  pomegranate juice.
❀ Write them on the back of an amulet.
❀ Write them in menstrual blood.

The personal growth tools in the last few chapters are designed to help you cultivate higher levels of power and presence which can be applied to the more advanced sacred sex rituals we introduce in the next section. As the journey becomes more physical, it need not become any less spiritual. Soon, you will learn to offer your sexual desire, arousal and orgasm to Spirit. This is how lovemaking becomes a prayer.

Pink

Five

The God-Goddess Within

The greatest lie in the history of religion is that God is a bearded old bloke sitting in the clouds judging us. It's equally dualistic to believe that God is a woman. Even though we all came to Earth through the miracle of our mother's womb, God is neither masculine nor feminine, but both.

Another dangerous distortion is that we need a priest, minister, rabbi or pope to mediate our relationship to God-Goddess. Whenever an organization mandates that we need any person beyond our self, it is disempowering to our innate and direct connection to Source. Tantra teaches us that we are extensions of the divine, and that we are perfect, whole and complete as we are.

OK, so if I'm a part of God, why am I so addicted to the Internet? Why does my heart hurt when I think of my ex? Why do I have such a weakness for chocolate? Because we are also human. We're part God and part human. But here's the catch: It's all God. Even the guilt, shame and fear. Even the blood, piss and shit. The judgment, insecurity and unconscious sex. It's all divine.

The only way to experience life's perfection is to wake up. Wake up to who you really are. Wake up to your own wholeness and completeness. This chapter offers the necessary tools to transform the most fundamental wound within each individual, which is the illusion that we need somebody outside our self to be complete.

The following pages are an initiation into Shamanic practices of embracing your inner masculine and inner feminine. Gods and Goddesses are self-sufficient—we don't depend on anyone else for our power and pleasure. You are your own other half—don't let a partner, or lack of one, prevent you from experiencing the magic and love that is within.

Now we will consider various cultural perspectives on the polarity between the masculine and feminine principles. These contrasting and complementary forces are universal; however it's important to consider that they have different qualities ascribed to them within different cultural contexts.

YIN-YANG

The Taoist concept of Yin-Yang is perhaps the best visual representation of the way feminine and masculine energies dance together to form the universe. The circular symbol consists of two equal portions, each containing an element of the other, illustrating the light within the dark and the dark within the light. Yin and Yang are the paradoxical energies that harmonize and battle within every organic system. The literal translation of Yin-Yang is two mutually correlated opposites, such as heaven and earth. This concept of unity in duality represents the paradoxical nature of the Universe not only in the cosmos but also in each of us.

YIN	YANG
Earth and Water	Air and Fire
Feminine	Masculine
Lunar	Solar
Dark	Light
Moist	Dry
Cool	Warm
Diffuse	Directed
Vague	Focused
Intuitive	Logical
Passive	Productive
Receptive	Active
Internal	External

SHIVA-SHAKTI

In Tantric cosmology, the whole universe was created because of the erotic interplay of Lord Shiva and Goddess Shakti. Shiva is the principle of awakened consciousness whereas Shakti is the principle of creative power. More personally, Shiva is the masculine and Shakti is the feminine within each of us and throughout creation. The symbolic representation of their sacred union is the Yab-Yum position, which translates to Mother-Father Pose. In Yab-Yum, the woman (Shakti) straddles the man (Shiva) and sits on his lap while he sits cross-legged in lotus position. The masculine form is passive and the feminine is active. United, the individuals are able to overcome the veils of illusion and false duality.

Shiva, the divine masculine principle, is often depicted as the supreme yogi sitting naked, "clothed in the universe"; or wearing a tiger skin, sitting in meditation under the tree of life or on his bull, Nandi. He is also called The Destroyer and The Supreme Lord. Shiva holds a trident that represents the Hindu trinity. He is in a continual state of samadhi or nirvana. Shiva embodies the principle of spirit consciousness and space. Represented by the Shiva lingam or a stone phallus, he is the stage upon which the play of life dances.

Three times when Kamala Devi was in ecstatic worship, she had the experience of being visited by Shiva. He appeared naked with ash all over his body, long dark dreadlocks and a huge unwavering erection.

Shakti means sacred force, power or energy. Shakti is the personification of the divine feminine. She embodies the creative, active and powerful, yet she has receptive qualities. She is infinite in her forms: Adya Shakti is the primordial power, Uma Shakti is the divine mother, Kundalini Shakti is the serpent in the spine, Maya Shakti is the creator of illusion and our physical reality, Parvati Shakti is Shiva's loyal wife or consort, and Kali Shakti is the fierce protector and destroyer.

SHIVA	**SHAKTI**
Masculine	Feminine
Un-manifest	Manifest
Formless	Formed
Consciousness	Energy
Changeless	Change
Truth	Illusion

Ardhanarisvara is the Tantric androgyne. Andros (man) and gyne (woman) come from Greek and imply a combination of both male and female qualities. This God-Goddess is the embodiment of the hermaphrodite archetype. The left side of his/her body is female with a breast, rounded hip and half a yoni, whereas the right side of his/her body is male with a Shiva lingam and one testicle. S/he symbolizes the balanced union between Shiva and Shakti, the active and the passive. S/he is the bisexual lover who can give and receive pleasure simultaneously.

Studying various Gods and Goddesses can deepen our understanding of their energetic qualities. Poring over images of archetypes, dancing, drawing and making offerings to these deities can further activate our connection to their teachings. For example, if we establish a special relationship with Quan Yin, the Goddess of Mercy, we become more in touch with the quality of compassion. If we make an altar to Laxmi, the Goddess of Abundance, we may be surprised by newfound financial independence. Praying to Krishna before each meal may fill our life with divine love.

True Tantric practice doesn't worship Gods and Goddesses as if they existed outside of us—it awakens the Gods and Goddesses within.

ANIMA-ANIMUS

Carl Gustav Jung made a major contribution to modern psychology when he presented the idea that the human psyche has both masculine and feminine components. Jung believed that human beings are psychologically androgynous with latent inner energies awaiting development. He called the inner feminine component the anima and the inner masculine the animus. He studied ancient alchemist treatises, which suggested that the biblical story of Adam and Eve was a parable to illustrate that within every man is a Goddess of his creation.

The anima and animus have both positive and negative qualities. For example, a positive anima (divine feminine) is tender, patient, considerate and compassionate. Negative anima (wounded feminine) is vain, moody, bitchy and controlling. A positive animus (divine masculine) is direct, rational, assertive and strong, whereas a negative animus (wounded masculine) is opinionated, mean and argumentative.

These qualities appear not only in the individual but also in the collective. Culturally, our unhealthy masculine shows up as the ego that wants to continue in self-importance and righteousness. He will unconsciously gather evidence, distort, select and provoke others to support a story that perpetuates the wound of his inner feminine. Together, the unhealthy masculine and the wounded feminine enact a vicious cycle of toxic shame that binds us in powerlessness.

These qualities cry out for healing. There is a deep collective calling for wholeness. The only way to break free from this prison is through willingness, compassion and empowered communication. We must gather our personal power and evoke divine support to instigate change and choice.

When the undeveloped aspects of our personality are given conscious attention and are accepted, they begin to heal. Developing this shadow side is necessary to become fulfilled as human beings.

RIGHT-BRAIN, LEFT-BRAIN AND THE CROSS OVER

It has long been established that the right hemisphere of the brain is more creative, intuitive, emotional and subjective thinking and is associated with the feminine whereas the left side of the brain is used for logical, analytical, rational, and objective reasoning and considered more masculine. To further complicate our understanding of gender polarity we must consider that the nervous system crosses over at the base of the skull so that the right hemisphere of the brain is more responsible for controls on the left side of the body and vice versa. Thus the left side of the body is generally associated with the feminine principle, whereas the right side of the body is associated with the masculine.

Further, there's been an explosion of brain research in recent years about the bio/physiological differences between the sexes, which has not been without controversy. One active area of debate is whether the corpus callosum (which connects the left and right cerebral hemispheres and facilitates inter-hemispheric communication) is larger in women, homosexuals and those with gender identity disorder.

Scientists, doctors, psychologists and sociologists have also produced a body of findings about inherent differences between genders which are often debated, suppressed or denied for political reasons. One generally accepted finding is that women have more sensual sensitivity plus are predisposed towards relationship and people whereas men inherently have better eye-hand coordination and are significantly more predisposed towards things and visual stimuli.

"Unless you have resolved your inner fight between the right and the left hemispheres, you will never be able to be peacefully in love—never—because the inner fight will be reflected outside. If you are fighting inside and you are identified with the left hemisphere, the reason hemisphere, and you are continuously trying to overpower the right hemisphere, you will try to do the same with the woman you fall in love with. If the woman is continuously fighting her own reason inside, she will continuously fight the man she loves… If this bridge is strengthened so much that the two minds disappear as two and become one, then integration, then crystallization, arises."
—Osho

A SHAMANIC PERSPECTIVE

A Shaman is a healer who straddles both the spiritual world and the physical world. A true Shaman embodies both the feminine and the masculine, fully. Shamans call on spirit guides to assist them in rituals and in learning the healing arts.

In the landmark book, ***The Invisible Partners***, John Sanford writes about how male Shamans call on female spirit guides who may act like a spirit wife to him. From a Jungian perspective, it's as if the Shaman cultivates a special relationship to the other half of his or her personality to the degree that it becomes a real living presence. In ***Shamanism***, Mircea Eliade says, "A spirit wife says to her Shaman husband, 'I love you, I have no husband now, you will be my husband and I shall be a wife unto you and I shall teach and help you myself.' The Shaman comments, 'She has been coming to me ever since and I slept with her as with my own wife.'"

Baba Dez underwent a deep process of reclaiming his lost inner feminine during his Shamanic training. Here's how Dez tells the story:

"It all started when I realized something was missing in my life. There was a feeling of separation, pain and suffering. As a man in this society, I was scared to feel. That's what the unhealthy masculine does: he denies the importance of the emotions. The emotional body is our connection to the divine feminine. The ego says, I'm fine, I'm great, and if anyone tells me that I'm not, I'm going to fight them to the death, or run away.

"That's what propelled me on my Shamanic reunion with my divine feminine. I began the total integration process with Diamond and River Jameson. I practiced Shamanic trance, dance, screaming, shaking, vibrating, eye blinking and finger tapping and doing different movements that would pull me out of my head and into my belly and body. These practices kept the mind busy with motor tasks so that I could shift out of normal consciousness into a state of expanded consciousness.

"That's how I started to feel everything that I hadn't been willing or able to feel in my life. And perhaps even past lives and/or genetic memory.

"So I gave myself permission to feel everything this culture has conditioned me to avoid, especially rage, anger, sadness and grief. Sometimes memories from my past would come up, and sometimes not. Sometimes I felt and moved through all the pain, suffering, anger and rage of all the women who have been blamed and exterminated for centuries, or the fear and guilt of the perpetrators. Whatever came up I let it move through my physical body, my emotional body and deepen my capacity to witness and feel. These practices started to build my power. Our power is directly linked to our ability to feel. When I finally had built enough power, I could consciously call my divine feminine back. I'd say to my feeling body, 'I'm sorry. I need you. I'm powerless without you.' The more I opened up to my emotional body, the more power I felt. The more power I had, the more she came back to me.

"Initially, the process is difficult and painful. When I was calling back my dispossessed feminine I was terrified. When she first came back she was pissed off. She had to move through layers of stored anger, victimization and resentment for all the years I didn't support her. That's what the wounded feminine looks like: she has the potential to hold a grudge and she has the ability to be relentlessly punishing. But eventually, as I supported her and consistently held space, she started to heal and release. And even though it was hard at first, my nervous system eventually reprogrammed and I started seeing more and more magic and ease. Now it's a joy. I call out loud with increasing power, 'Bring it on, bring it back, and come home to me!' I savor the process and look forward to bringing in the next pieces."

Exercise #15: Inner Marriage

Our late friend and associate, Robert Frey, initiated Kamala Devi into the following Shamanic visualization exercise:

PREPARATION: Take a relaxing bath or shower and dress your body in your favorite garments. Even though you will be doing this exercise alone, you want to prepare as if you were going on a date with your beloved.

METHOD: Now lie down, relax and start to breath into the right side of your body. Notice all the sensations you have on your left side. This is your masculine. Visualize in your mind's eye, or write quickly in your journal. Be honest. And don't judge anything that comes up.

1. What does your inner God look like?
2. What color are his eyes and hair?
3. What is his body type?
4. What kind of things does he say?
5. What is he wearing?
6. What is he holding?
7. What is he passionate about?
8. What kind of lover is he?
9. How does he react to any given situation?
10. How much space can he hold?

Now drop back into meditation. Breathe into the left side of your body. Begin to feel into your feminine. Ask yourself:

1. What does your inner Goddess look like?
2. What color are her eyes and hair?
3. What is her body type?
4. What kind of things does she say?
5. What is she wearing?
6. What is she holding?
7. What is she passionate about?
8. What kind of lover is she?
9. How does she react to any given situation?
10. How safe does she feel?

The intention behind this work is integration, not separation. The first time you do this exercise you may find that it's more challenging to visualize one side or another. You may find that your male is like an angry teenager or your female is shy and coy. As you repeat this practice and continue to do this work, your inner masculine and inner feminine evolve and become healthier.

Once you've personified your inner God and Goddess, you're ready to have them meet each other. Begin to visualize a safe and beautiful place in nature, like a park or beach that is fond and familiar to you. Imagine a romantic picnic spread with all your favorite foods. Notice the details, such as what color the plates are, or the liquid in the glasses, or the flowers in the centerpiece. Invite your inner masculine and feminine to show up to share the meal together.

1. How do your inner God and Goddess feel about each other?
2. What do your inner God and Goddess say to each other?
3. If your inner God were to give a gift to your inner Goddess, what would it be?
4. If your inner Goddess were to give a gift to your inner God, what would it be?
5. What do the gifts symbolize?

When you've concluded the session, you can have them thank each other and say good-bye, for now.

This exercise is meant to open an ongoing dialog between your feeling body, which is your feminine, and your thinking body, which is your masculine. You can revisit this exercise as many times as you like, for as long as you like.

ADDITIONAL NOTES: A lot of people start this work thinking their inner Goddess is going to be sweet and happy and that she's going to look like Cindy Crawford. That may be what their ideal woman looks like, but your inner feminine is not necessarily your ideal. When you do this exercise, the challenge is to hold space for whatever is real.

When Baba Dez first started this work, he found that his inner feminine wouldn't even talk to him. She was so angry for all the years she had been denied that she didn't even want to connect. With patience and willingness, he would listen and hold her until she finally understood that he was not going to ignore or leave her.

Kamala Devi's inner feminine was an enormous Hawaiian mama. She was so fat that she was disabled and she couldn't use her legs. Kamala thought, "Is this really what I look like inside? That can't be me!" Kamala wanted to disown her. But the more Kamala was able to hold space for the truth, the more her inner feminine began to transform. Each cycle became more transformative, and now her inner feminine is a fully expressed Goddess.

HEALTHY MALE AND FEMALE

The healthy masculine does three primary things: he witnesses without judgment, he creates safety and he holds space. It's important to note that all three are qualities of being, not doing. Action comes in response to his feeling. The healthy man stands fully present, with one hand on his heart and the other on his sword. All he wants is to create communion, and for everyone to be in peace. To this end, he is ruthless in his witnessing, creating of safety, and holding of space. According to the Toltec teachings, these are the attributes of a warrior: sweet, cunning, patient, ruthless, responsible and able to respond—not react—as reaction is a trait of unhealthy masculine. So when he's living in a place of harmony he is not distracted.

The healthy feminine feels deeply and vibrates with warm, attractive energy. Like a magnet, she is powerful. She's the power behind his sword. She is what he holds space for and responds to. She is the womb of all creation.

To sum up the relationship between the healthy masculine and the healthy feminine, Baba Dez has often been heard saying, "If every man gazed into the eyes of a woman giving birth, there would be no war."

With the exception of the biological functions involved in birthing a baby, men and women are essentially equal in mental capacity and can fulfill all the same social roles and behaviors. It eventually becomes futile to keep looking for differences between the masculine and feminine. With greater, more integrated awareness we realize that we can't have one without the other. The more enlightened we become, the more we begin to move toward the androgynous ideal. We become so integrated in our being that we're able to choose from the full spectrum of human experience and behavior, rather than being limited to the roles traditionally associated with one particular gender.

When men get in touch with their inner feminine, women will no longer be a mystery to them. They will find it easier to understand their wants and needs. And, of course, when women get in touch with their inner masculine, they will begin to relate better to men. Women who do this work are likely to manifest a man who's in touch with and will honor his feminine. This work helps us all attract and recognize a partner who's really ready to meet us.

ETHERIC LINGAM AND YONI

Have you ever been in the act of making love and experienced an intuitive hit that you know what it would feel like to be the opposite sex? Many women report feeling like they are penetrating their partners. And men sometimes experience what it's like to "take it" from their more active lovers. These energetic experiences are evidence of what we call etheric genitals. Within every woman there is an energetic lingam and testicles; within every man there is an energetic yoni, womb and breasts.

Though these experiences often happen by accident or only in certain circumstances, we can consciously cultivate a relationship with our etheric genitals and enhance our capacity for sexual pleasure and sexual empathy. Owning and activating the etheric lingam and yoni can lead to higher levels of sexual wholeness.

We live in a patriarchal culture that is violently out of balance and we don't want to perpetuate this discrepancy. Therefore, the following practices must be done with caution. There are many powerful career women walking around with a wounded feminine shadow. There are just as many emasculated men who don't have the capacity to hold space. The growth edge for these individuals is to first reclaim and heal their primary gender before integrating the bodies of their inner opposites.

For those who are ready to own their etheric bodies, we caution that these advanced gender-bending practices must be done in moderation and with the intention of integration. It is highly recommended that this work be done under the guidance and facilitation of a sacred sexual healer.

The following exercise is an advanced Shamanic practice that Dez trains Dakas and Dakinis to do. If the seeker is an empowered individual, Dez can shape-shift as friend, brother, son, father, lover, mother, daughter, sister, lesbian lover, or any other type of relationship called for.

Let's say that the seeker is a heterosexual female. Dez might start by sitting down and talking her through the exercise. The intention of this work is to hold space for her to explore the unknown and dormant aspects of herself.

Once she is ready, Dez would disrobe and ask her to lie down with him. He'd then let her explore his naked body as if it were her own. Most women haven't had the safety and permission to explore a man's body without the expectation to serve and pleasure him. So if she goes into the automatic response of trying to take care of him, Dez would stop her and have her take a few deep breaths. Then she would resume her exploration. She might touch his shoulders, his back, his lingam and testicles, paying special attention to the details and subtleties, hairs and muscles, and any other masculine features, like the veins on the backs of his hands. He'd then ask her to breathe this experience into her own body and imagine what it would feel like to be in a man's form.

Then, Dez might lie beside her and have her close her eyes. He'd then lead her through a meditation where she'd visualize facial hair or stubble growing on her face. She'd see her Adam's apple appear, her breasts turning into pectoral muscles, her vulva growing into a scrotum and her yoni morphing into a lingam. Then she'd take time to really feel what it's like to be a man, perhaps even visualizing walking down the street with a lingam between her legs, tucked into her pants. She'd imagine going to the bank or to work, just to get an idea of what it's like to move in the world in masculine form.

She would then be guided to feel what it feels like to deal with men's issues, desires and responsibilities. She may even get in touch with some of her own misogynistic thoughts and see how she, herself, objectifies women. This is a big eye-opener for women. They say, "My God, that's me!" And once she starts owning it, she can start healing and re-educating her inner masculine. Once we've moved through the wounding, there's a sense of integration and we can begin to own our etheric lingam.

Depending on how far she'd like to go, and how comfortable and ready she feels, she might choose to see what it feels like to energetically make love from her inner masculine. Dez would morph into his feminine so that the seeker could learn to initiate, penetrate and truly love. It's all part of expanding the vessel and ending the separation. Most women haven't energetically felt their lingam inside a woman before. Meanwhile, Dez would support her in staying present to what's happening sexually, emotionally, and psychologically, noticing everything that comes up for her inner male.

This exercise creates another embodied reference point. It ends the finger-pointing of that's for men or that's for women. It's all me! It's all my experience. Whether you are a man or a woman, there is no experience that you can't own, feel and know, if you allow it. After doing this work, some women may decide to be more in their feminine the next time they are penetrated because they've learned what a joy it is to penetrate.

It's extraordinary to be on both sides of the human experience. And this is one of the processes through which you become an extraordinary lover. This is how you make love to yourself as you make love with another. There is no separation. You feel what they feel. You then create the foundation to be able to merge in sacred union.

By the end of this ritual, it's likely she'd be in an altered state. To conclude the practice, Dez would morph back into his healthy masculine and she would open her eyes. He'd lean up against the bed to engage in a moment of eye gazing where he could meet her brother to brother. Dez can feel it if you're able to stay in your healthy masculine. He might say, "Welcome home, my brother. I stand shoulder to shoulder with you. Watch my back, and I've got yours. Brother, I will stand in presence, and in power, and I will fight beside you, for her." There is a special type of bond that men have with one another. Most women have no idea what it's like to show up as someone's brother.

After this initiation, women start to show up for themselves in a way they never have before. They stop looking outside themselves for the safety and protection of a man. They stop blaming others for misogyny and mistreatment of women.

This exercise helps both men and women start to understand how important it is to honor and serve their own emotional bodies, the feminine, the Goddess. Men, too, can become aware of their etheric wombs and yonis. As men find their wounded feminine and love her, women everywhere will be healed. As women own their dysfunctional masculine and transform him, men around the world will be healed.

The easiest and most exciting way to do this deep personal growth work is by practicing a masturbation meditation. In the next chapter we not only teach how to make love to your inner God-Goddess, but we detail a whole range of practices to help integrate, heal and manifest more magic in our lives!

A GIFT FROM APHRODITE

An Enlightening Personal Encounter with Baba Dez as Recounted by a Fellow Shaman and Sacred Sexual Healer: Anyaa McAndrew M.A., L.P.C., N.C.C.

It was a weekend in late April and Atlanta was in full glorious bloom. My friend and priestess sister, Cheri, was bringing Dez, a Daka whom she'd been raving about for months, to teach a Tantra seminar on the inner union of feminine and masculine. It was certainly a topic that sparked my interest, and by some miracle it was a weekend I was not facilitating a circle. I had recently felt called to teach Tantra to women, and I felt that this seminar would be important to my own work, so I signed up.

The unlikely group that assembled for the weekend showed up in fits and starts between Friday night and Saturday morning: four young men in their early to late 20s, two young priestesses from my circles, a young Tantrika priestess "wannabe," an older woman who found my website, two high priestesses from other circles—one a Dakini and one an adult entertainer—and a male healer friend of my priestess sister, Cheri. I wondered what I could learn with this mostly beginners group of students, but I was open to let go of self-image and see what might happen.

I found myself on Friday night with an interesting physical symptom. The lymph gland on the left side of my throat had been swelling up for the past three days. I had spent the day before with a group of friends. The ceremony we all co-created together moved us into a huge space of love, and I had simply assumed that the swollen gland was somehow a part of my process. But now, listening to Dez talk about the inner masculine and feminine, I was suspecting something additional. My feminine was in crisis and I was clueless about what she wanted to communicate. Our homework was to self-pleasure as a man, and then as a woman.

I was surprised at my response to Dez. In addition to being an absolutely mesmerizing man, he was speaking in a language and from a place I recognized immediately. The work he had done to come to his truth was the same work I had done on Maui many years ago with the same teachers. Dez had integrated Tantra with the emotional body, a piece that is missing from most Tantra teachings. He also immediately acknowledged me for the work I was doing with the priestess process and making space for the feminine, which IS the emotional body. Explosions of aliveness and remembering brought me to full presence. I was ready for this weekend to unfold!

My night became a healing crisis. I managed the homework and enjoyed the feelings and sensations of holding my testicles and lingam as a male, and my breasts as a female. But the pain in my swollen left gland was getting worse, and aching even when I didn't swallow. I knew if I did not reverse what was happening I would be sick all weekend. I got out my homeopathic remedies and went to work. I slept fitfully and every two hours got up to do another round. I noticed an emotional pattern that unfolded with the remedies that I downed: first self-doubt, then struggle and fight, then influence from outside forces, then impatience, then mental chatter. It read like the pattern of my life in relationships with men! I finally fell into a deep sleep and had a dream. There were two sets of jewels. One set could be worn but the other set had to be wrapped in tissue paper and kept in the back room. I knew intuitively that this was my inner feminine. Part of her was fragile and hidden. She was telling me that it was time for all of her to come out to be worn. The swollen gland softened and the pain dissipated over the next several hours.

Saturday was more intense as we looked at the truth of present-day relationships and their forms: how to create new forms, how to actually become our own inner masculine and feminine, sacred spot work, all blended artfully with honoring mind, emotions, body and heart. My conversations with Dez were sweet and honest. By the end of the day I found myself considering the benefits of doing an individual session with him. The homework was to honor the feminine, preferably in sacred spot work with a partner. Dez asked all of the single men who wanted to work with a partner to stay and be chosen by a single woman, and he himself sat down to be chosen! In a bit of confusion, I walked over to him and asked if he would like to create a private session with me. He seemed happy to oblige. After a brief stop for a change of clothes for him, we headed to my apartment, listening to music and talking nonstop.

We ate some dinner on the swing in front of the little lake in my backyard as I told a little of my story and set intention for our session. We saw a water moccasin swim by and wondered at the symbolism. I spoke of how I was completing the relationship with Jim, my ex-husband, as lover and friend, but that the Goddess has told me to wait for a new lover. I spoke of the swollen gland that was finally beginning to retreat, and what it had meant as a protection for my feminine. I spoke of my father wounds and my history with men. I spoke of wanting a deeper connection with my feminine and how the feminine is my path to enlightenment through my own surrender, my work with women and the Goddess. I heard some of his story and felt our kinship and soul connection. He looked at me through the darkening twilight and told me that he wanted me to know he truly "saw" who I was and how much work I had done and was honored that I had chosen him. My expectancy was building as my attraction to this man was fully confirmed. It had been so long since I truly felt fully met by a man of heart, and I silently thanked the Goddess for her timing!

I could not help but run Dez's astrology chart before we moved on, and quickly saw that his Moon, Sun, Mercury and Venus were exactly the same as my ex-husband, Jim. We moved to the hot tub and more conversation. It was then that I saw Dez reveal more of his own inner woman, as he told stories and shape-shifted back and forth between masculine and feminine. He told me he felt that our meeting was, in part, his own initiation as a priestess with me. I was in awe of this man's inner development. It slowly began to dawn on me that more was at work here in the archetypal realms, and exactly what it all meant was yet to be revealed.

We finally began our sacred spot work/play around 10 pm as we relaxed into an easy erotic open space on my bed. When I unveiled and lay before him, Dez declared me beautiful and began to move his hands on my thighs and belly and breasts in graceful massaging strokes. He chose spicy oil that had been formulated for me by a Hispanic Kansas City Magdalene priestess. We broke into giggles as the oil began to heat up our bodies and genitals! The attraction between us was natural and relaxed and somehow we both knew this was more than a sexual healing session.

Then Dez laid his long lean body behind and next to me and gently moved me into a guided journey back in time before my conception. He spoke of conscious parents preparing for me and calling me in, and a father who was always there for me. These were my Godparents in another dimension, and they loved me unconditionally.

Then asking my permission to enter, Dez moved his long fingers into me. He spoke of his love for the yoni and exclaimed his arousal at my inner landscape. My body responded to his periodic declarations of "Oh Goddess" and I moved as an instrument being played by his skillful hands. I rode the waves of pleasure while he probed the interior territory of my yoni. He made mudra connections with the swollen gland, commanding that what no longer served me was free to go while new space opened for the creation of my dreams. Gradually it became clear that both of us wanted more as we moved into deep kisses and soulful eye gazing. He suckled my breasts and moved his long erect lingam around my belly and the lips of my yoni. It was fully clear to me that I was open to this beautiful God entering every cell of me, but from my own inner masculine. I stopped and asked if this was where he also wanted to go. In one seamless agreement we asked the appropriate questions, decided about protection, and chose that we would not only be lovers, but that he would stay the night with me. I savored every inch of him entering me. Oh Goddess, it had been so long since I enjoyed a man who fit so well! We declared ourselves as soul friends, we laughed and moaned and flowed in delicious ecstasy. At some point he declared that he was seeding my new masculine within me and I understood. The Goddess asked me to wait until this very moment when a man of heart, one who held true space for the feminine by embodying his own feminine, could show up for me.

We loved until very late, and then again in the morning, knowing our time together was short. I reluctantly pulled away to shower and get him to the Tantra workshop on time. He slept a little longer while I enjoyed seeing his beautiful brown body against my white sheets.

I understand why the swollen gland on my left side happened. The feminine on this planet and in my own being had been far from honored, which had resulted in blocked throat chakra. But now, there was a new possibility as the Sacred Masculine stepped forward to cheer on the returning Sacred Feminine, within and without.

Today my heart is smiling as I carry this new seed in my womb. My masculine is standing a little taller and the world seems a little safer for my feminine, who feels she is truly blessed with a precious gift from the Goddess. She feels she can now wear those jewels that have been in the back room.

Six

Masturbation Meditation

Self-pleasuring begins before we're even born. When Kamala Devi was pregnant, she was so curious to know whether she was carrying a girl or a boy that she didn't even consider the old-fashioned option of waiting until the baby's birth. At eighteen weeks she scheduled an ultrasound. The ultrasound technician said the baby's heart looked good, the spine was straight, little finger buds were developing fine, but the baby had wrapped its legs around the umbilical cord and she could not see the sex.

Disappointed, Kamala went home and told all her curious friends and family what happened. Of course, this was the cause of a lot of jokes. Isn't it ironic that a sexual libertine like Kamala Devi would have a baby that is so modest? How proper of the baby to cross its legs and not flash its genitals. We've since heard similar stories from other pregnant friends. As it turns out, it's a common position for little babies to get into right around the time their genitals start developing.

Kamala imagines that if she were in a new little body, it would feel pretty good to rub freshly forming genitals against a squishy umbilical cord. Scientific studies with ultrasounds confirm that self-pleasuring starts while in the womb. In utero babies even get little erections. And when babies are born they feel exquisite sensation all over their bodies, especially in their sex center. All babies naturally explore their ears, noses and toes; why wouldn't they explore the most pleasurable bits of all?

This chapter validates how natural and healthy it is to self-pleasure and details several solo rituals to cultivate a juicy relationship with self.

BUT, YOU'LL GO BLIND!

Cultural shame around masturbation is so deep and complex that it's difficult to untangle. We are shamed in so many ways, some subtle and some gross and systematic. The shaming messages begin as soon as a child starts exploring his or her genitals too much for the parents' comfort. As sensitive young beings, we energetically feel our parents' discomfort. This exploration begins at such a tender formative age that even the gentlest instructions such as "touching ourselves is something we do in private" implies there is something secretive, taboo or not acceptable about masturbation.

Unfortunately, the majority of children are not taught with such considerate cautions. More often the messages sound something like:

- ❀ You'll go blind.
- ❀ That's dirty.
- ❀ Nice boys don't do that.
- ❀ If you play with it too much it will break.
- ❀ You're a disgrace.
- ❀ Only perverts play with themselves.
- ❀ You'll grow hair on your hands.
- ❀ If you break your cherry nobody will marry you.
- ❀ You'll go to hell if you masturbate.
- ❀ Can you think of any others?

Flip through your memory Rolodex and evaluate what you were taught about masturbation. How did your parents or other adult role models feel about it? Do you remember ever talking about it? Did you have to close the bathroom door and hurry? Did you ever get walked in on? Are you comfortable talking about it now?

Renegade spirit Betty Dobson single-handedly elevated masturbation from the ranks of "self-abuse" and "the solitary vice" to a healthy and therapeutic form of self-expression. Known as the Mother of Masturbation, she has helped liberate thousands of mainstream society members by giving them permission to masturbate, penetrate and vibrate themselves. She is a living poster child for the healing power of the orgasm. At age seventy-eight, she doesn't take any pharmaceutical medications and is spunky as ever. She has spent the past thirty years advocating masturbation since her self-published success, **Liberating Masturbation**. The groundbreaking book was later updated and republished as **Sex for One**.

SELF-LOVE

Masturbation is the foundation of all sexual activity. Masturbation connects us with our physical bodies, our emotional currents, fantasies and desires. A healthy masturbation practice allows us to become more aware not only of our physical anatomy, but also our energetic anatomy. We learn about how we function and flow. Masturbation increases self-confidence and intimacy and raises our awareness so that we have more power to share with others.

Self-pleasuring also allows us to satisfy our own sexual needs. Instead of growing desperate, clingy, and dependent on others to fulfill our sexual needs, masturbation affords us self-sufficiency, confidence and choice about when and how and with whom we make love. We do not buy into the illusion that someone else is responsible for our pleasure.

We'd like to make a distinction between selfish, selfless and self-love. Selfish people are primarily concerned with what they want and put their needs first. Considering our own needs and desires isn't selfish unless we do it to the exclusion of other people.

Selfless people are those who put others' needs ahead of their own. Many women are natural caregivers who make people-pleasing an unconscious habit. When we put others' feelings first, we often sacrifice our own needs and desires.

Self-love is when we're able to take care of ourselves first so that we have energy and reserves to serve others. Maintaining this healthy integrated choice is paramount. We practice self-love because we understand that we can only love another to the degree that we love ourselves. We cannot give to others that which we don't have. It's like pouring water from a clay pot—if we don't refill the vessel, it will eventually run dry. Self-pleasuring is one way to relax, replenish, rest and recharge before giving energy to others.

MASTURBATION MEDITATION

What is your authentic experience around self-pleasuring? Have you ever consciously observed your process? When most people get aroused, the sexual energy stimulates a mental salad of fantasy, memory, media images and feelings. They go into habitual movement toward whatever inspires climax. Many men are so intent on clicking through porn that they don't even feel what is going on in their hearts. Many women have a similar fixation with their vibrators. The experience ranges from release to emptiness, and the entire event is quickly forgotten.

What a bummer, because self-pleasuring can be a profound path towards self-realization. Masturbation is a spiritual practice, even more potent than other methods of meditation. When we learn to make love to ourselves, and really engage our bellies and hearts, we are making love to the essence of our beings, which is divine. If you leave the emotions and the heart out of your masturbation practice, divinity is not attained.

Though masturbation meditation can take many forms, we offer the following four basic methods for your enjoyment and self-discovery:

1. Sacred Self Healing.
2. Running Sexual Energy.
3. Inner Union.
4. Manifesting the Ideal Mate.

No two people masturbate the same way. Everyone has different preferences and aversions. Listen to your inner guru and see which meditation method brings you the most pleasure. The best method is the one that works best for you.

We recommend creating time to practice each method several times. Allow yourself to try the different practices at different times, and to change methods as you evolve. Ultimately, if you are sincere in your practice, one of these practices may lead you to realize your God nature. Short of that, you may learn more about yourself, awaken your senses, expand your awareness and/or experience ecstasy!

These masturbation meditations are spiritual practices and require willingness to personally grow. Once you begin this work, you will likely change the way you touch yourself and you will no longer masturbate with the sole intention of releasing. You may even change when, where and how you self-pleasure. Look at how often you normally touch yourself and for how long. If the reality is that it takes five minutes in front of the computer and you do it when you most need a sense of relief, or to vent your sexual frustration, then you will be drastically restructuring your masturbatory schedule. Though we sometimes celebrate the creative use of erotica, vibrators, tools and toys, we suggest you turn them off for now and set them aside. You can come back to them later from an empowered place of choice.

The first step to all of these practices is to create the ambiance. In order to get the most out of the experience, you must feel totally safe and relaxed. Select a room that feels comfortable, turn off your phone, lock the doors, play soft music, light candles or incense, deepen your breath, and if appropriate, say a prayer. Above all, take your time. No particular moment is more important than the next. If you find yourself rushing, stop, take a breath, and remind yourself to rejoice in the journey.

Masturbation meditation is not just a genital-focused exercise, it is a whole being experience. We suggest you start by caressing and exploring your entire body for a minimum of ten minutes before touching your genitals. This includes your own hands, ankles, knees, ears and low back, perhaps even giving your entire body a pass from feet to head. Experiment and see what feels good to you.

Throughout each of these practices, we encourage you to breathe into your pelvic region, to keep the belly soft, to keep the PC muscles active, and not to hold your breath. Nobody is watching or judging you, so allow your body to do whatever it wants. Give yourself over to God. You may discover that your body moves differently during masturbation, or perhaps you make different sounds than you do during sex. You can even exaggerate your movement, breath and sound to stimulate arousal and creativity.

SACRED SELF HEALING

Sacred Self Healing cultivates and utilizes orgasmic energy as a powerful healing aid. Select a specific injury, wound or sexual issue that you'd like to heal. While caressing and stimulating your body, breathe deeply and imagine the energy spreading from your sex center to the belly and the heart. Imagine your heart bursting forward with light or warmth. Send loving intention to whatever place in your body needs the most healing. As you breathe, engage the PC muscles at the top and bottom of the breath for additional potency. At the height of orgasm, direct your energy toward healing your specific wound. After you climax, lay still and breathe healing energy throughout your body. Drink lots of water and rest well on the days you do this practice.

RUNNING SEXUAL ENERGY

Running Sexual Energy helps develop relationship and familiarity with the inner realms and energetic body. Start with a simple breathing exercise such as breathing up and down your spine. Next, breathe into your different power centers, such as the chakras.

Running Sexual Energy can also take the form of an energy circuit to activate a certain polarity. The feminine breath is to inhale through the yoni and exhale through the heart. The masculine breath is to inhale through the heart and exhale through the lingam. Once you have learned to direct the breath through these energy channels, you can infuse the breath with sexual energy and arousal.

For this meditation, we suggest you create an energy circuit in the body and practice circulating sexual energy simultaneously with self-pleasuring. When you are very near orgasm, direct all your sexual energy into the heart and/or spread it around the body. This experience is challenging for a lot of people because the arousal will often dissipate when distributed beyond the genitals. Continue to self-pleasure, almost to the point of arousal again, but do not climax until you have circulated the energy throughout the energetic body at least three times. On the third time you can orgasm, or you may find that an orgasm feels redundant and you'd rather just rest.

By the way, Hartman and Fithian studied multi-orgasmic men and concluded that if a man is able to make love to himself for fifteen to twenty minutes, he's likely to make love to a partner as long as he wants!

Running Sexual Energy is a prerequisite to deeper Tantric rituals such as sex magic, where we masterfully mix breath, arousal and intention. It is also fundamental to the practice of ejaculatory mastery, because instead of ejaculating, you learn to redirect orgasmic energy, or "injaculate."

One of the common questions we get when men are first learning how to run sexual energy is, "What about blue balls?" To which Dez answers, "The energy wants to move. And if it doesn't move out the lingam, it'll build pressure in the testicles and can create a very uncomfortable sensation, sometimes even painful. If we learn to move the energy up and down the spine, it is no longer stuck in the testes."

The best part about the simple and powerful practice is that instead of depleting energy, we often find ourselves generating energy. Running Energy induces an extraordinary state of being so that we can enjoy longer-lasting lovemaking.

INNER UNION

In the preceding chapter, we developed a deeper relationship with the God and Goddess within. Now we will offer a powerful integration exercise to help you learn to make love with your inner aspects.

Our culture teaches us that there is an imaginary something outside of us that somehow is going to fill us. Masturbation is often centered on external imagery such as porn, or fantasy which can take us out of our power and away from our core. All fantasy actually occurs within us. So even when we are fantasizing about Angelina Jolie, we are really making love to ourselves. Like Jungian dream work, every character in the dream is really just an aspect of ourselves. As such, sexual fantasy can be a powerful metaphor to help us commune and communicate with the deepest aspects of ourselves.

The feminine breath is to rock your hips, inhaling as you rock forward and exhaling as you rock back. With the inhale, you draw sexual energy in through the yoni and breathe it up to the heart, with the exhale you exhale it out the heart. You can simultaneously stroke and honor the left side of your body. This breath helps us get into our soft, receptive feminine aspect.

Spend about half an hour getting in touch with how your inner woman feels, smells and moves. Learn to pleasure yourself as she would pleasure you. If you are a woman, be soft and sexy, to entice your inner masculine. If you are a man, listen to who this woman is and what she wants. Ask her what she really wants instead of doing whatever you want to her. Allow yourself to penetrate her divinity.

After at least half an hour, switch into the masculine breath. Rock the pelvis back and forth rhythmically with the breath, inhaling as you draw back and exhaling as you thrust forward. Imagine drawing loving energy into the heart as you inhale. On the exhale, thrust the love out through the lingam. The arousal of the healthy masculine energy may be more penetrative.

If you are a woman, you can connect with and cultivate your inner lingam, or imagine your fingers or wand are his lingam. What does it feel like to be made love to by a healthy man? Allow him to explore and stimulate your body through your own hands. Tune in to where you'd like this man to show up for you. Invite him all the way in, communicate to him, letting him know exactly what you want. Allow yourself to be pleasured by his great sex drive and intensity. If you are a man, step into your warrior power and make love to yourself with cunning, ruthless responsiveness, or whatever masculine aspects are alive in you. Feel how masterful and present the masculine can be.

Initially, this masturbation meditation involves about half an hour of foreplay, half an hour of making love to our inner feminine, and half an hour of making love to our inner masculine. With practice, once you begin to fully embody your divine feminine and healthy masculine, this exercise will not need so much preparation. Stepping into the masculine or feminine becomes second nature and only takes a few breaths or the wink of an eye. You begin to self-pleasure from whatever aspect most nurtures and serves your highest good. This is a profound practice toward total integration, so that we learn to stop looking outside ourselves for our other half.

MANIFESTING THE IDEAL MATE

Many seekers complain, "When I'm with someone I'm attracted to, I don't have any trouble feeling my sexual desire, but when I'm alone, I don't feel anything." This challenge arises because we're conditioned to be dependent on an external source to stimulate our desire. This sets us up for failure because if we can't cultivate our own desire, then we are not going to be desirable. Sexual desire needs to happen within our own temple first, especially if we want to manifest a partner. It can't happen "out there" until something shifts in the inner reality.

> *"The Yogi unites with his Shakti before he unites with his Shakti."*
> — *Ancient Tantric Scripture*

Ask yourself: "What would my life feel like? What would it taste like? What would it smell like if my lover were here?" Start to bring those dreams into your energetic field right now.

What's your day like now, and how would your day be different if you were living with your beloved? We all need to start living our lives now, as if we were with our beloved all the time. So if the desire is "we'd go for a hike," or "we'd have a beautiful sunset dinner, then we'd take a bath and make love," then the answer is to take ourselves by the hand. Go on a beautiful hike, watch a sunset, light some candles, take a bath and take yourself to bed. Pretend that your inner God or Goddess is making love to you when you masturbate. Get into the feeling of what it feels like to be right where you want to be. And then your ideal mate will naturally show up.

Practical wisdom tells us to make a list of qualities, attributes and interests that you seek in a new partner, and then slip it between the mattress and box springs. That's a great start, but this is not something to do once and then forget about. Deep inner work is required for us to project an attractive prayer field. Wherever we put our attention is what we're going to attract. So if we put our attention on what's working in our life and what we have to be grateful for—that's what's going to expand.

SPICE IT UP

As you work with any of the above meditations, it's important to tailor them to your unique style and to let them evolve. If you find yourself falling into habit, getting bored or unconsciousness, it's time to mix up the strokes and techniques. Here are additional suggestions to spice up your experience:

- ❀ Use a full length mirror.
- ❀ Try a blindfold.
- ❀ Vary your strokes.
- ❀ Caress lightly with one hand, touch firmly with the other.

❀ Vary your position.
❀ Use your non-dominant hand.
❀ Add anal penetration.
❀ Add a vibrator or tool or sex toy into the mix.

THE GREAT DEBATE

To vibrate or not to vibrate? That is the question. Many Tantra practitioners believe that vibrators can be habit-forming, which reduces our spiritual capacity to be in choice and liberation. There is also the sci-fi fear that once women start using vibrators, they'll replace the human component with technology and become dependent on machines instead of men.

Joking aside, some Tantrikas argue that vibrators speed up arousal so much and make women orgasm so consistently that women are becoming as goal-oriented as men. Perhaps the biggest point of contention is that vibrators can desensitize a woman's yoni. They've even been called "genital jackhammers." And the consistent and intense vibration on the clit is believed to cause numbness. The yoni is then not able to receive as much pleasure from the tongue, fingertips and lingam.

This raises the question of whether vibrators are creating body armor. This term refers to soft-tissue trauma that can be caused by abusive, forceful, uncomfortable or unconscious sexual experiences. This is contrary to the aims of Tantra, which include becoming more fully alive, aware of subtleties and sensitive to all forms of touch and pleasure.

These are all valid concerns. However, any belief system that manifests as a dogmatic "should" or a strong opinion, such as "women should not use vibrators" or "human contact is better than mechanical pleasure," shows that we're in judgment and not holding space for the potentially sexually liberating power of this tool. This is exactly what it is: a tool. All tools can either be used or abused.

Sacred sexual healers who advocate vibrators argue that they help women explore and stimulate places deep within the yoni that cannot be reached by hand. The consistent and intense vibration on the clit is known to bring many a non-orgasmic woman to climax. Vibrators also enable women to make self-pleasuring more accessible and efficient. They dramatically shorten foreplay and make quickies more satisfying. Vibrators can empower women with a sense of independence and self-reliance. And, of course, they provide pleasure.

There is a similar debate among sacred sexual practitioners as to whether or not it is beneficial for men to ejaculate while self-pleasuring. Some Taoist and Right-Hand Tantra practitioners are staunchly against masturbation. Taoist texts and the Kama Sutra warn, "If a teenage boy begins to masturbate before the age of sixteen his internal organs may become damaged." In contrast, we believe the most unnatural and dangerous practices on the planet involve suppressing the powerful sexuality of a blossoming being.

A WORD ON ADDICTION

With all the negative sex messages, pressure and perversion in our culture, it's surprising that so many people manage to have healthy masturbation practices. Sexual addiction is a compulsive pattern of unconsciously stimulating sexual guilt and shame through behavior we believe we have no control over. Masturbation addiction happens when a great need builds up and it becomes inevitable to climax, and then after the release, there is no lasting sense of well-being, so the cycle will repeat. Sexual addiction can show up as an excessive preoccupation with sex, masturbation or porn.

Addiction is any activity where we feel powerless to choose anything else. If someone is in sexual addiction and doesn't engage in sexual activity, such as self-pleasuring, the nervous system goes into agitation or shock, and the person gets irritable, angry and obsessive. Addiction is what we do instead of feeling our feelings. And it all goes back to the core wound, which may be abandonment, neglect, or rejection, whatever it is that we have not fully felt.

If you have a masturbation or sex addiction, we recommend working with a sacred sexual healer. Even though you can work through it alone, the insight and reflection of a Daka, Dakini or sex therapist will help you realize that you have choice and can help you reclaim the power you need to exercise that choice.

Without conscious awareness, masturbation is just a pleasuring of the body. Though there is nothing wrong with that, when we practice masturbation meditation we can engage the emotions and heart and self-pleasuring becomes so much more. It becomes a way to heal ourselves, build power and create inner communion. When we become masters of our inner relationship we can more fully commune with our partner, community, co-workers and the rest of the world.

In the next chapter we focus on the Tantric orgasm, which makes an important distinction between orgasm and ejaculation. You are about to learn how to take yourself or your lover to the edge, hold it, expand the pleasure, and circulate multi-orgasmic energy before spilling over and surrendering to a greater connection to your higher power.

Seven

The Tantric Orgasm

Have you ever seen rabbits mate? The male mounts the female and moves quickly like a little jackhammer. After about thirty seconds, his eyes roll back and he falls over. He completely collapses. He's down for the count. After several seconds he hops back up, up and away. It doesn't matter if the rabbits are exotic angoras, lop ears or common cottontails— they are just naturally programmed to procreate quickly and are totally defenseless afterward. We marvel over the similarities between these cute fuzzy animals and the stereotypical male.

Have you ever noticed how intimate and truly vulnerable we become after a powerful orgasm? Women feel tender, teary and nostalgic. Artists admit some of their most profound ideas and inspirations come through after orgasm. Unfortunately, there is tremendous social stigma around men being emotional. Men are trained not to cry, feel or reveal their romantic, loving affection.

Mainstream conditioning makes many men revert to their animal nature after sex, which is why they often collapse and snore. Since they don't have much experience keeping their heart open and feeling deeply, it's just easier for men to pass out and go unconscious.

This chapter is dedicated to men who want to learn the difference between animal sex and human sex, and for women who want to experience one of God's greatest gifts to humankind: the Tantric orgasm. We detail traditional Taoist visualizations for ejaculatory choice and offer a powerful new technique to increase presence, arousal and surrender when preserving the seed. We also offer teachings to help expand and multiply your orgasmic potential.

TO CUM OR NOT TO CUM?

Ejaculation control is an ancient Taoist practice also referred to as preserving the chi, retaining the seed, injaculating, conserving the life force, and ejaculatory mastery. We prefer to call it "ejaculatory choice." The subtlety of language is important because control connotes tightness and restriction, whereas choice implies freedom. When we're in choice, we're in power.

In this practice, instead of compulsively ejaculating, you may choose to ejaculate with intention and intimate communication. Once you have mastered this practice, you may make love for as long as you like, and you may choose for ejaculation to serve the highest good.

In ancient Chinese medicine, semen is viewed as life force energy. It is believed that every time a man ejaculates, he drains his vital power. In this belief system, if a man ejaculates too frequently, he suffers detrimental effects to his health. Conversely, cultivating sexual arousal without ejaculation can revitalize the organs and lead to longevity. Legend has it that these practices were originally developed for a Chinese emperor who had two thousand wives and ten thousand concubines. He was able to sexually satisfy all of them as long as he didn't ejaculate every time.

There are many physical and psychological benefits to the Taoist practice of not ejaculating.

EJACULATORY CHOICE

❀ prolongs the duration of the lovemaking session.
❀ cultivates greater desire and connection with your partner.
❀ eliminates the refractory period, so you're ready to make love at any time.
❀ leads to deeper and more intense whole body orgasms.
❀ cultivates the transcendental realms of lovemaking.
❀ can bring your lover to multiple orgasms.
❀ leads to greater overall health and vitality.

❉ increases power, not only in the bedroom, but in career, relationships and life in general.
❉ takes people out of the goal-orientation of climax and allows them to be present for every exquisite moment of lovemaking.
❉ dramatically increases one's capacity for empathy, compassion and intuition.

If lovers start their day with a morning practice and slowly make love without ejaculation, perhaps even holding still and going into meditation while they are still connected, they will continue to feel deeply bonded all day, even when they leave the house for work.

With all these wonderful perks, you may be wondering why everybody doesn't practice ejaculatory choice. Perhaps the biggest reason more men don't do it is: It ain't easy. It takes a tremendous amount of dedication, patience and willingness to rewire deeply rooted neurological patterns.

Further, this practice can stir up intimacy issues and threaten the relationship. We've coached a number of couples that have nearly broken up over it. While learning the technique, many men get tangled in their ego, overly focus on the technical logistics, and disconnect from their female partners. When they accidentally ejaculate, some men go into shame and contraction around failing. Men can get so focused on doing it "right" that they replace their goal of cumming with the goal of not cumming and totally lose site of the greater goal of connecting.

Women complain that they miss their old way of making love, and they feel dissatisfied because they are not able to make their lover cum. Women, in other words, can be just as focused on ejaculation as men. In a recent playshop, one participant shared that when her lover starts circulating his energy it feels like he is pulling away: "There he goes, doing that thing again."

Kamala Devi had a similar experience when she

reunited with a lover who had just returned from studying in Nepal. His Taoist teacher believed that a man gives energy when he ejaculates and a woman takes it. This theory supports why men typically feel relaxed or drained after lovemaking and why some many women get charged and can't go to sleep. When Kamala made love with this man and he controlled his ejaculation, she felt empty and neglected, as if he withheld himself from her. Instead of feeling honored, she felt their lovemaking was a power struggle and her lover was fighting to maintain his life force. In many cases, ancient practices that are designed to help men cultivate power for longevity and enlightenment often have very little to do with connecting with the woman.

When Kamala started circulating sexual energy with Dez, she was pleasantly surprised to discover that even though he practiced ejaculatory choice, she felt included in his process. Dez uses a powerful technique called "Breathing it Down to Mother Earth." It cultivates a deep sense of connection. We will detail this technique after laying a foundation of the more standard Taoist teachings.

EJACULATORY CHOICE

The first step, should you take on the challenge of learning ejaculatory choice, is to commit to the whole journey. This is not a process that can be learned overnight by just reading this chapter, or even in a month; it may take years of practice. Still, it's worth every minute, because it will open the door to whole new realms of sexual ecstasy. During the process, it's important to remember that there is no right or wrong, no mistakes and no failure. It's all just part of the learning. Expect to experience new emotions, ideas, fantasies, fears and frustrations. Be willing to accept whatever shows up as a natural part of the process.

Find a safe space and time for exploring your body with a relaxed and spacious attitude. When first beginning this practice, we recommend stimulating yourself in whatever way creates the most arousal. When you arrive at the edge of your pleasure, just before the point of no return, deepen your breath, slow down and become aware of yourself at that edge. Notice what you're feeling and especially how you're moving.

The first step is simply to increase awareness of your body's response system. Try to ride your edge, without going over it. The trick is that once you have a reference point of your edge, it's likely to expand. If you accidentally pass the point of no return, stay present and enjoy the ride. It's a process of trial and error and it will take multiple sessions. When you go over your edge enough times, you will eventually learn to stop and breathe instead of spilling the seed. Consistent daily practice yields greater progress.

This practice must be cultivated alone before bringing a lover into the mix. Relationship dynamics and the physical needs of another being can be complicated and interfere with the confidence and competence necessary to do this practice properly.

As you start learning, it's important to remember that this practice is completely different from what you're used to doing. There is so much momentum behind your current masturbation habits that it's going to take some serious unlearning. In effect, you're retraining your neurology. Rather than having a certain response to a certain bodily stimuli, you're cultivating a whole new bodily function. There are chemicals that fire in the brain to signal gratification and we have to rewire those neuro-pathways. Not an easy task. But the ability to hold your seed and dance with orgasmic energy is even more delicious.

THE UPWARD DRAW

Normally when we come into a peak state of arousal, the energy moves across and through the fastest possible outlet, the lingam. Because of our biology, the seed naturally moves out, horizontally, to procreate. As we evolve as spiritual beings, we're able to redirect the energy vertically up the spine.

There are many ancient and modern books describing the vertical direction of orgasm. We highly recommend

Healing Love Through the Tao: Cultivating Male Sexual Energy, by Mantak Chia. One simple but profound practice that Chia teaches is called the upward draw. This is a process of visualizing the sexual energy as water flowing and being drawn up the spine through the various energy centers that spin like waterwheels until the energy reaches the base of the skull and replenishes the brain. The objective of this practice is for the ascending masculine energy to meet and mix with the descending feminine energy in the heart center.

Because male energy is ascending in nature, many women feel that men are quick to transcend their heart and body and go into their head or other spiritual realms without staying connected at the heart. This is why we offer our Shamanic approach to forge a deeper sense of connection.

BREATHING IT DOWN TO MOTHER EARTH

Many people, when they move into their sexual excitement, become easily ungrounded or ethereal. This simple visualization roots us into the moment. When your arousal is at 80% you can learn to breathe it down to Mother Earth. Using a simple breathing and visualization technique, you direct your energy downward with your exhalation through the bottom of your lungs, abdomen and tailbone. Simultaneously, you imagine sprouting "energetic roots" or "grounding cords" through the floor, the concrete foundation, the earth's crust and into the molten lava.

Keep it simple in the beginning. With practice, this technique becomes as simple as exhaling to send your roots down to the earth's core. It drops your arousal down a notch. It's like, "OK, breathe." It gives you the opportunity to stop, check in and say, "I am here. I am fully present, planted, grounded, on earth."

When you're grounded and fully present, you can bring the earth right back up your spine and into your sex center. You can even visualize bringing lava up into your tailbone, grounded earth energy up your spine, and you can connect it right back into your pleasure center, which is your second chakra. And then you can take the sacred sexual energy that we call Kundalini, progressively up each chakra in the spine, bringing passion and presence into each energy center. Say to yourself, "I am fully present. I am grounded and I am in my pleasure."

As your arousal expands, you can take its energy up to your third chakra, which is the color yellow. Breathe and become present, grounded in your pleasure and power. Visualizing a radiant sun in your belly, you might choose to continue breathing there for a while, thrusting your hips or stroking yourself while focusing on that place of power.

When you're ready, move your awareness up to the fourth chakra to open your heart center. Expand your lungs and fill your chest with passion and presence, saying to yourself, "I am fully grounded, in my pleasure, powerful and in love." Take as long as you need to feel and enjoy your green heart chakra before moving up. (You can always breathe back down if you get too aroused when ascending to the next chakra.)

When you come to the blue throat chakra, you get in touch with your desire to speak truth. Say to yourself, "I am fully grounded, in my pleasure, powerful, in love and speaking my truth."

The third eye center is indigo and it activates your seeing and knowing. Be sure to pause and breathe and circulate energy here. Say, "I am fully grounded, in my pleasure, powerful, in love, and speaking my truth with clarity."

Take your time to reach the crown chakra, which is violet ascending to pure white. This center connects you to divine consciousness and all that is. Since this center exists beyond the mind, people have a hard time visualizing anything and may get lost.

As you cultivate a deeper connection with divine consciousness, you can breathe this connection back down through the chakras. God touches your seeing and knowing, and you ask to speak divine truth, "Let my love be divinely inspired, my power be a conduit for divine power, my pleasure be God's pleasure." The last step is to anchor divine consciousness into the earth so that we become divine conduits. This is the process through which humanity can begin to manifest heaven on earth.

At any point in the practice if you get lost or become too aroused, simply dip back down to Mother Earth. Another great benefit of this technique is that we become very present with the Divine Mother. This brief practice of breathing down before ascending to the higher energy centers can feel as if we are taking the Goddess with us. It is powerfully pleasurable and is more honoring than other methods men use to delay ejaculation.

Men commonly try to distract themselves from the moment in order to prolong their sexual endurance. When they get to the edge of their excitement, they stop and think about their grandmother or baseball or something that has nothing to do with sex. In their distraction, they lose their erection before starting up again. Distraction may prolong the lovemaking, but it is NOT masterful.

When you hear about Tantric masters who have sex for hours or all day long, what they're doing is raising the Kundalini and surfing the edge of their excitement. Just like surfing, this moving meditation gets you right into the wave. If you hold back you'll miss the wave; if you come in too fast you lose control and the whole wave crashes over you. You want to be right at the edge where it's coming through, coming through, coming through and you ride that edge as long as you can. With skill and practice you'll learn to place your single-pointed attention on the edge of desire, drop in, relax and enjoy the experience.

With ejaculatory choice, there's not only one wave, there's an ongoing ebb and flow. There are also peaks and valleys. As a Tantric lover, you might rest inside your beloved for a while. You may even drift off and traverse the inner realms, a kind of Shamanic daydream, and then come back and start moving and breathing again. And when it becomes intense, you can choose to make it subside again and then rise up again, moving in and out of that sweet territory. You may choose to make love for twenty minutes or twenty hours. You have the power and consciousness to decide when and how and with whom you want to ejaculate.

Exercise #16: Exploring the Edge

BENEFITS: This exercise is for couples desiring to practice ejaculatory choice. The intention is to explore and become intimately acquainted with the man's arousal levels. The focus is one-directional and completely on him. This exercise increases self-awareness, improves communication and cultivates power.

PREPARATION: Allow a minimum of one hour. Create a warm, comfortable space for the session to take place. You may choose to wear lingerie, use certain sheets, play music or employ anything that helps you create the right mood. We suggest you place lubricant and a towel within reach. The man lays naked on a bed, cushion or massage table. The lights must be on enough for you to see the details of his penis. If it makes him more comfortable, you can blindfold him.

METHOD: Your mission is to study your partner's lingam. Ask your partner to verbalize his percentage of arousal. As you begin to gently stroke his flaccid penis, he may start with ten, twenty or thirty percent. When you notice that he is getting chubby and isn't communicating, simply ask, "Where are you now? And now?" Use your hands, fingers, breasts and lips, but not your genitals, to bring him to his edge of arousal and help him circulate energy there. There is no wrong or right way to do this practice. Use your sexual intuition. Choose strokes that pleasure you, as well.

Pay close attention to what his lingam looks like and feels like at different stages. When he gets to 80%, you can invite him to breathe down into Mother Earth with you. Bring the energy back down ten percent before resuming the stimulation. For most men, the last twenty to thirty percent can happen really quickly, sometimes before they even know it. Stop and check in. How much more stimulation can he receive before going over the edge?

When he starts to get excited again, you may ask him to bring the energy up to each chakra, asking him to breathe with you at each center. It is not necessary to know the chakras to practice ejaculatory choice. Use them only if they are already part of your practice.

The intention of this exercise is to enjoy yourself, stay connected and learn about his body. Notice when he gets really close to the edge. Do his balls draw up close to the base of his lingam? Does the head of his penis change its color or shape? What differences do you notice in his penis when he gets excited?

Move your fingers down toward his perineum and ask him to pump his PC muscles. Notice what that feels like when he's 60% aroused versus 80%. Practice applying gentle pressure at his perineum when he is close to ejaculation and ask him to bring his attention back down to the root. Try clenching and holding the PC muscles together. These muscles are responsible for pumping the semen from the testicles into the lingam. Applying pressure there can block the flow and short-circuit the ejaculation. This is a handy trick to use if the session is getting too hot and you want to slow it down. Always remember to ask him for feedback on how it feels.

When he's at a high level of arousal you can also try squeezing the head of his penis and finding out whether this turns him on or takes him back down. What supports him in holding his arousal? And if the arousal becomes so great that it spills over, remind him to enjoy the orgasm. It is all part of the process. Reassure him: "Great work, we learned about where your edge was today."

VARIATIONS: This practice establishes good verbal cues that can be applied to lovemaking, as well. During sex you can ask your lover what percentage he's at. If he tells you he's at 60%, you can continue to undulate and stimulate; if he's at 85%, you can hold still and breathe deeply. This type of communication becomes an art. In time you may become sensitive to his arousal and you may not even need to verbalize.

ADDITIONAL NOTES: There is much to be gained in repeating this exercise. Remember that it is much easier to fall back into unconscious habit than it is to apply these new teachings, so we need to practice, practice and practice. Happily, much of the depth and pleasure occurs in the practice.

Single men who want to have this experience can ask a Daka or Dakini to facilitate this exercise in a session. Couples can also use a sacred sexual healer to coach them through this process. It's very helpful to have someone with experience walk you through it.

EC IN SACRED UNION

After the man has been practicing solo and his partner has been practicing holding space for him, it's time to put the pieces together and see what happens. In order for a couple to realize the potential of these techniques, they must align their intentions. A partner's support and understanding during this process is paramount to the success of the session.

Both parties must ask themselves, "Why do I want to practice ejaculatory choice?" As we mentioned earlier, it's a long, challenging path and if you forget why you're doing it, you're likely to get frustrated and undermine your progress. Ejaculatory choice can take months, even years, to master. We suggest you focus on the long-term goal of staying connected. Even if you miss the act of sharing semen, you'll share the intention of maintaining intimacy.

The next step is to begin an ongoing conversation. It's helpful to communicate in detail all of the philosophy and beliefs that you have around this practice. It's also necessary to discuss your wants. This dialog must happen before the lovemaking begins. It might sound something like: "When we're ready to start moving into intimacy, I want to see how long we can circulate the energy. I may ask you to stop and breathe with me, I may ask you to move slower or faster. I want to support you and stay with you. Are you willing to support me in creating a new experience?"

A lot of times when couples first move into sacred union, one or both parties go into other realms. One party can slip easily into a transcendental place while the other might go into an ego trip. Learn to let go of the need to look good or do it right.

Approach ejaculatory choice as if it were play. It is not a test. It is not a performance. If you get tripped up in your ego, stop and breathe. Remember to stay connected, no matter what comes up. Stop and breathe. Stop and breathe. Stop and breathe. Sacred union is a type of meditation. It can be an awesome opportunity for both partners to practice stillness.

During penetration, if you find yourself too aroused, give yourself permission to pull out. Ideally you stay connected during the entire lovemaking session; however, some men get so turned on inside a woman that the only way to avoid the point of no return is to pull out of her energy field altogether. If you find it's significantly harder to practice ejaculatory choice while inside your partner, you may want to check in with your partner to see whether she is wavering in her support.

Even if your partner is theoretically supportive, most women unconsciously pull on a man's seed. It's biologically wired into them and it's a natural part of procreation. There comes a point when the arousal is so great that many women don't even know they're pulling. Some men describe this experience as his lingam being milked by a suckling calf.

Women who learn to energetically push instead of pull can support a man in holding his seed. Alternatively, at the point before ejaculation, you or your partner may want to reach around and put pressure on his perineum to focus the attention and slow down the process. Deep breathing can also interrupt and slow the ejaculatory reflex.

There's a fine line between being engaged, connected and on purpose and being out of control and in your spontaneous joy. The ideal is to be simultaneously in choice and out of control. You have to experiment and engage in this process many times before it becomes your natural form of expression.

MULTIPLE ORGASMS FOR MEN

Multiple orgasms are orgasms that keep cumming. They are recurring climaxes within a short period of time without dropping below the plateau of sexual arousal. They are like a series of waves crashing on the beach.

In 1948, Kinsey estimated that about twelve percent of males at age twenty experienced multiple ejaculation without the refractory period. In 1978, Robbins and Jensen studied men who reported having three to ten orgasms before ejaculation. These multi-orgasmic men apparently used methods of ejaculation control and reported that the reward for holding off is not so much in the ultimate climax, but in the gratification of the continued sex play.

What exactly is the relationship between prolonging ejaculation and multiple orgasms for men? First we must make the crucial distinction between ejaculation and orgasm, as modern culture conflates the two. Men tend to ejaculate every time they orgasm and orgasm every time they ejaculate. But if men bring themselves back to a memory of masturbating before puberty, they may recall a time of orgasm without ejaculating. Many prepubescent boys play with themselves to the point of orgasm before semen is emitted. One friend reports, "I remember being eight or nine and thinking to myself at the point of orgasm that it felt like air was shooting out, and I thought, I bet when I'm old enough white stuff will shoot out, too." By practicing ejaculatory choice solo, we reclaim the innocent and exciting experience of cumming without ejaculating.

When we experience orgasm independent from emission, it forever enhances our experience of orgasmic energy. The experience is subtle at first. During self-pleasuring, if we are able to sustain a high enough level of arousal for a long enough period of time, we will notice a tingling, a shiver or a fluttering sensation at the base of the penis. Our heart rate will increase and our breathing may change and though it may not feel like the kind of orgasm we're used to, it is still an orgasm. We know it's an orgasm because the anus and

PC muscles contract involuntarily. With awareness, time and practice, multiple orgasms can be cultivated and strengthened, and eventually they will become even more gratifying than the ejaculatory release!

Paradoxically, it can be counterproductive for us to focus on achieving multiple orgasms because goal-orientation does not enhance sexual arousal. We must stay open to the possibility that every moment can be orgasmic. If we take ejaculation out of the equation, we can enjoy the entire ride instead of just the destination.

Along with slowing down and taking the time to self-pleasure, we must also re-learn how to feel. In order to access and circulate orgasmic energy, we have to expand our capacity to experience emotion. A man must learn to be expressive, vulnerable and sensitive to the subtle and ecstatic waves that move through his whole body.

MULTIPLE ORGASMS FOR WOMEN

When it comes to orgasms, women fall into three basic categories:

1. Anorgasmic–Women who never experience orgasm.
2. Orgasmic–Women who experience single orgasm.
3. Multi-Orgasmic–Women who experience multiple orgasms.

Kinsey's research concluded that about thirteen percent of women are capable of having multiple orgasms, while Masters and Johnson believed the percentage was much higher. They found that clitoral stimulation is more likely to induce multiple orgasms than vaginal stimulation, and they noted that each orgasm requires less effort to achieve than the first.

When we have developed the capacity for multiple orgasms, we can choose the degree of sexual arousal that we would like. Some women are fully satisfied during sexual intercourse with a single orgasm. Some women are sexually frustrated and unsatisfied if they haven't orgasmed in a while. Others are quite satisfied with the emotional intimacy during sex and do not need to orgasm at all.

Women sometimes seek the help of sexual healers because they are orgasmic but would like to cultivate multiple orgasms. We believe that unless there is some rare case in which a client is physiologically damaged, every woman is capable of multiple orgasms. Movement, breath, sound, relaxation and safety can all encourage the experience.

Women have to be willing and open to explore. We suggest you start by bringing more conscious awareness when touching and breathing, which can help cultivate the first orgasm. And then at the point of expansion and contraction, let go of the need to regain control. Multi-orgasmic energy is a quality of the divine feminine. Our job is to surrender and be washed in multiple waves of rich experience. Most women and men short-circuit this experience because they are afraid they're going to drown.

There is no specific breathing technique to aid women in experiencing multiple orgasms, only that it's important not to hold your breath. Each woman must map and chart her own territory, starting by noticing what expands her experience and cultivates orgasm in her unique body. It's not just about technical stimulation; it's about presence, safety and surrender.

WHOLE BODY ORGASMS

Both men and women are capable of whole body orgasms, though men tend to suppress this experience more because our culture does not allow them to breathe and sound and move as wildly as it does women.

A conventional orgasm is located or concentrated in the sex center, or genital area. A whole body orgasm happens throughout the entire organism, from the tip of the toes to the top of the head. If you are sensitive to subtle energy, you'll experience the orgasm radiating outward beyond the boundaries of your body. Whole body orgasms can be cultivated with expanding body awareness. By exercising both your physical and emotional body with yoga, movement, breath and meditation, you can reclaim your sensitivity and gift your radiant system with a greater capacity for a broader sensual repertoire.

Tantra teachers Kypris Aster Drake and Steven Jay Gilbert recently discussed orgasm on the **Sex Magic** documentary. Steven says that an orgasm used to be like a little sneeze that came out of his penis. As he started to deepen and cultivate his orgasmic response it became more like ecstatic vibrations that run up his spine. Now he feels these oscillating contractions all over his body, not just in his genitals. Kypris reports that she can orgasm at any of her seven chakras. She has felt them most strongly in her throat.

Steven recalls a recent experience when giving oral sex. Even though he teaches people to be more present during foreplay, he admits that oral sex often becomes about pleasuring the woman. But this time he was really enjoying the sensation of his tongue against the inner lips of her yoni and thought, "Oh, God, this feels really good." Then he got really excited and there was an explosion of excitement in his open mouth. Steven doesn't ever remember hearing about a mouth orgasm before he had one. He didn't even know the body could do that.

Kypris smiles and recounts the first time she had one. It was at a Japanese restaurant. The sushi was so amazing and she tried to maintain her excitement and be restrained so people around her wouldn't know what was going on. "It was like **When Harry Met Sally**, except I wasn't faking!" The camera crew interviewing her wanted to know where the restaurant was and exactly what she ordered.

By expanding our capacity for orgasmic energy, we can move into experiencing more transcendental lovemaking. This is a phenomenon in which we dissolve the boundaries of separation. The ego surrenders to the higher self and moves into a grid of connectivity to the rest of creation. When we expand beyond the physical and psychological limitations of the body, we actually start orgasming with the earth. This practice requires a strong, healthy sense of self so that one can reintegrate afterward. If you know who you are, you can merge your individual desire, passion and sexual energy with more universal forces. You can make love to the trees, rocks, stars and people. The possibilities are infinite.

FEMALE EJACULATION OR AMRITA

Amrita is a Sanskrit word. Like ambrosia, it means nectar of the Gods. In Tantric circles, amrita is the physical manifestation of feminine energy that is fluid. It's more commonly called "squirting" or "gushing" and refers to the clear fluid releases from a woman's urethra during orgasm. The fluid is odorless and sometimes slightly sweet in taste.

Only about ten percent of American women report having experienced amrita. We believe this is because women don't generally have the safety and spaciousness they need to really surrender into this experience. The collective consciousness has been inundated with guilt, shame and fear around being sexual. Negative emotions short-circuit the flow of amrita.

Many women discover their ability to ejaculate later in life. We've conducted an informal poll of teachers and peers and have found that most women who ejaculate are over the age of forty. Many women who have experienced ejaculation also say they can control it or stop it from happening. Others simply lay down the towels and enjoy the wet and wild ride.

Some women have their first experience during an intense orgasm and confuse the healing waters for urine. They feel apologetic that they have peed on their lovers, pointing to guilt, shame and misinformation about basic bodily functions. Some women have even gone to their Western doctors and been treated for incontinence during sex. Amrita is not urine.

Alice Kahn Ladas, Beverly Whipple and John D. Perry, authors of the groundbreaking book ***The G Spot: And Other Discoveries About Human Sexuality***, contributed greatly to our understanding of female ejaculation. They noted that during the first few seconds of stimulating the sacred spot, women often experience a strong sensation that they are going to urinate. The feeling often subsides and becomes sexual enjoyment. The authors theorized that most women, in their interest not to pee on their partners, unconsciously hold back their sexual response. They even postulated that this is why up to twenty-five percent of American females never have orgasms.

In ancient scriptures it is said that when the amrita flows, the earth and all of its inhabitants will be healed. Female ejaculation is a beautiful, healing experience. Many modern Tantrikas celebrate this event. To learn more about it, we recommend an excellent video, ***Liquid Love: The G-Spot Explosion***, starring Leila Swan.

Even ancient Taoist texts talk about three different waters or fluids that are excreted during female orgasm. First there is the vaginal lubrication, which oozes out of the ridges of the vaginal walls. Secondly, there are the fluids that are emitted from the Bartholin's gland during orgasm. Finally, there is the fluid that squirts from the urethra during a female ejaculation. This particular fluid contains a protein-rich formula like seminal fluid, but to date there is still scientific controversy over where this fluid is produced or stored. Various medical theories propose that it is fluid from the female prostate, amniotic fluid or even possibly spinal fluid.

Regardless of what it is, we encourage amrita by creating a safe ritual space for women to let go of guilt, shame and fear. The Sacred Spot ritual in Chapter 10 teaches how to create a space with the necessary trust, safety and excitement to allow the Goddess to burst out and flow forth!

Perhaps the most direct way to expand your orgasmic potential is to seek the support of a sacred sexual healer. In the next chapter we detail what a modern Daka or Dakini is and exactly how they might support you on your path toward fuller, more embodied enlightenment.

Eight
Modern Dakas & Dakinis

Mary Magdalene is the quintessential sacred prostitute. She is the legendary beauty at the Last Supper who anointed Jesus Christ's feet with essential oils and lovingly dried them with her hair. We know she was present at the Crucifixion and that she was the first person Christ appeared to after the Resurrection, but the Bible leaves out many intimate details about their relationship.

Religious and secular scholars debate as to whether she was his favored disciple, his wife, his Tantric lover or a common prostitute whom he saved from a life of sin. The Gospel of Mary is a Gnostic manuscript, rediscovered in Egypt in 1896, that confirms Christ and Magdalene had a passionate relationship and often kissed on the mouth. Mary's training in the sexual arts is often sourced back to the cult of Isis in ancient Egypt. This lends credit to the saying, "Prostitution is the oldest profession in the world."

What we call prostitution today bears no resemblance to the ancient erotic arts. Sacred prostitutes were teachers, healers, poets, muses and respected priestesses then. This is a far cry from the women in mini-skirts standing on street corners because they have no other options. The sacred prostitute is more closely related to the geishas of Japan, the courtesans of Venice and the royal consorts of most ancient Asian empires.

Recently, there has been a resurgence of empowered practitioners who are bringing life and honor back to this ancient healing profession. We are ministers of sacred sexual energy and we call ourselves Dakas and Dakinis. Individuals who come to us are spiritual seekers willing to integrate the sexual shadow into the light of truth. This chapter reveals the essence of our work.

SEEKING A PRO

Most people are afraid to ask for help because it feels shameful or they believe they have failed. If your issue feels irreparable, permanent and incurable, that's all the more reason to reach out. There are many options for people seeking sexual healing. Methods range from ancient to modern, from mainstream to alternative. Some methods are more effective than others, some healers are more experienced than others, and no one solution works for everyone.

We recommend working with a master practitioner who has a vast toolbox of therapies. Psychologist Abraham Maslow reminds us, "If you only have a hammer, you tend to see every problem as a nail."

We also believe that the majority of mainstream methods lack sensual and spiritual integration. Talk therapy, for example, simply has not proven to resolve deep sexual wounds. The more effective therapies include Gestalt, primal therapy, rebirthing breath work, voice dialog, transactional therapy, EMDR, bioenergetics, hypnosis and somatic bodywork. These practices are often adopted and utilized by sacred sexual healers whose services may also include erotic and sensual touch.

Conventional professional regulations restrict sexual intimacy between seeker and provider because of the prevalent belief that when sexual involvement begins, therapy stops. We do not agree that therapists automatically lose objectivity when they begin to move sexual energy with a seeker. In many cases, sexual touch and intimacy are the most direct way to guide someone towards a breakthrough.

Of course, we support the ethical agreements of professionals to protect seekers from possible re-wounding, abuse and trauma. We believe that these agreements create a safe context for deep sexual therapy to take place. We also recognize that strict and general rules can reinforce fear, guilt and shame, so ethics must be communicated and upheld artfully.

State lawmakers, licensing boards and professional associations are working together to mandate bylaws to ensure that professional therapy never includes hands-on healing, sexual touch, sexual conduct or anything that might be construed as sexual harassment. Examples of forbidden behavior include discussing a therapist's sex life; sitting too close; hugging, holding or lying next to the patient; and socializing.

Such strict rules can produce layers of emotional distance, which is counterproductive to the deep trust and intimacy necessary to work on sexual issues. What's more, learning psychological concepts, too much discussing, and too much talking can be a defense, serving to avoid rather than connect and release. Sexual trauma is often somatized in the muscle memory of one's body and staying in the head doesn't always get to the issues.

Working with a sex surrogate, Shaman, Daka or Dakini gives the seeker an embodied experience. Hands-on work may include coaching, modeling, guided journeys and deep experiential teaching. Sacred sexual healers often call in unseen spiritual forces, which can produce miraculous healings and awakenings.

WHO ARE WE?

We are massage therapists, couples counselors, yoga teachers, life coaches, sex educators, erotic escorts, dulas, midwives, doctors, acupuncturists, chiropractors, psychotherapists and other healers who are spiritually minded and know the profound healing benefits of sexual energy and erotic touch.

We know Dakas who are firemen, accountants, scientists, surfers and even gay gynecologists. We know Dakinis who are nurses, clerks, chiropractors and lawyers. We are extraordinary individuals who have a calling to integrate spirituality and sexuality within ourselves in order to pass this wisdom on to others.

Perhaps our greatest attribute is that of our own sexual intuition. Since the lineage of sacred sexual healing has been broken and many of the ancient teachings have been lost, modern Dakas and Dakinis draw their wisdom from energetic sources. Though there has been a revival of apprentice opportunities and priest and priestess training programs, many solo practitioners gather their teachings from dreams, visions, guides and spontaneous downloads. Our gift is cultivated through meditating, remembering dreams, listening to nature, listening to body wisdom and skillful listening to others.

BUT WHAT EXACTLY DO YOU DO?

The work of a Daka or Dakini ranges considerably. New practitioners may have a few standard services that they offer in session. Master practitioners have a kaleidoscope of services. Our mission is to assess where seekers are on their path, to guide them to their growth edge, and to assist them in the embodiment of their divinity.

"But, what exactly do you do?"

It's hard to answer such a simple question because the Daka or Dakini is a Shamanic shape-shifter who does different things with different people at different times. In an intimate conversation, Dez describes the details of what he does:

"To prepare for the session, I move into a grounded place with the intention of creating a safe container to be fully present and witness whomever I'm with.

"So I greet the seeker and together we set the intention to move in ease and safety. We agree to tell the truth, see and be seen, and communicate what we are feeling. We're calling in information, feelings and experiences that can make a difference in the seeker's life and we're willing to be with whatever comes in.

"I ask them, What is it that they desire? What do they want in the session? What do they want in their lives? What is working and not working in life? Biggest dreams? Biggest fears? What are the specific issues they want to work on?

"As they are speaking, I watch how present they are in their bodies and their speech. I watch what's happening for them emotionally and physically. As thoughts, feelings and memories come up, I notice where they're holding back. I look for past trauma, memories and blocks that will outline exactly where we need to go and what needs to be cleared or addressed during the session.

"From here we move into mental, emotional or physical work, whether it is information, touch or energetic release. I often work in different rooms depending on what we're working on. The temple has several healing spaces that are sacred, serene and nurturing. I use the room that creates the most ease. One room is sensual with burgundy and soft throws, while the other room is light, blue, sunny and open. The other is dark, rich and moon-like.

"Sometimes a session will start in a warm-water pool outside, or a tub or the steam room inside. And depending on someone's energy and their desire level, sometimes a session will be fully clothed, partially clothed or naked. The vulnerability of being naked will often bring up more issues to address.

"The seeker might lie next to me. I may hold them as they breathe and come back into their ease. I might have them feel and move through any trauma that is coming up.

"Another important element is supporting people in getting out of their mental prisons so they can connect with the wisdom of their bodies, bellies and hearts. The work often moves them to their core and brings them back home to a deeper sense of self, clarity and ease.

"Sometimes a session will start with a walk in nature where we'll have a conversation and move energy. It's often powerful to be outside and breathe and feel the red rocks or forest.

"Sometimes I shape-shift and hold the seeker as their mother or father or lover; sometimes I embody the sister or brother. I mirror and meet them in whatever way is going to be the most powerful for their healing.

"There's always a place in the session where the seeker feels full. We know we're complete because they feel gratitude and need time to be in solo process. Sometimes I'll stop and ask them, How are you doing? What are you feeling? Is anything else coming in?

"When they feel complete, I like to have them anchor in that state of expansion as a reference point. I ask them to notice the difference between how they feel now and how they felt when they came in. We are bringing in the difference that makes the difference. We acknowledge and thank our allies and the four directions for bringing in whatever needed to come in. We are in gratitude, we celebrate it and we ask for more. YES, I want more conscious awareness, both in session and in life. So the session ends in gratitude.

"Homework will often look like meditation. If a seeker already has a daily meditation or yoga ritual, I often ask that they touch into their deepest feelings as they begin a self-pleasuring ritual. It's so important to take time to feel and develop a relationship with your feelings because that is where your power lives.

"If someone is disconnected from their feelings, they dry up and shut down sexually. You can't shut down your feelings without shutting down your sexiness. If you keep your emotional body alive and awake you become more desirable and juicy.

"Another type of session is when someone shows up in a place of wholeness. Eventually when I continue to work with someone they show up in conscious awareness of their power. So rather than working on wounds and blocks, the session will move into the realm of magic.

"There is also great joy in training and supporting other practitioners. Now we're witnessing each other's divinity. You want to explore, deepen and celebrate your power with someone of equal or greater power. That's how we stretch and grow."

OUR SERVICES
Every sacred sexual healing practitioner offers a unique menu of services. Here are the services offered by sacred sexual ministers and priestesses at the Sedona School of Temple Arts:

Most sessions begin with a verbal intake that honors exactly where you are. We acknowledge the courage and vulnerability it takes to sit before a teacher and surrender to the need for help and change. Many sessions begin with a guided meditation, intention setting, and/or a few minutes of blissful eye gazing. The work is done clothed, partially clothed or nude, depending on your comfort level. Sessions include ambient music, candlelight, organic massage oils and sometimes a shower.

EROTIC MASSAGE, AKA TANTRIC TOUCH
In this ritual the whole body is considered sacred. The erotic touch experience may involve Swedish, Shiatsu, Lomi Lomi, sensual touch, light tender touch and/or deep penetrating touch, depending on your desire and preference. All parts of your being are massaged and honored. The lingam and/or yoni are honored and celebrated with clear communication and sensitivity. In some practices a similar session is known as whole body healing.

SACRED YONI HEALING OR SACRED SPOT MASSAGE
The seed of a woman's sexuality is in her heart. Sacred Yoni Healing uses deep Tantric practices to connect your heart to your yoni's pleasure. There is so much emotion stored in the yoni. Releasing conditioning, emotions, and trauma from the yoni clears the way for a whole new level of sexual experience and power. This healing process is like pulling weeds out of a garden to create space for beautiful flowers to grow. The seeker often journeys through deep Shamanic territory and into self-discovery and revelation.

PROSTATE MASSAGE

The previous ritual is also adapted for men wishing to reclaim, own and activate their etheric yonis. This gentle and slow massage can be performed externally or internally through the anus. There are many health benefits including the prevention of prostate disease. It can also be a pleasurable awakening of the male G-spot which is a spiritual sexual center. It is often combined with lingam massage and can be done to release shame and sexual trauma, and let go of deeply held emotions. Also known as prostate milking.

SACRED LINGAM HEALING OR VAJRA MASSAGE

The lingam or vajra is a sacred and very powerful part of our beings. It heals, loves, penetrates and pleasures. Most men have never been instructed in the art of using it properly or how to honor it as one of the most powerful tools and gifts in the universe. Difficulty in relationship and in getting and maintaining erection can often be healed through loving the lingam. We provide essential information to help clear out limiting and unhealthy conditioning, beliefs and telepathic agreements. You are initiated into a deeper level of what it means to embody the divine masculine and guided to realize your full potential as a lover. This ritual is also adapted for women wishing to reclaim, own and activate their etheric or energetic lingams.

PLEASURING YOUR PARTNER

Pleasuring your partner is about pleasuring yourself. We teach you how to focus on your own pleasure as you explore another's sensuality. Social conditioning has taught us to be a better lover by mastering an array of techniques. Tantra teaches us that the secret to better lovemaking is simply to focus on the pleasure in the moment. Through gazing into each other's eyes, breathing and running energy, the experience of lovemaking can move into an ecstatic realm. The heart and body can open to ejaculatory choice, multiple orgasms, and union with God.

TANTRA COACHING FOR COUPLES

Couples regularly experience conflict or karmic patterns in their relationship, and issues can easily become polarized. When couples seek outside help, they have the opportunity to broaden their perspective. We help untangle core relationship issues and provide tools to overcome future challenges. We also help couples take their sex life to the next level. These sessions provide an opportunity to experience a wide range of Tantric techniques and practices. They also may include a private question and answer session and homework/play assignments.

THE BATH CEREMONY OR BATHING RITUAL

Water is a powerful conduit for emotions and has healing, relaxing and cleansing properties. In this ritual, we prepare an aromatic sensual bath with essential oils, bubbles and/or sea salts. Surrounded by candles, incense, music and flowers, the seeker is bathed, scrubbed, stroked or held, any or all of which can bring back powerful memories of the womb and childhood. This is also a sweet space to discuss any questions or issues you have encountered on your spiritual path.

GOD-GODDESS WORSHIP AND ROLE PLAYING

Though schoolgirls, strippers and secretaries may be popular fantasies to play out with an erotic escort, Tantric role-playing focuses on the God and Goddess. Sacred sexual devotional practices involve honoring and worshiping the divine light within both men and women. These devotional practices take us out of ego and into service. We offer you the opportunity to learn various rituals and rites, and to display devotion through gifts and words and gestures to adore the God-Goddess.

TANTRIC TEMPLE DANCE

The Temple Dance is an erotic version of an ancient Balinese trance dance. It is mesmerizing to watch. The dancer channels movements based on the healing you need. Once your energy is raised, the dancer works with you one-on-one using touch, breath and undulation techniques to move the heightened sexual energy through your entire body. You may feel tingling sensations or waves of orgasmic energy flowing from your head to your toes. This session gets you out of your head and back into your body, paving the way for prolonged arousal and enhanced orgasmic response.

EROTIC TRANCE

During this session, you receive sensual or erotic touch without attachment to the giver. This is not about reciprocation or even connection; it is an opportunity to experience all of the sensations and feelings that arise and circulate in your body. Using breath and movement techniques, we guide you in expanding and circulating the sensations.

The Tibetan Big Draw has been popularized by Joseph Kramer, the father of Sexological Bodywork. This style of erotic trance begins with building up sexual energy through specific breathing practices, after which you squeeze your entire body for as long and as tightly as you comfortably can. The practice gracefully culminates with releasing into a pleasurable trance.

SHAMANIC JOURNEY

Drums, rattles, dance, sound, movement, smells, and/or medicines can be used to induce an altered state of consciousness wherein the seeker can experience other realms. Because these sessions are a non-linear co-creation between seeker, Shaman and spirit guides, they are difficult to describe in ordinary language. You must have a high level of willingness to face your shadow, demons and fears if you're going to experience the transformation that is facilitated through these rituals.

The Sedona Temple is an extraordinary location for doing this work because it is situated amongst the healing red rocks and energy vortexes. Baba Dez and the temple practitioners offer a combination of nature hikes, land journeys and vortex tours.

Dakas and Dakinis call on a super-conscious healing power and then anchor it into their own bodies before transmitting to the body of the seeker. In other words, Dakas and Dakinis use their bodies like vessels for divine energy. They become divining rods, bringing a high voltage of spiritual energy into their systems for the healing and benefit of the seeker. Both seeker and Tantra teacher are likely to experience kriyas during this process. Kriyas are somatic convulsions that accommodate more energy in the system. Kriyas manifest as shivers, tears, sweats, moans, convulsions, uncontrollable laughter, hot flashes, or chills.

SHOPPING FOR TRANSFORMATION

Seeking a Daka or Dakini is a very personal and powerful decision in one's life. It's not simply a matter of finding the person with the right amount of experience and expertise; it's a matter of resonance and chemistry, as well. We could no more tell you who would work for you than we could tell you what your favorite food should be. You may have to sample a few flavors before making your own decision. Before beginning the quest, we encourage you to take a thorough self-inventory and discern what you want from a sacred sexual healer. Here are some questions to help you take inventory.

PERSONAL ASSESSMENT

1. Would you like support for a specific issue or wound, or do you want to learn about sacred sexuality in general?
2. Is it important to you that the Daka or Dakini has years of experience, degrees and/or certificates?
3. Do you want to follow a spiritual path with a lot of lineage, or do you want to blaze your own trail?

4. Do you want someone who can work with you in other healing modalities, or are you interested primarily in sacred sex?
5. Are you looking for someone who can work with you in person, with hands-on sessions, or are you open to working over the phone or online?
6. What about style? Do you want someone who is like a spiritual guru or more like a sexy dominatrix?
7. Are you willing and able to travel for a session?
8. How much time are you willing and able to invest in sacred sexual healing?
9. How much money are you willing to invest in your full sacred sexual expression?
10. Are you interested or inclined to learn about the sacred sexual healing arts as a profession?

Now that you have a sense of what you are looking for, go to www.SedonaTemple.com and browse the available Dakas and Dakinis. You may also Google Daka, Dakini, Tantra or sacred sex in your area. Send e-mail inquiries to these practitioners to check their availability and to ask specific questions about their services. Many sacred sexual healers offer a complimentary telephone assessment.

Variety is the spice of life. Different practitioners will help you learn different perspectives, flavors, styles and teachings. Let go of your expectations; be flexible and curious. If your first experience is less than positive, don't get discouraged. Eventually, you will find the teacher with whom you resonate the most.

If it is within your means, we highly recommend that you arrange to stay for a while and drop into a deeper relationship. Three months is the minimum time it takes to begin an initiation. After about nine months, the teachings have had time to gestate in the body.

Throughout the process of working with a healer or teacher, we recommend that you meditate, pray, ask for guidance and listen to your intuition. Ultimately, it is up to you to be connected with your higher self and to be honest with your prospective teachers.

The next question, of course, is how much does it cost? Most practitioners don't list prices on their websites because their rates depend on the types of sessions, and the sessions depend on the seekers. Individual sessions with a Daka or Dakini last one to three hours, or can be scheduled for an entire weekend. Most experienced practitioners work on a donation basis with a sliding scale of $200-$500 per hour, depending on the seeker's income, the value received and the geographic location. Beginning practitioners often start with a requested donation of approximately $100 per hour.

Fees vary widely depending on the location. The same services offered in Austin, Texas, for $100 per hour may be $350 per hour in New York City. Discounted rates are often available when multiple sessions and/or packages are arranged. Working with two practitioners, such as a priest and priestess, can double the requested donation. The value of working with a Daka and a Dakini at the same time is exponential because it offers the opportunity to witness experienced practices by advanced practitioners of both genders. Some Dakas and Dakinis only take seekers who are willing to enroll in a series because that reflects their willingness and commitment to do the work.

ON BECOMING A SEXUAL HEALER

The call to be a Daka or Dakini is undeniable. At first, it may feel like a mere fantasy. It's fun to imagine communing with spirit guides and transmitting sexual healing to others. And, initially, it's harmless to start playing with this intention while making love.

As you gain confidence, you begin to hunger for more teachings. Workshops, playshops, retreats and conferences are wonderful playgrounds for learning, experimenting and exploring. Equally important are the contacts and community that are formed by participating in these circles.

We recommend working with a private Daka or Dakini in conjunction with the ecstatic group energy. Remember that the healing journey begins with self, so time is needed to understand and work through our own issues before trying to heal anyone else's.

After acquiring knowledge, experience, and tools, you may be comfortable enough to formalize your healing intention into a vocation. Many sacred sexual healers test, hone and refine their practices on family, friends and lovers before choosing this vocation. Upon becoming sacred sexual professionals, Daka-Dakinis often practice for free or for energy exchanges before asking for monetary donations.

> *"And the day came when the risk to remain tight in a bud was more painful than the risk it took to blossom."*
> — *Anais Nin*

When you are serious about becoming a sacred sexual professional, we invite you to join your soul family at the annual ISTA Conference in Sedona in the spring or to find a conference in your area go to the ISTA calendar of conferences online at http//schooloftemplearts.org. This is where you'll get to be in the presence of others who are in their spiritual and sexual power. During the weekend of dancing, lectures, playshops and wisdom circles, we gain the support of powerful allies and associates. The after-party is a great opportunity for people to let down their hair, network, hang out and play! It's splendid to get the reflection of so many individuals who have such a high degree of presence, awareness and skill.

There are also mentors and master teachers who will be happy to help you launch your practice. Baba Dez, Kamala Devi and other teachers at the International School of Temple Arts specialize in training sacred sexual healers and erotic entrepreneurs through private sessions, group trainings and apprenticeship programs.

TRAINING AND MENTORSHIP

Our curriculum includes:

❀ How to create and hold space through sacred ritual and ceremony.

❀ Bio-energetic activation such as movement, breath and sound.

❀ Ethics-appropriate instruction.

❀ Empathic listening to seekers' feelings and needs.

❀ How to handle emotional breakdowns and breakthroughs.

❀ How to shift from sex work or energy work to sacred sexuality sessions.

❀ How to stay safe, personally, publicly and legally.

❀ Advertising, sales, marketing, website awareness, networking, booking, billing and follow-up.

❀ Hands-on demonstrations of any of the practices or procedures described in this book.

Whether you want to become a sacred sexual healer or work with a Daka-Dakini, we can help you clear out negative sexual scripting, step into greater sexual expression, cultivate more personal power, and begin practicing magic.

In the next chapter we will introduce a systematic ritual that can bring your desires into reality. If you are ready to use your sexual energy toward fulfillment in all areas of life, then keep reading to learn the six simple steps to the SHAMAN Method of Sex Magic.

ETHICS: A TOUCHY SUBJECT

As healers and teachers we are potential role models in our communities as such, our behavior and ethics may reflect upon the entire field of sacred sex. And yet, we defy formulas and stereotypes because we are such a diverse group of creative individuals with a vast range of teachings that span the full spectrum of work from the sacred to the profane.

Even though Tantra Yoga may have existed for thousands of years around the world in aboriginal cultures without any regulatory body, modern society demands that these teachings be handled with a whole new level of consciousness. In recent years, the most hotly debated topic at the ISTA conferences has been whether we should form an organizing body to standardize a code of ethics which defines acceptable professional practices. This is an especially sensitive subject because of the controversial nature of working with erotic energy, sexual wounding and deep matters of the heart.

In America today, psychologists, medical doctors, lawyers and teachers have legal restrictions on dating and/or having sex with student or clients because of the psychological power differential. In many states if you are in one of these roles of power and have consensual sex with a student or client, it may result in losing your license, being disbarred or an automatic felony with years in prison. 100% of the responsibility falls on the shoulders of those in authority. Supporters of this law maintain that no meaningful consent can be given by the client/student because they have come to the relationship relinquishing power, and thus are vulnerable and not responsible. This position is also held by many gurus and spiritual teachers, ministers, yoga instructors and tantra lineage holders.

And yet, by design, tantra is nonconventional, and there is a vast body of teachings that cannot be transmitted through talk therapy. Even if a practitioner never dates or has sex with their seekers, there are multiple layers of ethical issues that inevitably arise in this work.

Baba Dez and Kamala revere every practitioner as self-sovereign and every individual has the absolute right to choose what level of sexual conduct is appropriate and desirable for themselves from moment to moment within the context of their relationship agreements. We maintain that it is the responsibility of each priest or priestess to do the necessary research and personal growth work to set their own code of ethics as long as it is congruent with their values, experience and skill. During our mentorship programs and teacher trainings we support practitioners to inquire deeply into their own capacity and evaluate more subtle complexities of this work.

When Kamala Devi practices sacred sexual healing in California, she does not have intercourse with her seekers, but does allow herself to fall deeply (sometimes madly) in love. During the initial session, she gives the seeker permission to surrender to their own heart. Because this intense experience can be disorienting, she preconditions her seekers by making an important distinction between personal love and transpersonal, unconditional love. Kamala puts her clients' physical, mental, emotional, and spiritual wellbeing as her top priority. She makes it is clear that she is not wanting anything from them, and holds them as responsible for their own feelings. She also teaches them how to cut cords and reclaim their own connection to source after the session.

It is important not only to set clear guidelines and agreements but to express them to our seekers at the beginning of their session so that we don't run unconscious assumptions, violate our client's expectations, and re-wound those who've come to us for healing.

If sexual and erotic energy of a personal nature arise between Sacred Sexual healer and seeker the practitioner may chose to:

* ❀ Set their feelings aside and focus strictly on a professional relationship with their seeker.
* ❀ Refer the seeker to another professional.
* ❀ Stop seeing them professionally and begin a personal relationship.
* ❀ Some lineages suggest a specific period during which the practitioner will not teach or see the seeker. At the end of that period, they are free to see the person in any consensual capacity. (3-6 months is a common period.)
* ❀ Discuss it openly and honestly co-creating a consensual relationship with that seeker where they resume healing concurrent with romantic relations.

❋ Seek moderation from a third party.

With time, experience and personal capacity, our ethical practices will evolve. Regardless of all our variances, most practitioners agree with established clinical health care providers to hold the following two directives as sacred bottom lines: nonmaleficence (do no harm) and beneficence (do your work in the highest good).

SACRED UNION: ETHICS, BLOCKS AND BOUNDARIES

Baba Dez wrote the following open letter in response to an international Tantra Festival which decided not to host him as a teacher because they don't allow their teachers to engage in Sexual Union with students.

Dear Ones,

Recently there has been some polarization in the global community around the issue of engaging in sexuality with those who are in a student or client role with a sex educator.

I receive a good deal of feedback in this area as I am one of those who chooses such a path. I make no apology for doing so and see it as an essential part of what it is I am teaching and have to offer. We all celebrate the Tantric path as one of Love, Power, and Freedom. Part of the embodiment of this path is seeing and then healing where I as a teacher can go along with the limiting cultural beliefs, judgments, and telepathic agreements around sex, love, and healing. Leaving these elements unhealed can perpetuate more separation, fear, and disempowerment in the world.

I hear and understand the reasons many people have difficulty with teachers and healers engaging physically with students and clients. There is probably no other area of human interaction that carries more shadow as well as potential for major healing and energetic shift. Everyone has some wounds in this area and some much more than others if they have suffered direct abuse. People are often in a very vulnerable place when they seek to work with sexual issues and students also have the power dynamic when they are engaging with someone who is in a teaching role. I do get this. And I choose to do what I do out beyond the rules and ethics that belong in the realm of therapy and classrooms. Love, consciousness, mediation, insight, breath, energy and body work all have their place in healing. So does sexuality including the physical act of Sacred Union. Evaluating the seeker/student and using guidelines and protocols, I let love choose who and how I connect with someone while at the same time being as conscious of how our interaction may affect and trigger response. It is tricky territory to traverse and requires years of training.

I do respect and understand why educators set boundaries and have rules about their interactions with students. However, to judge or ban all teachers that might teach and share Sacred Union with students creates a block where a healthy boundary is needed. Let's deal with teachers on an individual basis of professionalism, track record, and integrity. Professionally, if you fail in discernment around what and who it is appropriate to share with, or, if you are using this work to fill your personal sexual appetite, you will pay a high price for your lack of integrity and impeccability.

I ask to be treated with the same respect for my work which I undertake consciously, motivated by love and with the intention of providing a space for radical healing and empowerment. I have worked with thousands of clients over many years and had the privilege of being the difference that mattered at crucial times in their lives, often precisely because I was prepared to move the way love called me to move.

I also attract a good deal of controversy as a result and need to discern between projection and any elements of my own shadow. It is a razor's edge out beyond the safe boundaries of mainstream ethics. This is why I walk it impeccably and continue my own growth by engaging in review with trusted peers and allies.

Yes, it is appropriate that schools and/or groups take action and confront teachers, guides, and practitioners that leave a trail of traumatized, manipulated, and abused students and clients behind them.

To address ingrained puritanical Victorian values, let us start to heal our own shadows and projected issues of fear, guilt, and shame around sexual intimacy and Sacred Union. Then Sacred Union can be one of the beautiful ways to address wounding, deep healing, activation, initiation, and celebration.

For thousands of years Temple teachers, priests and priestesses have been sharing Sacred Union with seekers, and students. It is one of the beautiful ways to addresses wounding, deep healing, activation, initiation, and celebration. Where do we send these people that are wanting to learn and celebrate the sacrament of sacred union with a teacher of this art? Until I can tell them where else they can go … I cannot ignore them or dismiss them.

Each of us who work in this field know we are one in essence and driven forward in our work by the same dynamic and evolutionary force of love. I join with you there even while celebrating the necessity of sometimes walking alone into the fire of my unique contribution.

We are One Heart
Living In Love, Power, and Freedom,

Baba Dez

Red

Nine
The SHAMAN Method of Sex Magic

A mainstream movie recently made headlines because of its willingness to reveal "the secret" of manifestation. Though masterfully marketed, the wisdom in this movie is nothing new. Nor does it contain the most guarded of secrets.

Modern-day success leaders such as Jack Canfield, Wayne Dyer, Abraham-Hicks, Tony Robbins and Brian Tracy offer powerful teachings about how to direct our desire and intensify our emotion in order to achieve any goal. What these teachers don't speak to, however, is how sexual desire works like rocket fuel, launching us toward the reality of our wildest dreams. This is the secret beyond the secret: sex magic.

Simply stated, sex magic is a spiritual practice that uses sexual desire to manifest tangible effects in the physical world. One of the most powerful experiences that we have as human beings is orgasmic energy, and if we can pair it with intent, then we can direct the most powerful manifesting force available on earth.

Sex magic is nothing new, either. It has a long, shadowy history that includes pagan fertility rites, the cult of Isis, the worship of Ishtar, Hellenistic Gnostics, Shamanic sex trance, the Great Rite of Wicca, the Order of the Knights Templar, Masonic magicians, and Aleister Crowley's Ordo Templi Orientis. Many of these teachings are oral traditions given only to the highest initiates. Documentation of these procedures and practices is murky and often shrouded in secrecy.

We dedicate this chapter to sincere seekers who want to learn a practical method to fuse their sexual arousal with conscious intention in order to more fully manifest their life's purpose.

DOES IT REALLY WORK?

In a recent playshop called "Sex Magic for Manifestation," Dez shared examples of things he has manifested using sex magic:

"Through the years, I've experimented to see what works, and what works even better. I started playing with sex magic rituals in Hawaii in the '80s. It was clear that the more I stepped into my emotional body, the more powerful the manifestations became. I practiced building my power, feeling my desire, circulating my sexual energy during my three years of celibacy. When I was up in the mountains in Colorado, I got really clear that I was ready for a partner, I was ready to engage with society and I was ready to contribute to the planet.

"And so, I asked spirit to show me how. That's when I manifested my partner, Heidi. And I manifested a small loan, my first tablet press and a supplement company called Pure Planet Products. Over the next ten years Heidi and I manifested a multi-million dollar company that contributed to greater health on the planet.

"Once we had the company up and running, we would spend our mornings working from home. We'd wake up and work from our morning office, which was our bedroom. We'd handle emails, hang out, do business over the phone, have breakfast, and make love—a lot.

"We'd sometimes practice sex magic for our business. I remember one particular morning we talked to our sales manager about how we needed a new distributor in Germany. So, Heidi and I discussed it. We began to envision exactly the kind of distributor we wanted to manifest, we talked about what it would feel like to work with them, and we took that clarity, intention and desire and merged it with our lovemaking, which amplified and intensified it. Then we created an energetic field and visualized sending it across the ocean to the European continent and landing in Germany. It was an invitation for this distributor to come co-create with us.

"I can't remember the exact timing, but within 24 hours, we were in our afternoon office, which was at the manufacturing facility, and I remember the phone ringing and the secretary saying, 'so-and-so is calling from Germany,' and I remember looking over at Heidi, and she looked at me, and we just smiled, thinking, Here comes our distributor.

"He turned out to be an amazing person. He had tremendous success with our product in Germany. He came and hung out with us, and we went to Germany and hung out with his family. And even though we sold the company in 2001, he's still a distributor and a really good friend.

"The interesting thing about our meeting is that he just happened to be looking for some green food products to represent when he found a bottle of Pure Planet product on a shelf in New York. He picked up the bottle, saw a phone number on the back, and called to ask if we needed a distributor in Germany. That's when I thought, holy shit, this stuff works."

THE FIRST INGREDIENT IS INTENTION

Intention is the art of directing our conscious awareness. We focus our power into a single statement of your desire, the way a Tai Chi master directs his energy into the tip of his sword. Intention is core to sex magic.

Intention starts with learning how to make a clear declaration of our desire, goal or vision. Usually, intentions are personal and are stated in the present tense. Some examples are:

❀ I intend to release the illusion of separation between my beloved and myself.
❀ I release all that which no longer serves me and bring in that which does.
❀ I intend to earn $100,000 in annual income in exchange for environmentally friendly work.
❀ I am co-creating a *New York Times* best-selling book.
❀ I am manifesting a new set of tires for my truck.

You may be tempted to energize all of the above, but we have found that this work is most effective when you prioritize and activate one intention at a time. Further, we have found that our desires are made more powerful when aligned with the intentions of others. To align our intentions with our beloved's, or our family's or our community's has a magnetizing effect.

As experienced practitioners and teachers of sex magic, we are compelled to caution novices: "Be careful what you ask for! This practice produces results. Make sure you really want something as compared to intending something that sounds good, or something that someone else wants for you." We often ask a battery of questions to ensure that a seeker's goals are consistent with what the mind, body, belly and heart really want.

In order not to misuse this powerful practice, we insist that you begin by formulating an intention in the highest good of all. For example, "May this or something better manifest for the highest good of all." Or, "If it aligns with divine will, then make it so." Wise practitioners of sex magic will take a vow to do no harm.

Instead of being a mental exercise, this is an embodied emotional process. Get in touch with what your goal would smell like, taste like, feel like, sound like and look like when it is realized.

This is not always a calculated verbal exercise— allow for non-logical wisdom to come in via your senses. An occurrence in one of our playshops illustrates this point. While participants were taking time to envision what they wanted to create, one man reported having a body epiphany, wherein he kinesthetically experienced exactly what it would feel like to attract the kind of clients he wanted. Amazingly, the woman he was talking with didn't know he was a carpenter, but she reported smelling sawdust!

Now ask yourself: "What do I most want to manifest?" Stay open. Allow the intention to come into your entire being.

THE SHAMAN METHOD OF SEX MAGIC

During our recent trip to Hawaii, Dez and Kamala hiked up the side of a volcano through a tropical rainforest to the house of a hermit who lives off the grid. We sat at his altar eating fresh passion fruit and drinking hot tea as rain splattered the windows. We warmed ourselves in front of a wood-burning stove and spontaneously downloaded the six-step process called The SHAMAN Method of Sex Magic.

Each letter represents a step in the practice. Every step is important to have a successful ritual. It is up to you, however, to tailor each step and select the specifics that are authentic to your unique nature and style.

S IS FOR SACRED RITUAL

Consciously or unconsciously, we are involved in rituals all the time. Brushing our teeth is a ritual that we do on a daily basis. But a ritual is not sacred unless we charge the experience with presence and intention. The more present we are, the more Spirit can show up and meet us with magic.

The SHAMAN Method of Sex Magic elevates the act of lovemaking from the realm of the ordinary to the realm of the extraordinary. We suggest the following special preparations to create the sacred sexual ritual.

Invite a partner—or yourself—to participate in the ritual and schedule it. Putting a date on your calendar will set synchronicity into motion. The more you plan for a ritual, the more powerful it becomes. If you're creating the ritual around a special event, the planning may take months.

There is a special window of time between when the ritual is planned and when it actually happens. Use this time to commune with the universe and notice the signs that are offered by your guides and allies, both seen and unseen. Notice how the magic starts to come in.

On the day of the ritual, we suggest eating live foods to keep your physical energy vital. Bathe and massage your body with oils or lotion. Wear your best scents, jewelry, lingerie and/or fine garments. Be sure to keep your energetic reserves high. The magic is not as powerful when your body is tired or your immune system is run down. We're bioelectric beings, so you may have to replenish your energy during the ritual, as well, by drinking something with electrolytes or snacking on nourishing fruits and nuts.

Select a sacred place to hold the ritual. There are many places on the earth that are charged with the intention of beings that have been there for hundreds, even thousands, of years. You can practice this ritual in nature, in a temple, or in your bedroom. Many Tantrikas consider their beds their altars.

Preparing the space where the ritual is going to be held and cleaning the space is part of the process of preparing for the ritual. You can do an energetic sweep, or a thorough scrub down.

Next, you may gather sacred artifacts to use for the ritual. A sacred artifact is any aesthetic object that symbolizes the meaning of what you want to manifest. In the selection process, you naturally engage the creative hemisphere of the brain that calls forth more super-conscious energy.

Sacred artifacts may include a photograph, a painting, candles, flowers, ribbons, shells, grains, foods, leaves, incense, feathers, water, wine, blood, milk, hair or Tarot cards. We also recommend that you incorporate objects that delight the senses, such as music, incense, oils, fur, feather boas, or soft silk robes or sheets.

In preparation for the ritual, we recommend writing down your intention on a piece of paper or an index card. You may also engage your creative side and draw a picture and decorate it with color and crayons. It's OK if the image is abstract or looks like a stick figure. The point is to have fun while creating it.

Take a few deep breaths and infuse each sacred artifact with your intention while placing them in the space where you'll be practicing the ritual. Select a prayer or invocation for opening the ritual, asking for guidance and protection. Choose something that has relevance to your personal spirituality. For example, you may call in the four directions, your guides, gurus, ascendant masters, Gods, Goddesses, higher power, or whatever raises your vibration.

H IS FOR HOLDING SPACE

After you've set up a beautiful environment and called forth your allies you can begin to create a safe container by holding space. In this step of the practice, you and your partner sit facing each other, getting as close as you can for comfortable conversation. Drop into deep belly breaths and feel what is going on in your body, belly and heart.

You may start with eye gazing as long as it feels relaxed and natural. Gaze into your partner's eyes and experience the beauty and power of the God or Goddess who is willing to co-create a new reality with you. This is the time to drop into your God self. Ask your ego to step aside for the duration of the ritual.

Holding Space is an aspect of the divine masculine within each of us. We like to think of it as giving ourselves total permission to be in the fullness of your experience. If you have to laugh, laugh. If you feel like crying, cry. It's all accepted as part of the process. There are four aspects to creating a safe container that allows for the full spectrum of experience:

1. Intentions
2. Boundaries
3. Fears
4. Desires & dreams

We recommend holding space for each other using a dyad method. In this method, you take turns actively listening, then actively communicating. When you are the listening partner, listen without judgment or intent to fix or change your partner.

Let's take a moment to explore each component:

1. Intentions. The ritual begins with a declaration of the purpose. When you and your partner are completely present, you can read your intentions to each other. You can verbally reflect them back to each other or simply conclude by saying, Thank you, Aho! Amen! or So it is!

2. Boundaries. Next, you and your partner check in with each other about the logistics of the lovemaking ritual. This helps you stay in a place of ease and presence during the lovemaking instead of being distracted by technical questions. This is the time to share boundaries and discuss physical logistics, which may sound like:

❀ How long did we schedule the babysitter?
❀ I have to put in a birth control device before we start.
❀ I bought a new type of condom.
❀ What type of lube would you like to use?
❀ Can we get under the blankets until we warm up?
❀ I hurt my back.
❀ I'm on my period.

3. Fears. Notice what fears arise as a result of declaring your desire. This is the part of the ritual where you voice all of the concerns, doubts, limiting beliefs, and roadblocks that challenge your intention.

Many of us have been conditioned by Hollywood to have certain concepts of what it means to be romantic or spiritual. We may see the candles and incense and flower petals and think the ritual is supposed to be pretty and perfect. However, this is the time to move beyond romantic fantasy and honor that we all have fears. Tantra is about both the dark and the light. Truth is beyond concepts of what is perfect or what is flawed. From this perspective, fear, sadness, anger and grief are beautiful, as well. The good, the bad, and the ugly…it's all welcome here.

If you proceed into sacred union without expressing and releasing your negative thoughts, emotions and beliefs, the results of this ritual will be compromised. At best you'll get no results; at worst, you'll manifest your unspoken demons. What is unconscious, ignored or denied will show up powerfully in your manifestation to be reclaimed, owned and healed.

For example, if you are afraid that you're not going to be able to get aroused, then you speak that truth. The mind will say, "I'm supposed to feel sexy and turned on right now, maybe

I should fake it." As we learn to hold space, we give ourselves a green light to be real and truthful. Accepting what is present creates space for our feelings to flow and shift.

Be ruthless in your attempts to simply listen without getting drawn into the other's drama or story. This powerful practice of supporting and hearing the other holds the space for your partner to safely express, to be received, and to release charge. When your partner has completed, simply say, "Thank you for sharing." Then switch roles. Now you, the active listening partner, become the active communicating partner, sharing whatever concerns, doubts and fears you have about manifesting your intention.

This is also the time to check in with each other's energy levels and determine how long the session is going to be. Whether you spend an hour doing the ritual or five hours, it's important to be on the same page so that neither person is wondering, "When is this going to end?" The idea is to create an agreement field with as many specifics as necessary so that you both can surrender completely. It's important to honor your body's needs. It's hard to focus on magic when you are hungry, cold or have to pee!

4. Desires and dreams. This is where you expand your excitement around materializing your desires. Take turns articulating how it will look, feel, smell, taste and sound to realize your vision and to live with the manifestation of this new reality. Again, conclude this segment by saying, Aho!

Once all of these aspects have been voiced, we continue to hold space nonverbally throughout the rest of the ritual.

A IS FOR ACTIVATING THE KUNDALINI

Now comes the fun part. We get to run passionate energy up and down our spines and circulate it from the tops of our heads to the tips of our toes. Activating Kundalini energy magnetizes our intention to move into sacred union and manifest as sacred sexual beings.

In the Shamanic tradition, we use breath, sound, movement and visualization to activate the Kundalini and awaken the divine feminine. While there is a wide range of exercises for activating the Kundalini, we always start by grounding and connecting with Mother Earth. This is important because we want to bring our manifestations to earth to support our dreams and desires.

During this portion of the ritual, you and your partner sit in Yab-Yum, or stand or lay together facing each other. Ideally, you face your partner and not only breathe together, but actually share breath. This practice varies greatly depending on your comfort, experience and training.

Do whatever last minute preparations you need, such as slipping off your underwear or preparing the contraception. Now, move gracefully out of your mind and into your body.

Focus on your root chakra and begin deepening your breath. Begin to undulate your pelvis and/or pump your PC muscles with each exhalation. Simultaneously, visualize sprouting roots from the base of your trunk and sending grounding cords into the earth. Send your breath all the way to the bottom of your belly, and then to your spine, through the floorboards, through the crust of the earth, through to the molten center of the earth.

Continue moving and breathing and move the Kundalini up to the next chakra. Together, chant the bija mantra associated with each chakra three times. Bija means seed in Sanskrit. Encoded within the mantra there is a sacred geometry or a spiritual gateway. You don't have to understand how it works in order for it to work.

Exercise #17: Chakra Sounding

BENEFITS: Activating the ancient wisdom within the Chakra system.

METHOD: Simply focus on one specific chakra and chant the corresponding sound. During this practice, continue breathing and moving. Be true to yourself and stay open to spontaneous guidance. Breathe your intention into each of these power centers.

During this practice, continue breathing and moving. Be true to yourself and stay open to spontaneous guidance. Breathe your intention into each of these power centers.

1. Focus on your root chakra, connect with Mother Earth, see the color RED and chant LAM three times.
2. Focus on your sex center, connect with your passion, see the color ORANGE and chant VAM three times.
3. Focus on your solar plexus, connect with your power, see the color YELLOW and chant RAM three times.
4. Focus on your heart, connect with your experience of love, see the color GREEN and chant YAM three times.
5. Focus on your throat, connect with your truth, see the color BLUE and chant HAM three times.
6. Focus on your third eye, connect with your seeing & knowing, see the color INDIGO and chant OM three times.
7. Focus on your crown, connect with the divine, see the color VIOLET and chant AUM three times.

Once you reach the seventh chakra you can call the divine back into your body or spread orgasmic energy throughout with spontaneous breath and sound.

When the Kundalini moves, let her move you. This means, if you feel yourself wanting to take off your clothes, take off your clothes. Listen to your body. She may want to move closer, hold tighter, or sound louder. Whatever she wants, let her have her way. You don't have to do it right. It's OK if you skip something or miss something. She is very generous and forgiving. You honor her by being in the moment and staying in the flow.

More experienced practitioners may also visualize the color and experience the dynamic qualities of each chakra. Advanced practitioners may apply specific practices from their initiation.

VARIATION: More experienced practitioners may also visualize the color and experience the dynamic qualities of each yantra. Advanced practitioners may apply specific practices from their initiation.

VARIATION METHOD: Simply focus on one specific chakra in your body and chant the corresponding sound.

MMMM IS FOR MERGING

Are you ready for more magic?

After we've activated all the chakras, we can merge with self, merge with each other, and merge with Spirit. So, if everyone is open and juicy and ready, we merge the lingam into union with the yoni, the jewel within the lotus. The lightning bolt strikes the sacred temple!

This is where we fully engage and share ourselves with another being. We support, reflect and bounce our energy off each other, building and heightening desire as we go. We cultivate our orgasmic energy, infuse it with our intention, supercharge it with our will, and offer it up to the collective or the cosmos.

As orgasmic energy builds, we use the breath to draw it up the central channel to the third eye. When the orgasmic energy comes to a peak, we affirm our intention in the mind's eye, holding a single-pointed visualization of our desire between our eyebrows. We see ourselves in the ideal situation, playing it on the screen of our mind's eye. Visualize the picture as vividly as possible. It can be a still image or a short movie.

Use your breath to augment the orgasmic energy and mix it with feelings of accomplishment. Pleasure will start to cascade in. Inject it with your intention and offer this vision to the universe by breathing the image up through your crown chakra. Use your breath to direct your orgasmic energy into the cosmos.

When your intention is sincere, your being is in alignment, and it is divine will, you can rest assured: what you desire is on its way!

A IS FOR AFFIRMING

At the conclusion of the lovemaking session, after circulating the orgasmic energy through numerous peaks and valleys, we can slowly transition into a cuddle or a spooning position. Just lay still, holding each other in whatever position is most comfortable. The afterglow of sex is one of the sweetest, most powerful points of the sex magic ritual because our hearts are open and we are expanded.

Our conscious awareness has been sent out into the universe and now it's time to gather it in again. To do this, we suggest taking three deep, slow breaths into each chakra, progressively from the crown to the root, and bringing the energy back down to the earth.

7. Take three breaths at the crown and bring your connection to the divine back into your body.
6. Take three breaths at the third eye and invite Spirit to realign with your seeing and knowing.
5. Take three breaths at the throat and ask for divine help in speaking your truth.
4. Take three breaths at the heart and ask the divine to touch your ability to love.
3. Take three breaths at the power center and ask God's will to touch your will.
2. Take three breaths at the sex center and ask for the divine to touch your passion and guide your creativity.
1. Take three breaths at the root chakra and pray for spirit's help to bring heaven onto earth.

After a few deep breaths down into the feet and toes, while you are still in blissful Shamanic trance, reaffirm your intention by re-reading it or re-declaring it out loud. This makes it a declaration to each other and to the universe. And so it is!

Now we rest in the wisdom that we have created. Ah, yes. We are present to receive our manifestations. We receive this magic and we vibrate it in. But before we close this sacred ritual, there's one more step.

N IS FOR NEXT STEP

Next Step is the last piece of The SHAMAN Method of Sex Magic. Here, we consider the next empowered action we are going to take to bring our dream a step closer to tangible, actual reality.

So you have created a rip in the cosmos and your intention has been heard. Now it's your job to bring this intention down. Ask yourself, "What is something I can do this week, or even today, no matter how small as long as it is doable?"

A lot of so-called spiritual people do a lot of ecstatic practices on the energetic realm, but they don't know how to anchor their work on earth. They may be blissed out, but they are often lost or looking for what to do next. They are usually the people we hear complaining, "Why don't I have abundance?" It's like the old adage, "You can pray for the winning lotto numbers, but at some point you've got to buy the ticket." Or as Julia Cameron, author of ***The Artist's Way***, has been known to say, "You can pray to catch the bus, but if you see it going down the street, you better run like hell to catch it!"

In this last phase of the sex magic ritual, you and your beloved honor one another by holding each other accountable for taking action. Each of you deepens your breath and asks, "What is the next step that I can do, this week, to help manifest my dreams?" And then stay open to receive.

Even though you are going to commit to a tangible, doable step, it doesn't have to come directly from your logical mind. Stay open to receive wisdom from your belly and heart. You have just undergone a cosmic activation of your energetic circuitry, so if you shut down your intuition, then the entire ritual is for naught. Your mind might rush in and try to tell you what to do, but that's just your conditioning. Stay open and wait until your gut or your intuition speaks. You have to feel it.

It might come in loud and clear, it might be a garbled whisper.

If nothing comes in, ask Spirit for divine inspiration. "Spirit, how can I serve you?" And wait for your operating instructions. When you're ready, communicate whatever comes in. "So, here's what I'm going to do… What are you going to do?" Create agreements and support each other in keeping those agreements.

Perhaps Spirit wants you to turn on your phone so that you receive the call that says come pick up your check. Or, maybe it's time for you to:

❀ Make that phone call…
❀ Write that proposal…
❀ Clean out your studio…
❀ Get your art supplies out of storage…
❀ Send a newsletter…
❀ Build that webpage.

It may be the one thing that you most want to avoid! The next step is to figure out one step that takes you a little closer to your dreams. Just one. We move forward one step at a time. Sathya Sai Baba says that if we take one step toward God, God takes twenty steps toward us.

Next Steps are like operating instructions from the divine. Stay open to receiving them, even after you have closed the ritual. Next Steps may come in fifteen minutes or days after the ritual, so keep the lines of communication open and alive. Talk to your partner or support network about thoughts and ideas and inspiration that keep coming in. Sometimes even our friends and family members will get a piece of information or inspiration as a result of our rituals. So notice the omens that happen around you, and listen to the unexpected ways the universe might speak to you. Stay open to receive.

We end the ritual now with a closing prayer. Sit up tall and take a few breaths. Feel your gratitude.

Acknowledge yourself, your beloved, your gurus and your guides. "We thank God-Goddess for being with us, we thank our allies seen and unseen. We praise, honor and send glory to the four directions, the spirit above, the spirit below, and the spirit within. Thank you for helping manifest our dreams and desires. We hereby recommit to reclaiming our power, to opening and receiving more teachings, and to serving ourselves, each other and the planet."

Aho!

VARIATIONS

These four variations of the primary ritual may be embellished or combined. You may do them as simply or as elaborately as you desire. There is no right or wrong way to do them. However, if you are not enjoying yourself, you can't be doing it right!

The four variations of the primary ritual are:

1. Autoerotic Sex Magic.
2. Homoerotic Sex Magic.
3. Non-Literal Sex Magic.
4. Group Sex Magic.

1. Autoerotic Sex Magic. Sex magic starts right here, within the individual. We do not need an external partner to experience the power of this practice. When we practice alone, it still is beneficial to speak the intentions out loud, if possible. And during the holding space segment, still take the time to check in with yourself.

Check your calendar to see what your other responsibilities, obligations and commitments are. Allow enough time so that you don't feel rushed.

To create safe boundaries, you may want to shut doors, close window coverings, check where the neighbors are, and ask for your family's cooperation.

Other preparations include turning off your phone, checking your batteries or getting an extension cord for your vibrator.

It is valuable to have a special journal for this practice. Many magicians call their journal "Book of Shadows." This is where we write down our revelations, our next steps and any other inspiration that comes through.

2. Homoerotic Sex Magic. This practice is in no way specific to heterosexuals. The practice is nearly identical for two men, two women, bisexuals, or any couple that wants to practice creative gender-bending.

When it comes to the segment on merging, penetration can be naturally practiced between men, simultaneously between women with fingers or toys, or it doesn't have to happen at all. The "jewel in the lotus" and the "lightning bolt" are merely metaphors. We can just as easily unite with our etheric yoni and lingam.

3. Non-Literal Sex Magic. Sometimes, due to health challenges or other reasons, practitioners do not want to engage in actual sex. Sex magic rituals do not have to play out in three-dimensional space to be effective.

In ancient Tantric scripture, many rituals were intended to be metaphors for meditations. Advanced practices often involve elaborate visualizations instead of tangible accoutrements. Practitioners of Right-hand practices, such as ***Dakshinachara***, and other white Tantric sects do not engage in explicit carnal practices. They visualize the entire ritual, from lighting the candles on the altar to merging in sacred union. Nor are all intentions spoken out loud; they simply can be intended.

Non-Literal Practice is for more experienced and advanced practitioners. If you are just beginning on this path, we suggest you start with the literal practice of lighting candles and stepping through each of the six steps because it will help you create a reference point in your nervous system. Then, as you progress, you will be able to evoke the same feelings, sounds, smells and tastes.

Each time we plan and prepare for the sex magic ritual, we get better at playing it out in our mind's eye. Then, when we practice the ritual in real time, we feel it more richly in the different levels of our being. Hours and days down the road, it still vibrates in us and we remember.

If for some reason your health does not permit you to do the full practice, consider participating in as much as you physically can. As already mentioned, this practice does not require nudity or penetration and can be equally effective with soft penetration.

4. Group Sex Magic. This is an advanced and powerful practice. Because of the alchemical mixing of different seekers and their intentions, both the rewards and the shadow can be seriously magnified.

Group sex magic can also be complex to coordinate, and carefully selecting the right combination of adepts is key to the success of the ritual. People should be screened for their experience in both ritual and group sex. Other considerations include gender, sexual orientation, intention, emotional maturity and schedule availability.

The next question is whether the event will be facilitated by a priest/priestess or spontaneously run by group dynamics. We have found that group sex rituals are often better when facilitated in the beginning, and then opened to spontaneous flow. We have also found that ending with a closing circle makes for a better group sex experience.

WHY ISN'T IT WORKING?

The reason that the main title of this book is *Sacred Sexual Healing* and is subtitled *The SHAMAN Method of Sex Magic* is because wholeness is the prerequisite to magic. There is a tremendous amount of work that we need to do to be sexually whole before we have enough power available to fully manifest magic.

We can rebuild our power and move deeper into the place of magic by committing to our sacred sexual healing journey. The work never stops—it just gets juicier. We've found that the more power we build, the more magnetic and attractive we become.

If you are practicing and not getting results, it's time to seek a sacred sexual healer who can help you work through whatever needs to be shifted, help you cultivate presence and power, and help you get the results you desire.

As Dakas and Dakinis, the vast majority of seekers that we work with are consciously or unconsciously leaking their power and energy through emotional wounds, sexual wounds and self-esteem issues. The practices described in the early chapters of this book help us heal the spaces and the places where we leak power.

In the beginning, the work may feel overwhelming, but God-Goddess never gives us more than we can handle. Take it slowly, and if it's too much work, ask spirit to slow down or bring it on more gently. We suggest praying, "Divine, please support me in bringing back all that needs to be brought back so I can heal in a gentle, playful, more empowered way."

Early on, when we were first experimenting with sex magic, we realized that the results were only as clear as our conscious awareness. When we have unconscious energetic stuff going on, like denial of our shadow, incongruent emotions and other energetic misalignments, it affects not only our ability to manifest, but also the quality of the actual manifestation. Anything that is not aligned with pure intention undermines and short-circuits our ability to attract.

Kamala Devi tells the following story to illustrate how the effectiveness of sex magic can be compromised when we are not congruent in our mind, body, bellies and hearts:

"My beloved, Michael, and I had been practicing a sex magic ritual that had its roots in Huna from Hawaii. We mixed our sexual energy with a powerful incantation and the Ha Rite. Together, we overcame health issues and manifested other relationships, exotic travel and much spiritual evolution.

"We were living in a small surf shack in La Jolla at the time, and we talked about buying a house. The market was good and we had the means, so it seemed a very logical investment. We started using sex magic to visualize a meeting space for the community, with hardwood floors, a fireplace, a hot tub, and a great room to teach workshops.

"We found the perfect house, put a bid in right away, put our deposit down, and signed an eight-page contract. There were a number of unexpected delays. Over a two-year span, we

183

went through legal meditation, we had issues with unethical lawyers, and we even went to court.

"This was very confronting to my ego, because while training to become a Bliss Coach, I had studied the law of attraction with all the top success teachers and speakers. Michael and I were such great manifestors. I couldn't believe we didn't already have the house.

"So we went into deep reflection to ask why this house kept delaying. When we were really honest, what we came up with was that we were not emotionally ready to own land. Both Michael and I are travelers. We had been to China and India and all over Southeast Asia, and deep in our hearts, we romanticized the life of gypsies. California real estate might be a wise financial investment, but in the pit of my stomach it felt like shackles to the emotional body. That's why we were coming up against so many blocks! For sex magic to work, we have to be congruent with mind, body, heart and belly.

"So we shifted our focus to conscious conception and started doing sex magic to usher a new soul onto the planet. When I was about six months pregnant, my chemistry and my hormones shifted and my womb said, 'I'm ready for that house.' California real estate started sounding pretty good to a first-time pregnant mama.

"As soon as it was no longer just my head, and my womb said my baby wants to be born here, then, of course, we got the house. After such a big delay, it actually happened quite suddenly, which is perfect because we had enough time to move in, detoxify the house and prepare for a beautiful home birth!"

CONSCIOUS CONCEPTION

Many children are conceived and brought onto this planet even though they are not consciously intended. In most cases, there is little intention behind impregnation; it's just something that happens. The focus is often on physical pleasure and then it's, "Oh my God, I'm pregnant!"

Modern parents "trying" to conceive rarely stop and

consider, "What's behind this? What's the agenda? Is it because that's what we're supposed to do? Is it what Mother wanted or what the church recommends? Is it just something people have done forever, or is it a biological imperative?"

Bringing a new human into the world can be done as consciously as the sex magic ritual, creating a ritual with a prayer behind it and a deep love of wanting to contribute to humanity. When we have developed our own divinity as sacred sexual beings, then that consciousness can lead to conceiving and anchoring more of that divinity here on earth in the form of bringing in a divine being. We can only do so if we are grounded in our own divinity.

The beauty of The SHAMAN Method of Sex Magic is that it has a cumulative effect. Each time you practice, you reclaim more power and reap greater results. It is a spiritual snowball, gathering might, potential and momentum.

We bestow many blessings on those of you who are ready to partake in these practices. We pray that your wildest dreams come true. And once you are practiced and masterful at manifesting, we invite you to join us in manifesting peace on earth!

In the next chapter, we transmit a detailed initiation into a transformative sexual healing ritual that awakens, honors, and reclaims the sacred spot within both men and women. Read on to attain the key to unlock the ultimate gateway to your sexual awakening.

Ten

The Sacred Spot Ritual

In the sunny hills of La Jolla, Tantra teacher Francoise Ginsberg leads an all-day workshop to initiate people into the art of touch, including Sacred Spot Massage. Kamala recalls dancing with her beloved under a large eucalyptus tree in the backyard before the men and women are separated into different rooms to receive the deeper teachings of this intricate ritual.

The women then created a "red tent" atmosphere, sitting in a circle, passing a talking stick and sharing intimate details about their relationship to their G-spot. On this day, several women spoke about having religious experiences the first time this secret button was pushed. Others described discomfort, as if they were going to pee whenever their partner touched it. Some women wept and admitted that it hurt, describing it "like broken glass" when anything rubbed against it. One amazing 78-year-old woman listened in complete awe. Astonished, she shared that in all her years, she had never heard of the G-spot. Kamala is still in touch with this beautiful woman, who now sings, "I can't wait to reincarnate so that I can start to play with my G-spot earlier."

Sacred spot refers to both the G-spot in women and the prostate in men. This chapter discusses both. We integrate insights from Taoist, Tantric and Western medical techniques to heal, map and awaken the sacred spot. Original downloads from Baba Dez's twenty-two years of experience practicing Sacred Spot Massage are offered here in writing, for the first time.

G IS FOR GODDESS SPOT

Though the sacred spot was written about in ancient sacred sexual scriptures, the G-spot is named after the German gynecologist, Ernst Gräfenberg, who hypothesized its existence in 1950. In Tantric circles, the "G" affectionately stands for "Goddess."

The G-spot can be located two or three inches inside the yoni. It rests just behind the front (anterior) wall of the yoni, right behind the pubic bone, above the bladder, and is about the size of a lima bean. Its precise location varies between women because the anatomy of the yoni is so varied. It has a distinct texture unlike the rest of the soft tissue. When stimulated, the spongy G-spot hardens, swells and creates a heightened internal sensation that leads to a deeper experience of orgasm. Despite all of the direct experiences reported by a vast number of women, there is still scientific debate as to whether or not the G-spot actually exists.

Early explorations of the body lead women to discover their clit more easily because it is external and sensitive to even the slightest touch. The clit is wonderful for stimulating orgasm, and many women cannot reach orgasm without it. There's a certain familiarity and reliance that women have on their clit, whereas it may take years before a woman actually discovers and establishes a relationship with her G-spot.

Some lucky women discover their G-spot during their first experiences with penetration. The sacred spot is not only embedded deep into the vaginal wall, but often requires firm pressure in the non-stimulated state. Some women's G-spots aren't easily accessed, and when they are, the experiences range wildly.

BODY ARMORING

There is a big buzz about the G-spot in pop culture, books, videos and radio shows. Many sex educators feel the G-spot is overly hyped. One issue that is rarely discussed with the attention it deserves is sacred spot stagnation. The soft tissue of the yoni's inner sanctum is sensitive toward any type

188

of trauma, whether physical, emotional, mental or spiritual. In the absence of love and nurturance, yoni muscles harden, energy stagnates and body armoring forms. Tears that have not been cried out loud are silently frozen in the sex center.

Body armoring is another term for stuck emotion and unprocessed trauma that is lodged in the body. Just as chronic tension can show up in our backs, and stress shows up in our neck and shoulder muscles, women somatize stress and trauma in their yonis, which can show up as numbness or pain during sex and often more serious disease and dysfunction.

To heal these wounds, Daka-Dakinis provide sacred sexual healing rituals to reactivate and reclaim the yoni. For some women, Sacred Spot Massage is uncomfortable or painful; for others, it can be ecstatic. This ritual is designed specifically to peel away the layers of armoring. Each time this ritual is repeated, it dissolves another layer of armoring. The more women do this work, the more vital and alive their entire sexual system becomes. Eventually the ritual evolves from healing to magic.

The sacred spot rituals that we're about to describe can be practiced by men or women, at home, between lovers, friends or spouses. While we will give you intricate details and precise instructions for how to perform the ritual, if neither of you have done this work with a professional, we highly encourage you to do so. A Daka and/or a Dakini can artfully guide you through new and tender territory while holding space for the full spectrum of emotions that may get stirred.

PRESENCE, PRESENCE, PRESENCE

Let us start by meditating on the profundity of what we are about to do. Not only is the yoni an amazing and exquisite anatomical creation, it symbolizes the source of all creation, the mother's womb, from where we all came. We are grateful to all the vulnerable and devoted women who offer their bodies to experience more healing and pleasure on this planet. The intention behind this ritual is to invite the divine feminine to more fully embody this unique and magnificent temple so that we may honor her.

Before beginning, take time to contemplate, crystallize and communicate your individual intentions. This ritual is not only about healing, it also is about reclaiming, remembering, activating, celebrating, and sourcing power for divine service.

The G-spot massage may be performed by a woman or a man. In order to manifest your intentions, both parties need to make the following preparations.

The first step is to communicate and create agreements about the logistics of when, where and how long the ritual will be. One-and-a-half hours are the minimum amount of time needed for the ritual; three hours is the suggested maximum. (Amongst advanced practitioners, there may be timeless rituals that go on for days.) We have found that keeping the ritual to three hours or less ensures that the ritual is potent and on purpose, and that both giver and receiver are able to maintain their vital energy. Not to mention, when this session takes more than three hours, it becomes a challenge to schedule it regularly. There is great value in doing this work in frequent repetition.

The next logistical preparations involve securing clean sheets, towels, pillows, blankets, lubricant, massage oil and, optionally, rubber gloves. Energetic preparations include anything that is mood-setting or that stimulates the senses, such as music, candles, flowers, incense and special lighting.

Pay close attention to how warm the space is. Having different layers of sheets and blankets helps, as does lighting a fire or using a space heater so that the ritual may be practiced in the nude. It's vital for the receiver to feel warm and relaxed if she is going to open fully.

Cleanliness is a big concern. Both giver and receiver may shower or take a ritualized bath before the massage begins. Be sure hands are washed, fingernails are trimmed and rings are removed.

Some of the more challenging preparations entail letting go of expectations and getting present. We may want the ritual to be ecstatic, but it may just as likely be excruciating. Instead of getting turned on, receivers can get turned off. Their mind wanders, they get bored and they go into resistance. When we arrive at the ritual with all kinds of preconceived notions, we undermine our ability to stay in the moment. Healing happens in presence. Be prepared for anything to show up at any moment.

There is only one hard and fast rule: sexual intercourse is not a part of this ritual. The yoni is to be honored without any expectation or obligation to return the favor. This practice is strictly one-directional.

The ritual begins with sitting and facing each other. Straighten the spine, deepen the breath, and sit quietly for a few minutes. Feel yourself becoming more present.

If it feels right, the giver may call in the four directions and their allies. We also recommend saying a special prayer for guidance and support from awakened and ascended Dakinis, such as Vajrayogini or Mataji. These aspects of the divine mother are powerful allies to guide us through the ritual.

Once the invocation is complete, the giver may ask, "What is alive in you? What is dormant in you?" And then hold space for whatever comes up. This is the time to communicate intentions, boundaries and fears. Clear communication helps establish trust and rapport.

Certified sexological body workers often access the receiver's ability to express boundaries. "On a scale of one to ten, how comfortable are you at expressing your boundaries?" If the receiver says one or two, the giver might spend the session working on boundaries and save the sacred spot work for another day.

It is vital for the receiver to feel safe enough to voice when something is uncomfortable, and to ask for what she wants. We suggest discussing and agreeing on clear and simple verbal cues, like yes, no, hold, more pressure, less pressure, slower or stop.

"Hold" is an important word because it allows the receiver to breathe into whatever she is feeling in the moment. It is important for the giver to be patient while holding. Being careful not to change the pressure or the angle, the giver may simply breathe.

When given the instruction "stop," the giver gently stops. Stopping abruptly or pulling out can activate the receiver's abandonment story. The receiver, on the other hand, doesn't have to say stop every time something is uncomfortable or hurts. Releasing pain from the yoni sometimes means we have to feel it, be with it, and move through it.

In Sacred Spot Massage, we are opening a channel for the receiver to move through whatever is necessary for the highest healing to come through. When Tantra teacher Cynthia Lamborn practiced this ritual on a British television special, she instructed the receiver to free-associate. Even when the receiver has a memory of drinking chocolate milk as a kid, such random associations may have healing value. So, no matter what comes up, bring it on!

People assume that Sacred Spot Massage is about activating orgasmic energy or discovering new pleasure places in the yoni. Although those may be great side benefits, the primary benefit to this ritual is that the receiver feels she is being met with presence, perhaps for the first time in her life.

PREPARING THE BODY TEMPLE

We now move into massage, which may take place on a bed, on pillows or on a massage table.

The receiver starts by breathing deeply and relaxing. The giver starts by gathering the energy and getting clear guidance. The giver, when ready, warms his or her hands and places one hand on the receiver's heart, one hand on the receiver's abdomen. The intention is to send loving energy into the yoni and up toward the heart.

If experienced at running energy, the receiver can create a complementary link by breathing in through the yoni and out through the heart. She may continue this breathing as long as it feels comfortable. The breathing practices and energy circuits are not necessary, but they help keep the practice clean and the intent pure.

The giver begins with gentle, slow caresses on the body, facilitating comfort and arousal by massaging thighs, hips and the solar plexus. It will be awhile before the yoni is touched, though the giver may massage the inner thighs and perhaps even vibrate the yoni with an external abdominal massage. The giver holds the space neutrally with no expectation of arousal.

When the receiver becomes aroused, an energetic prayer field generates around the pelvis, inviting and welcoming deeper touch. We encourage the receiver to undulate and sound on her exhalation.

Typically, it is recommended that the whole body is honored for up to forty-five minutes before shifting the focus onto the yoni. We don't like to prescribe time frames because when we are truly in the moment, it may take minutes or it may take months to enter the yoni. Depending on the rapport and readiness of the receiver, we take as long as needed before moving toward the sex center.

Baba Dez often practices vibrational, psychic or energetic work inside the yoni before he physically enters. He may rest his hand on the yoni, and with her permission, enter inside her energetically. The feminine emotional body is very sensitive to subtle and vibrational presence.

Throughout the practice, the giver is monitoring the receiver's face. Ideally, eyes are open and both parties are completely present. If the receiver closes her eyes, the giver still watches for nonverbal signs of tension such as wincing, clenching the jaw or crinkling the forehead.

SACRED YONI HEALING

Tibetan Buddhists have a tradition of circumambulating sacred objects. This is where pilgrims walk with reverence and devotion clockwise around sacred mountains, stupas and great teachers. Even the Buddha was circumambulated. Thus, before the giver enters the sacred temple of the yoni, he or she must circumambulate around the temple doors.

Begin by slowly massaging around the outer labia and visualize energy running from the yoni to the heart. Use

193

forefingers and thumb to gently pinch, squeeze and roll all the way around the outer lips. You may check in about the pressure. When pressing and massaging, be careful not to pinch the urethra or the clit, as these areas are sensitive.

When the receiver is ready to transition to inner massage, the giver can press his or her palm against the opening and breathe into the heart circuit. This creates a beautiful opportunity for the flow of nonverbal communication. If the yoni is ready to be entered, she'll press herself against the giver's hand. Then, permission is asked to enter. "May I enter?"

If you are the receiver, this is a time to be really clear and honest about what your body, belly and heart desire. If your desires are conflicted, then don't permit entry. You have 100% permission to say no or to delay entry. "Actually, I'd prefer if you stay on the outer labia for a while longer."

When you do wish to be entered, say, "Yes, I'm ready for you to enter me." Nodding your head or saying "Mmmm" doesn't carry the same power as making eye contact and saying, "Yes, I'm inviting you in." This is a profound opportunity to heal our communication around sex.

YONI MAPPING

Yoni Mapping is a process of going around the inside of the yoni and reactivating all the stagnant points. Using lubrication, the giver slowly slides one or two fingers in up to a couple of knuckles, depending on size and comfort. After locating the sacred spot, the giver gently bends his or her fingers toward the pubic bone. Then, simply hold and breathe.

An analog clock is an ideal metaphor for beginners learning Yoni Mapping. The sacred spot is located at twelve o'clock, the perineum is six o'clock. The process is to start at twelve o'clock, hold, breathe and check in on how it feels. Then the giver can gently, slowly shift his or her fingers to one o'clock. Hold, breathe and check in. And so on, progressing through each of the twelve time stations.

In Taoist texts, there are eight major reflexology

spaces around the yoni. The number nine is sacred in Taoist philosophy, so if there are eight points around the yoni, the ninth stroke completes the circle. We like the clock metaphor because it is easier for people to remember the different times on a clock than to the specific reflexology points. Whether you use the convention of eight or twelve, you start and end at the same spot, which happens to be the sacred spot.

The holding may progress to gentle stimulation, and light stroking, depending on what feels good to the receiver. When stroking, move the fingers slowly from the back of the yoni to the front opening. You may ask if the receiver can feel the points of contact, sometimes her body language will be sufficient.

Rest between areas. This is essential because sexual healing occurs in the deep meditative times of stillness as much as during sexual stimulation.

Receivers, your mission is to stay acutely aware of how you feel. Does it hurt? Is there pleasure? Are you numb? Is there any other quality or texture that describes your experience? It is best to articulate what you feel at each of the twelve places.

The giver may make mental notes of what the receiver communicates verbally or nonverbally at each time station. Perhaps she gets numb or uncomfortable at four o'clock. Perhaps she gets really tense at seven o'clock and holds her breath. When there is tension, stop and breathe. When the tension relaxes, continue on. Perhaps she reports a painful memory around ten o'clock. Everything after is spacious and sweet. When the giver comes back around to twelve o'clock, he or she may ask, "Would you like me to massage at four o'clock, seven and ten?"

Be prepared for emotional release. Touching different spaces and places triggers memories that evoke fear, sadness, grief, joy, and sometimes even bliss.

When Dez discovers a place inside a woman that is so desensitized that she can't feel it, he has a special way of reactivating her. He'll slowly back out, gently tapping his finger back to a place where she can feel him, which might be on the inner lips or the thigh.

He'll ask, "Can you feel this?"

"Yes."

And then he'll continue tapping, slowly, with micro-movements toward her numb spot. "Can you feel me here?"

"Yeah."

He'll tap all the way back inside the yoni to the spot where she couldn't feel him touching her, which supports her to reconnect that spot with sensation. He'll move around to different places inside of her yoni, methodically bringing her awareness into places that were numb before. It may take several sessions, but eventually she will reactivate her entire yoni.

To give an idea of how masterfully this work can be done, Dez often visualizes that the light from the tip of his finger is being breathed up into the womb and the heart. Sometimes the circuit is so juicy, his whole hand lights up.

Once we have done enough emotional clearing and are complete with the healing, we can move into massaging to activate arousal and sensual pleasure.

SACRED SPOT MASSAGE FOR WOMEN

Most women have a limited concept of how much pleasure they are capable of experiencing. The following practice can actually expand our container for ecstasy.

All your intentions, up to this point, have been to create a safe place for the receiver to go to her edge, where she can experience more concentrated pleasure. From here on, the practice takes a lot of breath and presence. Every time she starts to contract or hold back, remind her that it is OK for her to let go and surrender more.

The sacred spot does not usually respond to light touch; it often requires medium-to-firm pressure to elicit its potential. Initially, the receiver may feel that she has to pee. (This is why we have you empty the bladder during the preparation stages.) The sensation of ejaculation often is confused with the desire to pee. When the sensation passes, the woman can access new depths of pleasure.

No matter how aroused the receiver gets or how much she wants to consummate the ritual with sexual union, it is important for the giver to stay focused. The giver may receive a lot of pleasure from giving, but this is not an act of mutual sexual stimulation—it is an act of service.

Women are especially wired to want to please others. They have been scripted to believe that they have to share their arousal or give back in some way. Some women are not used to receiving this much attention, and they may become self-conscious and uncomfortable. Remind the receiver that she deserves this love and attention. All she has to do is relax, breathe and receive!

The slow, steady presence of the giver is the greatest gift anyone can give to a woman. Eve Ensler, creator of *The Vagina Monologues*, traveled across the U.S. interviewing women on what their vaginas would say if they could talk. The recurring message from many different vaginas of every shape, size, race and age was the following two words:

"Slow down."

So, for the purposes of this ritual, slow down, slow down, slow down!

Whether or not you go into climactic release is completely up to you, but the focus of this ritual is not on orgasm or ejaculation. This is a profound opportunity to learn how to circulate orgasmic energy rather than release it. Orgasmic energy can be circulated and distributed to and through anywhere in the body. When pure sexual energy is celebrated and circulated in a sacred context, the whole body is healed.

CLOSING THE RITUAL

After the breathing has returned to a relaxed rate and the energies in the room have settled, the ritual comes to a natural close. As you settle into stillness, the giver may ask the receiver, "Would you like me to pull out or stay inside?"

In either case, it is important for the giver and receiver to stay energetically connected. There is a sweet Shamanic journeying that can happen in the stillness after intense sexual activity.

Next, the giver places one hand on the receiver's heart and one hand outside and on top of the receiver's yoni. With breath and clear intention, not with words, the giver helps the receiver anchor all the new sensations back into the body. The receiver then places her hands on top of the giver's hands and the giver slowly slides his or her hands away. The receiver is now holding her own heart and yoni. As she breathes, she reclaims the power of her own body.

When everything feels complete, the giver may ask, "Is there anything else that you need in order to feel complete?" Once the receiver is complete and fully back in her body, the final step is to decompress.

Find a comfortable position sitting face-to-face or in Yab-Yum, or lie down together. It is important for the receiver to move slowly as she transitions into a new position.

After a successful session, the receiver usually feels and looks rejuvenated. Her cheeks are flushed, her skin is radiant and she looks as if she has shed ten years of stress. This work can be like tapping into the fountain of youth.

Now it is time for the receiver to articulate her feelings about the experience. Some healers disagree—they believe it ruins the trance. They also believe nothing should be added and nothing should be taken away from the experience by talking. We believe it is important for the receiver to speak and to connect with the cognitive-verbal part of her brain. Not only does this help her integrate her experience, it transfers her experience from the sub- or super-conscious into conscious awareness. Therefore, the giver may ask, "What wisdom did you receive from this experience?"

After a recent yoni healing, one woman said that she truly gets how sacred her yoni is and that she is going to treat it with a lot more reverence and be more selective about who she lets enter it.

Givers remain givers to the end of the ritual, simply listening and holding space for the sharing. And if the receiver has nothing to say, then the giver may ask a few questions. Questions help the receiver return to cognitive-verbal brain. After the ritual, soaking in a warm salt bath, though not required, helps you rest and integrate the healing. Additionally, be sure to:

❀ Drink lots of water.

❀ Ground yourself fully before driving off in your car.

❀ Be gentle and nurturing with yourself because your emotions may be sensitive and raw.

❀ Follow up with your giver within the next couple days.

DIVINATION

When women are standing in the place of wholeness, they can be transpersonal telepathics. We can't move into divination until the sexual wounds are addressed and healed, and blocks are removed. When a woman has fully released the energetic grips of guilt, fear and shame, her yoni is like an oracle. Honoring and entering it, we can uncover the secrets of the universe. Ancient temple priestesses practiced great rites for this purpose.

Divination is an ancient ritual where people have gone to access information that supports individual and collective growth. Inside the womb there is truth. Inside the womb, we can journey to anywhere in the universe. All of creation is in the womb. It is the hologram. This ritual is a way to source the magic.

With this intention, the receiver goes into a trance and travels. The giver is holding space so the receiver can travel to other realms without losing herself. When the divine masculine steps into his ability to create safety, witness without judgment and hold space, he is like a midwife. He helps her open and create. He reminds her, "It's OK. Breathe, breathe, you are safe." And when it's time to come back, he guides her home.

Without a healthy masculine aspect to hold space, a woman will either short circuit from traveling that far, or lose herself and disconnect from reality. At one level, this is a simple ritual to help women reacquaint themselves with their divine feminine. At another level, this is super serious magic.

Sacred spot work can be extraordinarily vast and deep.

When we first start this work we are reaching into our lives and we are healing our personal trauma. And then, as we become whole, we start to reach into the collective womb where we can access the wisdom of the universe. Just as we send our intentions into the heavens, we can go just as deep into the womb. We know that outer space is limitless, and through this ritual we touch into the infinite depths of inner space.

Historically, this ritual has been misunderstood and sometimes misused, abused and used with ill intent. It is paramount for both the giver and receiver to be in the purest state of surrender and service before engaging in this work.

Dez has sourced memories in the collective consciousness of power struggles within ancient temples, involving priests and priestesses pushing personal agendas. This ritual was even used with threat and coercion. Dez has felt the tears and deep sadness around the betrayal and abuse of these rituals. This is why practices like this have gone underground and been kept secret.

We believe that if the intent is not pure the gifts and magic will dry up. And, those intentionally misusing these tools will have to contend with a ruthless and purifying fire of their own karmic creation.

KEEPING THE CONTAINER

After we initiate seekers into these practices, we ask that they practice at home with their partners. It is not uncommon for them to come back saying, "We prepared for the session by lighting candles and listening to music and she just cried the whole time," or, "We got into a big fight," or, "He fell asleep!"

Make no mistake about it: your stuff will get stirred up. These practices strongly oppose the mainstream current of sexual conditioning. This ritual creates a rip in the psychic agreement. What you're saying is, "I'm here, I'm present, I'm ready to receive, Oh, boy!"

Well guess what? All of the wounds, the separation and anything and everything that needs to be healed will rush into the ritual space. There could be a lot of tears, anger and rage. It is not always pretty. Just remember that it is not bigger than you, it is only all you. You can hold space for it.

Without conscious awareness, you can get distracted and go into addiction. Addiction is an avoidance of our power, so notice whenever you choose any substance or activity that distracts us from reclaiming our power. Particularly notice whenever we make choices not to feel our feelings. Remember, the emotional body is the seat of our power. Again, anything that comes up during the ritual is perfect, even addiction.

Another frequent issue that arises is when the receiver becomes so aroused that she wants to make love. Some women beg, plead, demand, seduce, and manipulate to get sex. If you, the giver, acquiesce, you are enabling her. The urge for penetration during this ritual is often a mask for not wanting to feel so vulnerable, or not wanting to believe that she deserves all the attention. If this comes up, and it will, we suggest you close the ritual, create a little distance between you and the ritual space, like go to the kitchen for a snack, and then if its appropriate go into the bedroom to make love.

A ritual is a contract with spirit. All we have to do to fulfill the contract is show up and honor the intention of the ritual. The container is not the room we do it in; the container is the intention to offer ourselves fully to spirit for healing and transformation.

Remember to close the ritual. If you forget to close the ritual, or you get distracted, you leak the potency of the spiritual contract.

THE "HE" SPOT MASSAGE

"Women's response to direct stimulation of the G-spot is identical to the response of males when their prostate is stimulated," according to Beverly Whipple and John Perry, authors of ***The G Spot: And Other Discoveries About Human Sexuality***. The similarities are so striking that even sex educators refer to both glands as the sacred spot. In some Tantric circles, the prostate is affectionately known as the "He" spot.

The prostate is about the size and shape of a walnut and is surrounded by a thick fibrous capsule. It produces twenty to thirty percent of the total volume of seminal fluid released when a man ejaculates. It is located directly beneath the bladder and in front of the rectum and can be reached internally by inserting a finger into the anus and reaching back and up toward the navel.

Externally, the prostate can be massaged at the perineum, which is midway between the testicles and anus. Feel for a pea-sized indentation, which is called the Million Dollar Point by Taoist Tantrikas. In Oriental acupuncture, this point is known as the Jen-Mo or Conception Meridian.

Increasing numbers of men over the age of fifty suffer from enlarged prostates, which causes painful or difficult urination, erection and ejaculation problems. Traditional doctors would massage their patients' prostates to cure or prevent disease. These days, however, most doctors only check the prostate, and if they find a problem, they prefer to cut it out or prescribe pharmaceuticals.

BENEFITS OF MALE SACRED SPOT MASSAGE
- ❀ Shrinking a congested prostate gland
- ❀ Improving urinary flow
- ❀ Increasing sphincter tone
- ❀ Relieving prostatitis
- ❀ Improving overall prostate health
- ❀ Curing impotence and erectile dysfunction
- ❀ Developing ejaculatory control
- ❀ Relieving stress
- ❀ Releasing emotion

❀ Promoting personal growth and exploration
❀ Increasing pleasure
❀ Optimizing sexual health
❀ Expanding orgasms

Energetically, He-Spot Massage directly affects the root chakra, and therefore is an opportunity for men to release huge amounts of tension and fear that are often at the core of lower-tract cancer and other diseases and ailments. This massage ritual also clears blocks and opens a channel to receive a flow of energetic support from the earth.

Tantra teacher Rundy Delphini facilitates a beautiful half-day workshop called Women Healing Men, during which he teaches internal prostate massage. Delphini maintains that one of the great benefits of this work for couples is that it creates equality in relationships. He goes on to say, "I believe that very soon the world view of masculinity will change drastically and a man's character will be measured by his ability not only to love but in his ability to allow himself to be loved, by his kindness, his humility, his gentleness, his receptivity, and his vulnerability. A man secure and centered in himself is a gift to the world."

BEFORE THE RITUAL BEGINS

Preparation for the male sacred spot ritual is essentially the same as the preparation for the female sacred spot ritual, except of course it's performed on a man. Another difference is that for prostrate massage, we prefer using tight-fitting latex surgical gloves and copious amounts of water-based lubrication. Gloves are recommended for anal play not only because they are hygienic, but also because they protect the soft tissue from fingernails. Also, the smooth latex surface slides more easily than skin.

We recommend having a bowel movement before you begin, if possible. Some men like to clean their rectum with an enema. Though not necessary, a warm bath helps the receiver relax, explore his own body and prepare for the experience.

The ritual begins with a prayer, invocation or meditation on how profound and vulnerable it is to be sharing this deep, often guarded and often forbidden space within the man's body. This is also the time to declare the giver's intention to honor and serve and the receiver's intention to surrender and feel. The receiver must be reminded that he is safe to feel and communicate whatever comes up during the process. It is OK to stop the practice at any time. It is OK to take a break and resume later.

It is also important to have a sense of humor and not take the ritual too seriously. Claire Cavanah and Rachel Venning are the founders of Toys in Babeland and the authors of **Sex Toys 101**. They offer this mantra for the prostrate massage ritual: Relaxation, Lubrication, Communication! The massage is typically conducted in one of these four positions:

1. The receiver lies face up with hips propped high on pillows, knees bent up, feet on floor.
2. The receiver reclines in a seated position with knees drawn up towards the chest and angled outward.
3. The receiver kneels with his hips high and his elbows resting on a couch or something firm.
4. The receiver lies face down with his hips propped high on cushions.

Depending on body type and physical capacity, the receiver should choose the position. The giver must have a clear view of the anus and genitals, and must also choose a comfortable position, like kneeling or sitting on cushions. The disadvantage of the latter two positions is that eye contact is compromised.

SACRED SPOT MASSAGE FOR MEN

Giver, you have much to remember during and throughout this massage! Keep your breathing deep and your movements slow. Use generous amounts of lubricant and reapply as needed. Periodically check in with the receiver to see how he is feeling and to ask if there is anything else he would like to make the experience more comfortable.

The giver starts with one hand on the receiver's heart and one hand on the receiver's perineum. To gather energy and create an energetic circuit, the giver and receiver breathe deeply together for a while. Deep belly breathing helps activate the emotional body and is recommended throughout the practice.

The massage begins on the hips or abdomen. The intention is both to help the receiver relax and soften, and to warm up and stimulate arousal. When the receiver is ready, the giver can begin an external genital massage.

Initially, we suggest focusing on the base of the penis, testicles and perineum because arousal relaxes the sphincter and makes the prostate swell, making it easier to work with. Press and massage the conception point halfway between the testicles and the anus. Feel into the area behind the balls. Most men are surprised to discover that a third of the penis actually resides inside the body. The internal and external penis may be massaged simultaneously behind the testicles and along the perineum.

Using lubrication, the giver may softly massage the outside of the anus in a slow, rhythmic, circular motion. There are many pleasurable and sensitive nerve endings around the entrance of the anus. As the sphincter relaxes, it will naturally open. The giver may help dilate the sphincter with slow, gentle touch.

As the receiver relaxes, his sphincter may naturally draw in the finger of the giver. Or, the receiver may push out on the exhale, which softens the sphincter so that the giver can gently enter the anus with the well-lubricated pad of the first finger. Once inside, be sure to pause, hold and breathe. This allows the sphincter to adjust to the new sensation. Also, be aware that there is a bundle of sensitive nerves just one finger pad in and up the anus. This is the root area and it can be highly emotionally charged.

Next, the giver slowly slides the finger in about an inch or so and bends the finger toward the receiver's navel to feel for a soft walnut-shaped bump, which is the prostate. The receiver may feel pressure deep inside and at first it may feel uncomfortable. Keep breathing. In order to increase comfort and pleasure, some people like to stimulate the lingam simultaneously with the prostate. To do this, the receiver may masturbate, or the giver may use the more dexterous hand for the lingam and the other hand for the prostate.

Once the receiver is relaxed and comfortable, the giver may explore different kinds of touch and pressure. Instead of in-and-out movements, like those used in vaginal penetration, try side-to-side or circular movements. The receiver may also ask the giver to hold still while he undulates his hips or pumps his PC muscles. Receiver, you may feel free to explore and experiment.

Many men begin to access strong emotions or experience past traumas, especially if this is the first time they have done the ritual. Giver, when this happens, let your divine masculine step in and hold space for the receiver. Receiver, you have permission to cry and release these emotions. And, you may stop or pause the session at any time.

Though ejaculation and orgasm are not the focus of this ritual, stimulation of the prostate may create a new and powerful urge to ejaculate. Many men report a whole different experience of ejaculation when the prostate is stimulated. The receiver may ejaculate while either he or the giver stimulates his lingam. Or, the receiver may ask the giver to "milk" his prostate, which entails the giver stroking the receiver's prostate until a small amount of semen flows from the flaccid penis. This is pleasurable and helps overcome negative social conditioning. (In the dominant and submissive subculture, this practice is referred to as "sissy milking.")

If the receiver chooses to ejaculate, we recommend enhancing the experience by visualizing light and energy rising up his spine, and by circulating the orgasmic energy throughout his body when he orgasms.

To end, the giver can gently withdraw his or her hands, take off the gloves, and place one hand on the receiver's heart, the other on the receiver's perineum. The giver holds the receiver as he absorbs the healing power of his anal awakening. Then the giver slowly withdraws his or her hands and the receiver quietly rests in his newfound sense of surrender.

We recommend closing this ritual with a verbal decompression, as it helps both the giver and receiver come back down from the high of the experience.

Remember to wash toys, fingers and other body parts with soap and hot water after touching the anus, and before making contact with the vagina, mouth or food.

TABOO

Most heterosexual men are uncomfortable around the idea of a prostate massage. There have been many negative shaming messages about the anus. Homophobic men are often afraid to explore this area of their body for fear that if they enjoy it, they might discover they are gay. Clinging to these limiting notions may prevent us from realizing our full sexual range. Other fears involve associations with the anus being unclean, unnatural, perverted, disgusting or uninteresting.

Many religions have condemned anal sex, and object to any form of sex for any reason other than procreation. Similarly, legal authorities have outlawed anal sex, thereby systematizing prejudice against homosexuals.

The guilt and shame projected on the anus and anal sex in this culture reflect an insidious unconscious belief that our bodies are not our own. Puritanical thinking and judgment pervades the unconscious collective. Laws support, perpetuate and reinforce this thinking, evident in punitive sanctions for anal sex. We live in an atmosphere where we are not free to touch, explore or pleasure our own bodies.

Energetically, the prostate is associated with the root chakra, which is where humans hold their fear and aggression. Some of the primary imbalances in the world include abuse of power, war, competition and degradation of Mother Earth. These are all manifestations of the unhealthy root chakra. As long as the taboos on our first chakras remain intact, the world will not be able to relax and heal.

In the next chapter we introduce three different types of sexual paths. We offer various perspectives, practices and paradigms for non-monogamous relationships. And, we discuss how alternative relationships can serve your sacred sexual liberation.

Eleven
The Sacred Path of Poly

As early as kindergarten and all through grade school, Dez felt something was missing. He looked around at the way people were relating and saw a lot of lying, cheating and deception. He was an intuitive young man and even before he understood relationship dynamics, he sensed the underlying confusion, separation and suffering. At the core of his being he knew that something was askew.

He started asking, What does it mean to be a boy, a man, a woman, and what does it mean to be in relationship?

By default, many people adopt the predominant cultural paradigm of monogamy, and then find themselves lying, cheating and sneaking. This dysfunction makes it clear that people often choose relationship paths that do not match their true nature. Conscious individuals, by comparison, have the personal power to choose an alternative path that aligns with their desire.

Sacred sexual relationships take these primary forms:
1. The Sacred Path of Celibacy.
2. The Sacred Path of Monogamy.
3. The Sacred Path of Polyamory.

No one path is higher than the other. Some people walk all three paths at different times in their lives. Every individual has to find the path that suits him or her at various points in life.

This chapter is dedicated to anyone willing to explore a variety of new perspectives and possibilities in regards to responsible relationship. Since there is a marked lack of support and resources for people practicing non-monogamous alternatives, we offer our personal experiences, new definitions, and a road map for common challenges.

To begin, ask yourself if the way you do relationship is working. Does it serve you? Are you fulfilled? If so, excellent! If not, here are some ideas to contemplate, explore and even emulate.

WHAT IS POLYAMORY?

Deborah Taj Anapol popularized the term polyamory in her landmark book, ***Love Without Limits***. In a weekend training, Kamala remembers Taj saying, "Raise your hand if you're married to the first person you ever loved and are still with that person today. Go ahead, raise your hand." Nobody raised a hand. "Then I can deduce you probably have loved more than one person. Polyamory means 'many loves' or the ability to love more than one." Taj clarified that it doesn't have to be all at the same time.

Polyamory.org also defines polyamory as "loving more than one," and adds that loving may be sexual, emotional, spiritual or any combination of the three, according to the desires and agreements of the individuals involved. The term polyamory is also used to describe people who are currently involved in one or less relationships, but are open to more. Intimacy and the nature of the connection between individuals and groups of individuals vary greatly. The Sacred Path of Polyamory emphasizes openness, communication and consent. Deception or denying problems in the primary relationship by escaping to another lover can be damaging to self and others.

BUT ISN'T THAT SWINGING?

The relationship between swinging and polyamory is controversial. Most people agree that polyamory has more to do with emotionally intimate, long-term relationships than with one-night stands. Swinging is generally viewed as a form of monogamy in which two primary partners agree to have casual sex with other couples or singles, no strings attached. Swingers may continue to sleep with the same people for years, but they usually don't go on romantic dates and/or process deep emotional issues together.

Baba Dez believes swingers are a category unto themselves. They have their own organizations, newsletters, conferences and contact networks under the label "lifestyle." The interactions of many swingers, as seen online, is often sexually explicit and overly concerned with superficial appearances. Swinging is rarely practiced as a spiritual pursuit. Most polyamory and Tantra practitioners, by comparison, do not approve of recreational sex.

Kamala, in contrast, considers swinging to be a subset of polyamory. As long as the individuals are practicing responsible and honest communication, it is only a slightly different love style with a stronger emphasis on sex. The poly and swing communities, in Kamala's point of view, are allies under the umbrella of open relationships. We have seen many friends and clients who started out swinging and have matured and transitioned into intimate emotional connections. We have also seen many poly people have sexual awakenings that allowed them to let go of their judgment of sex for sex's sake.

POLY-TANTRA

At first glance, polyamory and Tantra are not inherently related. We view polyamory as the practice of responsibly loving more than one, and Tantra as a spiritual path toward being in love all the time. People can practice Tantra without polyamory; people can practice polyamory without Tantra. Tantra, however, dramatically improves our experience of polyamory because it offers philosophy, practices and tools that make loving more than one person easier, deeper and more ecstatic.

For several decades, Baba Dez has been walking the sacred path, which at different times has been celibacy, monogamy and polyamory. In a recent interview, he discussed his practice:

"I currently enjoy many relationships on many levels. I have been friends and lovers with some women for almost thirty years. And with others, I have only recently been blessed by their presence in my life. The 'now' keeps unfolding and it is exciting to see who keeps showing up.

"When I'm with women I feel attracted to, I pay attention to: What is the nature of this attraction? What is the feedback from my heart, my emotions and my body? What is the truth? Where does my desire meet theirs in each new moment?

"How do I share in a way that feels safe, real, honoring and supportive? How ready, willing and able am I? How ready, willing and able is this other person? I notice where I would want to make the relationship into more or into less than what it is. Making more out of a relationship happens because we want something so much we distort reality.

"When we decide to only have sex with a soul mate or life partner, we may find ourselves in delusion about what a relationship truly is, because our need for sex is so great that we subconsciously make someone fit our criteria for life partner, just so that we can have sex with them. Over time we wonder how we got involved with this person. 'What was I thinking?'

"On the other hand, we sometimes make less out of a relationship because we are afraid of the depth, intimacy and sweetness. To avoid the possibility of rejection and loss, we minimize a relationship, convincing ourselves that this person is not for us because of a mental list of reasons. We unconsciously push a beautiful relationship away and even end it because we are afraid of the possible loss. Often there is even relationship addiction where people become compulsive about the quest or conquest.

"When I start entering intimate territory, it is essential for me to stay connected to my belly and my heart. I let go of what things look like and stay open to what everything feels like. This is how I avoid undermining my relationship with God, self, or my beloveds."

AN INITIATION

Kamala's introduction to polyamory happened in her final year at college. For her senior thesis, she wrote and directed a lesbian-themed stage production, ***Passion Flower***. Her girlfriend at the time was a petite brunette who stage-managed the show. After rehearsal, Katherine and Kamala would walk to the local coffee shop to study together. Even though Katherine had not yet "come out," she and Kamala were lesbian lovers for about six months.

Meanwhile, Kamala found herself inexplicably drawn to Cain, a man she met at a poetry reading. Since Katherine and she were graduating from college and didn't know what would become of their relationship, Katherine was open-minded about Kamala's interest in this man.

Cain admitted his attraction to Kamala was mutual and volunteered to paint the set for Kamala's play. Katherine and Cain worked together amicably to get ready for the production.

Cain took Kamala car camping. More specifically, he drove her out into the desert and spent the night cuddling with her on the hood of his car.

The next evening, Cain disclosed, "When we were lying there, holding each other under the stars, I had a strong impulse to tell you that I loved you."

"I'm so glad you didn't. That would've really freaked me out," Kamala admitted.

"Why? What's wrong with love?"

Though her heart told her she was falling in love with him, she couldn't believe it. "Because, I love Katherine," she said.

But that didn't stop Cain, who replied, "What does it matter who else you love? I love you like I love life. I tell my mother that I love her like the mountains and the sky. Why can't I love you like that? There's enough room in my heart for everyone."

This concept seemed so strange to Kamala, and yet felt so real. She went on to deconstruct her definition of love and discovered that her belief system viewed love as exclusive, while Cain's view of love was inclusive. Kamala talked to Katherine about this new definition of love over a bowl of wonton soup.

Relieved, Katherine exhaled and said, "I've been watching you fall in love with him for months and I was wondering when you'd finally admit it."

After graduation, Katherine moved to LA and Cain moved to Hawaii. Kamala followed Cain to the islands, but continued to date Katherine when she returned to the mainland during the holidays. During their two-year relationship they shared a number of other lovers.

WHY POLY?

During a Tantra and poly playshop, a skeptical student asked, "One woman is complicated enough…why would anyone want more?" To answer this reasonable question, the class brainstormed this partial list of benefits to polyamory:

* Increased personal freedom
* Stronger communication, trust and truth
* More community and greater sense of belonging
* Opportunity to practice non-attachment
* Greater sexual exploration and fulfillment
* Opportunity to work through jealousy and possessiveness

Many people have a hard time explaining their personal and spiritual reasons for loving more than one person. Kamala Devi sums it up with, "It's just the shape of my heart."

Another skeptic in the playshop asked, "It takes all my energy to have just one relationship. How do you deal with multiple lovers?"

The answer for Dez is that he doesn't engage in relationships that drain his energy. He chooses to be sexually intimate only with people who bring and build power. Clear, conscious, powerful lovers support and cultivate more health, joy and energy, which make it easy to maintain multiple intimate relationships.

POLY JARGON

Poly relationships are inherently complex. From the outside looking in, they can be confusing. Because of their multifaceted and dynamic nature, non-monogamous relationships even warrant their own language: Poly Jargon. Some people venture to call it a science: Polygeometry. Following are some helpful terms and definitions:

PRIMARY. The partner who has seniority or the strongest bond.

SECONDARY. The second relationship in terms of time or priority.

THIRD. The person in an ongoing relationship who is not as active or intimate as primary or secondary. Note: Many people don't use the above terms because they imply hierarchy.

TRIAD. Three people involved in a loving relationship with any combination of intimate bonds.

TRIANGLE. A relationship in which all three people are intimately involved with one another.

TERTIARY. This is a less frequently used name for the second person in a triangle or a threesome.

VEE. A three-person structure where one person has two lovers, but those two lovers are not as closely connected with each other. Geometric arrangements involving four persons can be described as an "N" or "Z".

PIVOT POINT. The person who is closely connected to two individuals who are not particularly emotionally involved with each other. This is the person at the bottom, or hinge, of a "V".

CIRCLE, FAMILY, or INTIMATE NETWORK. These are more politically correct terms for non monogamous relationship structures because they imply equality and community.

POD. This playful term is a dolphin reference for any group of three or more polyamorous lovers.

OPEN RELATIONSHIP. A committed partnership, sometimes a marriage, where both partners are open to sexual and/or intimate relationships with other people. This term includes polyamory and swinging.

POLYFIDELITY. A relationship of more than two individuals who have made a commitment to keep sexual contact exclusive within the group. In other words, they don't practice polyamory with outside partners.

POLYGAMY. A marriage in which individuals have multiple spouses.

POLYGYNY. A marriage in which men have multiple wives.

POLYANDRY. A marriage in which women have multiple husbands.

GROUP MARRIAGE. A single-family unit in which all members are considered to be married to each other.

LINE MARRIAGES. Intergenerational marriages intended to outlive the original members by adding new spouses. This is seen as an ideal way to care for the children and the elderly in a family unit.

COMPERSION. A poly term for the ideal experience of pleasure when one sees or hears about his or her lover making love to another person. The opposite of jealousy.

People in any of the above definitions may also use the labels heterosexual, gay, lesbian, bisexual, queer, trans, dominant, submissive, etc. The above jargon is all just a list of labels. When we consider the complexity of human sexual behavior and preferences, we appreciate that people can never be defined by mere words. Many conscious individuals refuse to use labels. As a matter of respect, we should never assume that a label fits anyone unless that is how the person self-identifies. Labels are only tools to help us talk about these concepts, to connect with others who have similar interests, and to create a sense of identity and community.

BUT DON'T YOU GET JEALOUS?

The most commonly-asked question is, "What about jealousy?" The answer is, "Jealousy happens." It's like that bumper sticker: Shit Happens. Jealousy not only feels like shit but, like shit, it is a natural human experience.

Different people experience jealousy to different degrees. Some people never feel any jealousy. It's like they never got that part installed at the factory. But those individuals are rare. Ironically, some lovers get furious with each other because a lack of jealousy is equated with not caring.

Jealousy is so common and so natural, you may as well befriend it. Instead of avoiding, repressing, or denying jealousy, we recommend you take a conscious look at what's driving your jealousy. Breathe deeply and look for the deeper teaching.

Dossie Easton and Catherine A. Liszt dedicate an entire chapter to jealousy in the ***Ethical Slut***. This book is considered by many poly people a bible, and it suggests one way to work through your jealousy is "by envisioning the worse possible scenario that you can imagine. Go ahead, wallow in it. Elaborate it until it becomes ridiculous."

Jealousy is a complex emotion involving fear, anger, and sadness. Your emotional work may start with asking yourself basic questions like:

❊ Why do I feel hurt, angry, betrayed?

❊ What am I insecure about?

❊ What am I afraid of?

❊ What do I really want?

When we consciously look at what underlies jealousy, we may discover our unmet needs. People who practice compassionate communication maintain that needs are hidden underneath all the emotions. Kelly Bryson, poly pioneer and author of ***Don't Be Nice, Be Real***, a guide to Compassionate Communication, teaches what he calls "freedom-based relating," coaching people how to identify their needs and how to get their needs met without sacrificing the needs of others.

In the Sacred Path of Poly, if we're having a hard time working through our jealousy, we may ask our partner for help, providing our partner is willing and able. While it is tempting to blame or attack our partner for whatever he or she did, it is essential to understand that nobody can make anybody feel anything. Each of us is responsible for our own emotion and for recognizing which needs are not being met.

If our partner is unable to listen, or gets defensive or tries to fix us, then we call someone who knows how to listen in a way that encourages the full truth. This may be a friend, a coach, a sponsor, a Daka, a Dakini, a teacher or a therapist. The most effective listeners simply listen, witness, and hold space. Sometimes the most powerful response is simply, "Thank you." Other compassionate responses are, "I can imagine how you might feel," or "That's understandable."

In sum, once jealousy has been recognized, felt and

responsibly processed, we can experience ourselves more objectively, independent of our fear and projection based on emotional backlog from our wounded past. The ultimate aim is to be fully alive and dance in the pleasure of the moment.

HAVING NEEDS IS NOT NEEDY

Mainstream culture teaches us that your entertainment needs can be met by going out. Your intellectual needs can be met by books or classes. Your physical needs can be met by going to gyms and playing with workout buddies. But for some reason, your intimate, romantic and sexual needs should only be met from one person!

Tragically, many people live their entire lives sacrificing their needs because their primary partner can't meet them. Another problem we observe is couples believing that their partners are responsible for their happiness, financial success and/or orgasms. This kind of thinking is a red flag, pointing to the need for self-work.

The ultimate primary relationship is always self or Spirit. No matter how empathetic and intuitive your partner may be, only you know what you truly want and need. Nor is it possible or desirable for any one person to meet all of your needs. We don't have to become completely self-sufficient, but how can we expect anyone else to meet our needs if we don't want to take care of them ourselves?

No matter how evolved our consciousness is, all humans have needs. We must learn to listen to our body, belly and heart to learn what they are. It's easy for our sophisticated minds to grasp poly theory, but it's hard for our wounded inner child to catch up.

This is why we advocate giving your little kid a gigantic double scoop of compassion. Let the inner child know that all feelings and needs are as yummy as rocky road ice cream and underneath all of the messy emotions, there are basic human needs. We all have the need to feel included, secure, special, provided for, considered, honored, appreciated, desired, respected, accepted, loved and loveable.

There are also many contradictory needs that compel people into poly, such as the need for freedom, truth, sexual expression, variety, novelty, romance, excitement, spontaneity, and abundance. As we practice accepting basic needs, we cultivate a greater capacity to accept the less desirable needs such as the need to look good, to be in control, to be deviant, to be held, to be touched, to touch, to merge sexually, to rebel, or to shock. Whatever your needs are, we invite you to breathe deeply and accept them. Judging ourselves is counterproductive to our evolution.

Poly is a profoundly abundant state of mind. Consider the possibility that you can have all of your needs met, as long as you are not attached to getting them met by one person. The universe is infinite and it can provide for infinite desires. So, own your desires, make clear requests to get them met, and be willing to receive.

TOP TEN POLY CONCERNS

In coaching poly individuals, couples and pods, we have observed certain recurring issues. Following is a list of some common concerns:

1. I'm afraid someone else will be better in bed than I am. I just don't want to be left out, spending the night alone while they are out having sex.
2. Or worse, what if my partner leaves me, divorces me or abandons me for another person?
3. I'm OK if my primary has sex with someone at a play party, but I don't think I'd like it if they actually established a relationship.
4. Or, they can have an intimate relationship but I want to be the only person they penetrate.
5. We only have so much time as it is. I don't want to have to share my primary by splitting my time with someone else.
6. If my primary meets someone in our community and dates her, then everyone is going to find out and think

I'm not satisfying him.

7. I worked so hard to train my husband to be a good lover and provider. If he meets someone now, it's like giving away all my hard work.
8. What if I get stuck with all the mundane roles such as working and taking care of the kids, while my wife goes off to have romantic sex with someone else? Why do they get the milk for free when I had to buy the cow?
9. But I want to raise a family with kids and I don't think that polyamory sets a healthy example.
10. And a litany of little things like, Who will I bring home for Thanksgiving? Who sleeps in the middle? Whose names are on the floral-patterned checkbook?

NEGOTIATING AGREEMENTS

It is up to each individual to decide what he or she is comfortable with in relationship and then to negotiate agreements and boundaries with each of his or her partners. This negotiation can look like a graceful dance or a crunchy compromise. In any case, it is always a co-creation.

Assumptions about relationship agreements are neither advisable nor acceptable. Clear communication is absolutely vital in poly. Many people are afraid even to start a discussion with their partners for fear of rocking the boat, but we strongly encourage you to "get over it." If you are able to speak the very thing that you are afraid of saying, you will be free. It takes great courage to negotiate a relationship agreement. The co-creation is an art which leads to greater understanding of self and others. Ultimately, when we have spoken and/or written agreements, everybody feels safer and can move forward with a greater sense of trust and freedom.

If you are not currently in relationship, it is still valuable to explore your needs, desires, triggers and bottom lines. This personal growth work will help you attract an appropriate partner or partners in the near future.

Here are twenty questions to help get clear about your true desires in relationship.

20 Q'S FOR SETTING BOUNDARIES

1. What are your relationship boundaries? What are you currently allowed to do, or what do you allow yourself to experience?
2. What would you like to be able to experience that you are not currently allowed or allowing yourself?
3. Does your primary relationship always come first? Are certain times or places always reserved for primary partners to be alone together?
4. Do you agree to stop if poly is hurting the primary relationship? Do you stop a certain relationship, or stop being poly altogether?
5. Do you engage with poly-friendly partners? Are you allowed to date "outside the species," meaning people that have no poly experience?
6. What's your position on recreational sex?
7. Is it OK to sleep with personal friends? How about ex-lovers? Are there any specific people who are off limits?
8. Are you "out of the closet" about your relationship choices? Who are you allowed to tell and who do you want to keep it from?
9. Do you prefer to connect with your partner and his or her lovers all together, or do you prefer one-on-one connections?
10. Do you require informed consent among all parties?
11. How about advance notice of potential sexual partners? Does your primary need to meet your potential new lover before sexual contact occurs?
12. What are your safe-sex standards? Be specific!
13. How long before you must share new developments with your primary partner? Do you communicate immediately, within one day or within one week?

14. Do you have a time restriction as to how often you are allowed to date others, like once a week, once a month, or vacations only?
15. What is your curfew? Do you allow overnight dates? Is it OK to sleep with a lover if your primary is sleeping alone?
16. Are you allowed to bring home your lovers? Is it OK to behave sexually with other partners in front of your primary? Can you have sex with a new partner in your primary partner's bed?
17. Can you call, email or go out with lovers without consent of your other lovers?
18. What is your absolute bottom line, which is to say, what boundary, if broken, might seriously jeopardize your relationship?
19. What are the consequences if your agreements get compromised? Is there flexibility and forgiveness or is it an ultimatum?
20. When are these agreements open for discussion? Is it OK to discuss the agreements at any time for any reason, or would you rather wait for a periodic review such as during the full moon, quarterly or every six months?

Perhaps the most important thing to keep in mind when creating relationship agreements is that with more experience, comfort and support, your rules will change and evolve. It is inevitable that some agreements will have to be revised and that some agreements will become unnecessary.

The examination, discussion and process of creating agreements can be a profound part of our growth. Once we have worked out the details of our agreements through journaling or dialog, it is time to put our agreements in black and white.

Creating a written contract can be fun! It is a declaration to the universe that you and your partner(s) aren't subject to unconscious mainstream conditioning. It may be as formal or as poetic as you like. Some contracts are written like marriage vows with statements such as,

"I vow always to share sexual energy as an expression of my love and affection." Or, "I vow never to withhold my love from you or anyone else."

Once you and your partner(s) have written the contract, sign it and save it so you can retrieve it and review it during periodic relationship discussions.

TERMS OF AGREEMENTS

Here are examples of terms and clauses that people have used in their poly contracts:

SINGLE-SEX POLY. When bisexual individuals in a poly arrangement agree to date one sex and not the other sex.

PRIOR APPROVAL. When a couple agrees to open the relationship but they want to meet any new partners before moving into sexual territory. Often, the primary partner's comfort level is a decisive factor before moving into sexual territory with someone else.

VETO POWER. When the primary partner is given the power to approve or veto any outside relationships. If the primary partner does not approve, then the new relationship is not allowed to continue.

CONDOM COMMITMENT. When condoms are not used in the primary relationship, but are used when having sex with other people. In other words, the couple practices safe sex with everyone else.

FLUID BONDED. Any relationship in which partners are allowing the exchange of bodily fluids and having barrier-free intercourse.

FLUID MONOGAMY. When couples use condoms with all relationships except the primary relationship.

TELL-ALL POLICY. When individuals in a poly relationship agree to inform each other of the full intimate details of their involvement with other parties.

NEED-TO-KNOW. When partners agree to an open relationship and promise to inform their partners about any information that may affect the primary, such as when they start sleeping with someone else. This differs from Tell-All Policy in that there is no need to report unless asked.

DON'T ASK/DON'T TELL. When individuals would rather not know any details about their partner's outside relationships.

SOFT SWAP. When intimate behavior such as kissing, petting, and oral sex are allowed with multiple partners but penetrative sex is allowed only with the primary.

PACKAGE DEAL. When a couple only dates and has sex with others when they are together.

NON-EXCLUSION. When primary partners are always invited to join each other's dates and sleepovers. In other words, nobody spends the night alone unless it's by choice.

NO DRAMA. If a relationship has a repeated pattern of emotional crisis, creating undue chaos, and challenging other relationships, it can be considered drama, which by this policy is not tolerated. The No Drama policy can also take the form of placing a limit on how often and how long relationship issues are discussed. Compulsive emotional processing can be counterproductive and addictive. Polyamory requires more communication, but there is such a thing as too much processing.

Creating agreements can help new lovers feel safe. As you evolve and become more adept you may decide to keep looser agreements or fewer rules. However, we caution seekers to take it slow. When seekers dive into the deep end of polyamory too quickly, they often end up bonking their heads. If you are new to poly, we suggest you move only as fast as the slowest link in your relationship chain. If the relationship is meant to be, everyone involved will grow together. If it is not meant to be, you may grow apart. Separation can be a profound opportunity for spiritual growth.

We must give ourselves and our partners permission to communicate, renegotiate, forgive and accommodate. Remember, rules are made to be broken. We are human, after all. Ideally, communication occurs before an agreement is broken, but we've experienced incidences when this is not possible. We are not suggesting license for anything goes. We simply recognize that as a subculture, polyamorous people tend to be renegade spirits who rebel against rules. It is not uncommon for individuals, couples and pods to outgrow their agreements as fast as they can discuss them.

KAMALA DEVI'S POLY PROFILE

Kamala first met Michael at a Tantric puja led by Francoise Ginsberg in San Diego. He was at the door volunteering to greet people. When he welcomed Kamala, he flirted with her by drawing a little heart on her nametag. She didn't think much of it because she suspected he flirted with everyone.

As the evening progressed, a gorgeous strawberry blond caught her eye. When that woman slipped into the bathroom, Kamala took the opportunity to follow her. Viraja was even sexier up close, so Kamala expressed her adoration and scored her phone number.

At the end of the puja, Kamala found herself connecting deeply with Michael. Feeling her attraction for him, she immediately disclosed her orientation toward women and polyamory. This was a sort of a test. She figured that if he had a problem with her sexual orientation, she wouldn't bother getting involved. Michael passed the test by saying that he used to have a bisexual girlfriend and really enjoyed the freedom and open-mindedness that he experienced with her. So Kamala and Michael exchanged numbers. Kamala didn't find out until later that Michael and Viraja had also exchanged numbers earlier in the evening.

Kamala's first date with Viraja was sweet and promising. Her first date with Michael was fireworks and fantasy. Her second date with Michael was a Tantric camping trip at Canyon de Guadalupe, where Viraja happened to be cooking dinner for the group. Viraja and Michael admitted that they had a not-so-successful first date during which Viraja kept trying to get Michael to admit he was gay. After a good laugh and sharing organic bean soup, the triad stayed up until dawn exploring one another's bodies.

It's been six rich years since that unforgettable night. Viraja and Kamala have moved in and out of various types of relationships and remain soul sisters. They were even pregnant at the same time and are now aunties to each other's sons. Incidentally, Viraja met and dated Dez about a year before Kamala met him. So we thank her for introducing us. Without Viraja, this book may never have happened.

Today, Kamala and Michael are ecstatic to be co-creating a conscious Tantra and poly family, of which Dez is a big part. Different lovers may have different definitions, boundaries and practices, but our underlying mission is to bring out the best in each person. As Gods and Goddesses walking on this earth, we listen to our guidance and move in and out of spiritual practices, sacred rituals and relationships that serve the highest good of all.

BABA DEZ'S RELATIONAL PROFILE

Baba Dez started his relational journey with multiple lovers in high school, and continuing through his late twenties. He then moved onto a spiritual-shamanic celibate path for three years while he was traveling and teaching in New Zealand, Australia, and Colorado.

While practicing celibacy, Dez observed the temptation to suppress and disconnect from sexual desire. He learned the importance of embracing his sexuality and staying connected to his power even when celibate. (When our sexuality is not embraced on the celibate path it can result in compulsive behaviors, such as the extreme cases of abuse amongst catholic clergy.)

After his celibate phase, Dez experienced eight powerful years on the sacred path of monogamy with Heidi. His experience was sweet, focused, and magical while the lessons were deep, transformative and profound.

Dez now finds himself moving fluidly in and out of all the relational paths and into a realm he calls "The Sacred Path of No Path."

He explains, "Although I find myself often experiencing months of celibacy, monogamy or polyamory, I really don't identify with any of these relational containers. Each path has its own rewards and challenges. I find that if I have a deep desire or repulsion toward any particular path, it is an indicator that there are gifts for me in walking that path...at least for a short while.

"Sweetness and ease are always good indicators of whether or not we are on the right path at the right time. The point is, walking any path with presence, integrity, and impeccability will bring growth and rewards."

Ultimately, individuals must walk the path that matches the shape of their heart. Many people who discover they are not monogamous find it challenging to swim against the mainstream current alone. Whether you are celibate, monogamous, or polyamorous, we encourage you to surround yourself with individuals who are spiritually and sexually positive. It takes courage to reach out and accept support from healers, friends and family, but once you dip your toes into the stream of a sacred path, you will find teachers to help guide your way. If you continue to move towards the messages from your body, belly and heart, you will know when it is safe to dive in.

Epilogue
Blossoming into Wholeness

The lotus flower is the definitive metaphor for the spiritual journey. Artists, poets and philosophers often marvel at the pristine beauty that springs from such dark muddy waters. Unlike some interpretations that the flower rises above the filth and troubles of the world, we appreciate that it draws its power from rooting deeply into the muck. We all start our path from our connection to earth.

As a bud, the lotus looks like hands in prayer. The great stalk stretches toward heaven and the flower only unfurls when kissed by God's grace. Similarly, it's the spontaneous rising of the Kundalini that allows us to blossom to our sacred sexual Wholeness.

Petals open, like luscious lips, and return to the pond as they fall. Eventually, the naked core is revealed and the precious pod drops seeds back to the mud, giving rise to future flowers. At the end of every great journey there is a homecoming, or a return to the source.

Many flowers are not allowed their full expression. They are often cut off as buds and sold in the market as offerings. Though the tall flower bud look elegant in a vase, it has no connection to its roots and may never realize its potential.

Sacred Sexual Healing isn't about sacrificing your truth for someone else's pleasure or striving for a blessing that is out there, beyond reach. It is about staying connected to source and surrendering to the pleasure and play of the divine force within.

Sexual wholeness requires a tremendous amount of personal power and devotion. If you are to change the direction of your life, you must be consistent with your new practices to overcome the momentum of your previous choices, which still carry you in the old trajectory. In order to get out of the rut, you must create a new groove. Each time you practice the rituals, exercises or teachings in this book, you will be guided toward your full expression.

Change takes presence. Be gentle. Be flexible, be persistent, be brilliant. Be yourself.

About the Authors
How the Book Was Conceived

The tropical fingers of the island's breeze tickle Kamala Devi's face when she steps onto the rain-sprinkled tarmac. She's returned to Hawaii after eleven years of traveling the world before settling in San Diego, and it feels like coming home. She's only staying a week for the whirlwind filming of a documentary tentatively titled ***Sex Magic***.

Baba Dez Nichols pulls up in a red Impala. The door flings open and there's a professional cameraman recording Dez as he greets Kamala with hugs and kisses. He is a tall, slender Shaman with long honey-colored hair who looks ageless, timeless and sometimes even androgynous. He throws Kamala's bag in the trunk as she squeezes in. The black lava fields whirl by in the rain as they drive to the nearest health food store to buy the fixings for dinner.

Kamala first met Dez at the annual Daka-Dakini Conference in Sedona. Dez first started this national conference for Tantra teachers and professional sacred sexual healers in 2010. It is now called The ISTA Conference of Sexuality and Consciousness. The event is a forum for some of the most experienced teachers and practitioners in the field to gather and exchange ideas, practices and support.

Kamala agreed to lead a talk on "Self Promotion for Erotic Entrepreneurs." She originally thought her purpose in coming to the conference was to promote her Tantra novel, ***Don't Drink the Punch***, but as soon as she gazed into Baba Dez's eyes, she realized the real reason her soul was called to the conference was because it had a contract to reconnect with a community of sacred sexual healers.

Each day overflowed with the sharing of sacred sexual secrets, and afterward participants went to Dez's home for a sensual party. Dez owns a stunning nine-bedroom house and a two-story school building one block away built into the red rocks of Sedona. Throughout the year the school serves as a retreat center for sacred sexual healers to gather, study and practice. During the conference after-party, people dance in the living room, soak in the hot tubs, massage in the watsu pool, steam in the sauna and cuddle in the backrooms.

Kamala recalls that first night when she was invited to dance and play with Dez and his girlfriend, Maya. Though tempted to spend the whole night connecting with the gorgeous couple, she was eight weeks pregnant and decided to return to her hotel to rest her body.

That weekend was a powerful gestation time for both Kamala's baby and her career. Kamala came to know a multitude of sexual practitioners who were walking parallel spiritual paths. She left her first conference in a deep state of grief, tears streaming down her face as she drove to the airport. She lamented all the years that she didn't know about this gathering. She grieved for the loss of sexual freedom that came with being a new mother. And, of course, she wept because the pregnancy was making her cuckoo-hormonal.

Kamala's baby boy is now a year old and she left him at home in San Diego with her husband, Michael, in order to join Dez in Hawaii. This is the longest she's been away from her son and just thinking of his pudgy little cheeks makes her heart ache. But what postpartum mother wouldn't dream of an all-expenses-paid trip to paradise with her Tantric lover and no baby to wake her at 4 a.m.?!

Kamala likes to think that she is living the American dream: She has a house in Pacific Beach, a baby and a devoted husband, Michael. She is also living the American fantasy: She and Michael have a handful of Tantric lovers, they throw popular community events at their home every month, and on the weekends they attend dinner parties, sensual gatherings and

Tantric rituals. Sure, jealousy presents itself, but as a Tantrika, Kamala accepts every emotion as an opportunity to evolve and become more fully alive. Kamala is grateful to be surrounded by an open-minded community of fearless individuals like Baba Dez who models how we can transcend unconscious social expectations and truly live our dreams.

Dez pulls the rental car into an unpaved driveway of a stunning cottage on a private beach with more windows than walls. Kamala immediately strips into her bathing suit to dive into the warm turquoise surf. After swimming, Dez and Kamala climb low-hanging trees, play in the outdoor shower, melt into each other while making love and practice yoga on the beach during sunset in front of the camera.

Everyone gathers around the dinner table for a blessing before savoring raw zucchini pasta, cucumber and seaweed salad with ginger, and tropical fruit smoothies. The feast was shared by the Dynamic Duo film crew, Eric and Jonathan; Sam, a gorgeous surfer musician who is the host of the house; Das, a white-bearded yogi mountain man; Natasha, the extraordinary raw food chef; and of course Dez and Kamala.

This unlikely family has gathered to support the creation of Dez's documentary Sex Magic. It's the story of Dez's life's work and includes stories of numerous other sacred sexual healers. They have been following Dez around for more than a year, going to his lectures and conferences and getting a second-hand initiation into sacred sex.

Both Sam and Das are long time friends of Dez, dating back to when Dez had moved to a remote coffee and taro plantation on the big island to do organic farming in his twenties. Living close to nature spawned a deep connection to Mother Earth. He lived an alternative lifestyle off the grid, paddling canoe in the ocean and growing his own food, his hands in the dirt every day. That's when he had his first sexual awakening.

One day after he was done working in the gardens, he and his girlfriend went inside to shower. Relaxing in each other's arms, moving slowly, sweetly, he felt a quickening in his heart. He got very present and while making love, he stepped into an alternate reality. It was a peak experience with colors and visions. Afterward, he shared that he had a taste of something very powerful, describing it as radiance and exaltation. The intensity of his experience scared her and he could feel her pulling away. She thought he was crazy. Even though it wasn't externally validated, he felt it was true. It has since brought up significant questions that have compelled him on his Tantric journey.

He continued exploring, opening, discovering and deepening in Hawaii. He saw that the underlying motivation of all humanity was to love and be loved. He asked himself, How can I be the best lover possible? How can I expand my love for other beings, the planet and myself?

He met Charles and Carolyn Muir when they were just starting their work back in the '80s. He was later introduced to a progression of amazing beings and was blessed by their interactions and the books that fell into his hands. Though his introduction to Tantra was mostly technical, it was catalyzing and powerful. Sacred Spot Massage and learning to delay, redirect and circulate his ejaculation were two of the most significant and unselfish gifts he has given himself and his lovers.

Then his path took a Shamanic turn and he began learning about the emotional body. For years he worked with the Multi-Dimensional Research and Expansion team, a group of Shamans, life researchers and doctors in Colorado. It was at this time around the age of thirty-two that he experienced three years of celibacy. The challenge was staying connected to his desire while circulating his sexual energy with his inner feminine, cultivating power instead of shutting down.

Next Dez was called to experience monogamy. He entered into a committed relationship and learned about the power of sharing intention and ritual. During this time he saw the connection between healthy living and a healthy planet. Nutrition became a passion and he experimented with how different foods, sleep patterns and exercise could make a difference in one's overall well-being. He and his partner manifested a successful supplement company called Pure Planet and sold spirulina and green foods.

After eight years, the relationship was no longer serving them in their individual paths, so they shifted out of monogamy while maintaining a friendship and strong love. They sold the supplement business and Dez went back to teaching sacred sexuality.

He discovered that when sacred sexual healers faced professional challenges, they had nowhere to turn for support. Many teachers of the Tantric arts were trying to brand their work and market it, unconsciously perpetuating competition, separation and isolation. So, in 1991 he started the annual Daka-Dankini Conference out of his home in Sedona with eighteen women practitioners. Over the years, the conference has grown to accommodate hundreds of participants and has a multi-speaker format featuring some of the pioneers and powerhouses of the industry, such as Charles Muir, Betty Dodson, Deborah Taj Anapol and Mantak Chia.

After dinner the cast and crew go to the back porch to watch the moonlight play on the crashing waves. A casual discussion about ejaculation control arises. Natasha and Sam are both curious and eager to learn from Dez and Kamala. By the time lights and cameras are set up, the informal talk has been formalized.

Dez shares that most Taoist practitioners believe that men have a limited reserve of chi (life force), which is wasted when a man ejaculates, while orgasmic women can tap into an unlimited source of this energy. In order to access these infinite reserves of vital chi, men can cultivate a relationship with their inner feminine.

Though Kamala has had numerous lovers who practiced holding their ejaculation in order to preserve their life force, she gained a whole new appreciation of these teachings when making love to Dez. Most men have a difficult time staying present with their partners as they transmute their sexual energy, but Dez has a deep reverence for the Goddess, and teaches men how to touch into the essence of Mother Earth while circulating the orgasmic energy throughout their bodies.

Kamala's personal initiation to Tantra was by a man who had a similar androgynous capacity. Prior to beginning her Tantric path more than ten years ago, Kamala was secure in her identity as a lesbian. She had been almost exclusively with women for seven years when she was seduced by a Tantrika who happened to be in a man's body.

She remembers the first night she and Cain slept together, both wearing boxers. He commented about how small her twin bed was. She quipped that it was better for cuddling. As they got situated, Kamala realized what an adjustment it would be to sleep with a man. She remembers how logistically challenging it was to accommodate his big arms, big legs and big head. After she managed to wrap her arms around his broad chest, he apologized by saying, "I hope I'm being respectful of your space." Kamala reassured him, "It's OK. It's not your fault that you take up twice the space as most women."

Eventually Kamala got over the physical differences and dropped into an extraordinary energetic connection. This is how she realized that this man was more of a Goddess than any woman she had ever dated. She learned to soften into her own Goddess and balance her overly butch inner masculine. This relationship opened her to bisexuality, polyamory and her devotion to Tantra.

Kamala followed her lover to Waimanalo, Hawaii, where they lived in a crazy drumming commune in a pegboard shack with their pet chicken, Stu. By day, Kamala lead botanical garden tours on a cattle ranch and by night she directed gay and lesbian theater. Meanwhile, Cain worked on his book, danced and modeled naked for art classes. Month after month, they expanded in sensual exploration of erotica, role playing, gift giving, foot washing, partner yoga, ritual sex, sensual feasting, anal sex, cross dressing, performance art, massage, meditation, spanking, dreamscape and gender bending. It was a spontaneous sexual awakening that unfolded without a curriculum or a guru.

During a regular Tuesday drum rehearsal, the Tahitian neighbors roasted a pig and everyone danced under the stars. Kamala remembers dissolving into the dance. She laughed whole belly laughs at the absurd significance of life, until she wiped the tears from her eyes to see who was laughing. After every ounce of being had been spent, she crawled home to make love. She melted from her earth-suit and merged with the force that animates her. At some point she drifted into a dreamless sleep and when she awoke, it was to a whole new level of consciousness. This experience went unnamed for years. It's not that the enlightenment was confusing, or even a secret—it's just she didn't want to try to understand it or explain it away.

In fact, she wasn't ready for the other potentially transformative teachings Cain had to offer, so she left the relationship to ground herself with something less ego confronting. Her Tantra quest led her through Europe, Southeast Asia, China and India. All her seeking led her to a Tantric Shaman named Michael. Together they are building an eco-friendly temple in San Diego and anchoring Tantra into their expanding community.

Now Kamala Devi lays her naked body against soft white sheets while feverishly typing the rough draft of ***Sacred Sexual Healing*** into her laptop. Baba Dez's head is propped against the bamboo headboard and he shares his ideas for the book. His feet are tucked in a fluffy down comforter, which matches the billowing drapes that cover a half-dozen open windows. The rain outside is pelting the tin roof and is almost as loud as the waves crashing on the front porch. Much of this book has been created by Kamala typing while listening to Dez or transcribing past lectures. This morning she struggles to type as fast as he speaks memories from his childhood.

"I grew up in West LA. Like everyone, I learned how to function in dichotomy: good and bad, right and wrong, all that is sweet, and all that is bitter. I felt myself and others disconnected from the Earth and each other, I wanted to believe that the world could be healed, people could get along and this could be a really loving beautiful place. But everyone said: If you're going to survive in this world, you've got to get real. I remember when I tried to communicate my frustration, I was shamed. How can you be right and everyone else be wrong? And since my dreams were not acceptable or in alignment with mass consciousness, I let go of the dream. In a world of so much disconnection and dysfunction how can heaven happen? Sometimes I was given drugs to calm me down so I was not 'so sensitive.'

I was fortunate enough to manifest an uncle who was half Native American. He took me out to the desert where I had my first spiritual awakening, which came through my connection to the Earth. This is how I got my nickname Desert, or Dez for short.

"I began to drink deeper in the sweetness and the bitterness of feeling. Now, I can feel into my deepest visions and desires that my little boy had. I am reclaiming my emotional body from when I was seven or eight. Now, I am holding space for myself to dream again, meeting myself like never before."

Dez takes a few deep breaths and blinks back the tears. Kamala closes her computer and the conversation subsides into warm caresses and conscious kisses. Kamala feels her feet curling around the backs of Dez's calves. Her arms roam his tan chest and she begins to trust him with more of her body weight. She abandons her mental state and submits to her arousal. Soft lips and wet tongues start to explore each other's curves and corners. If the camera crew were in the room, they would likely pan away to show the sun breaking through the stormy sky.

As the rain subsides they are able to tour more of the island. Dez arranges for a ritual hike into a cave where the lava dried in the shape of a yoni. It's a sacred site where Hawaiians did fertility rituals. It takes a fair amount of driving around, hiking and looking for it before they find themselves at the mouth of the cave. They take some quiet time to gather their offerings and pray before the journey. The mosquitoes come out and they are hungry.

The cast and crew lower themselves into a tube made of black pumice. Eric has a huge flood lamp, which provides just enough light for the next few steps. The walls and ceiling are dripping from the morning rain; the jagged black rock is wet underfoot. When the lamp is turned away, the cave becomes pitch dark, a black hole. The space is eerie with shadows flickering against the walls. There is a heavy feeling that the place is still inhabited by generations of ancestors.

With a reverent tone, Dez shares a little history of the site as they walk. There are beds in the cave where men and women make love, babies are conceived and sacred rites are performed.

They continue through the tube in single file. Kamala and Natasha are instructed to sit down in the dark and to get comfortable. Light is then cast upon the yoni. In that moment, it's as if Mother Earth shape-shifted into the form of Pele the volcano Goddess spreading her lava-formed legs to reveal herself. Mother Earth has a yoni. She has labia, with red and wet inner lips. Kamala is moved to tears by the mysterious depth and beauty before her. She places her offerings at Pele's clit and cries some more. When she recovers from sobbing they begin chanting:

Mother, I can feel you under my feet…
Mother, I can feel your heartbeat…
Mother, I can feel you under my feet…
Mother, I can feel your heartbeat…

The song resonates in the cave acoustics and settles into a powerful sacred sexual healing trance.

Kamala has a lot to heal. This year she underwent the tremendous rite of passage from maiden to motherhood. Pregnancy was the happiest time of her life and her baby held on for three weeks after the due date. The home birth was twenty-one hours of breathing, moaning, chanting, dancing and soaking in the hot tub, without any drugs. Instead of intense pushing, Kamala used a Tantric breathing practice called Cobra Breath to birth her beautiful baby boy. He slipped onto earth at sunset. Michael proudly caught him and untangled the umbilical cord twice from his neck and once from his belly.

When Devin Echo squeezed out of Kamala, it's as if he took all her happiness with him. He looked up at his mommy smiling and cooing while she spent most of her days curled up in her pajamas crying.

Midwives and doctors recommend that a new mother not have sex for at least six weeks while the birth canal is on the mend. No sex. Not even masturbation. Six weeks. Total celibacy. For most mothers this might sound like a welcome vacation, but not for Kamala. During pregnancy, sex had become her daily prayer. It was how she rested, rejoiced and reconnected to the divine vessel she inhabits. Six weeks with no sex felt like a death sentence.

Even worse than the pronouncement of celibacy was the pain she felt when urinating. The baby's head had bruised and torn her urethra when it came through.

There are countless people who after any kind of sexual trauma let their sensuality silently slip away as they pretend to enjoy sex, but secretly numb out. This could have been all too easy for Kamala, if she didn't know first-hand the pleasurable potential and divine depths of a woman's womb. The birth canal is the mouth of a sacred channel that connects Mother Earth to Father Sky. This vessel is open to the degree that we feel fully alive. When we feel wounded, numb, guilty, fearful or shameful, the channel is obstructed and energy cannot flow. There is a kink, dam or block in the channel. In postpartum depression, Kamala felt the darkness of this disconnection, and thus agreed to co-author a book about Sacred Sexual Healing with Dez.

This book is based on Dez's life's work and he is committed to empowering the broadest possible audience with its message as soon as possible. Dez had been envisioning, proposing and pitching a book for several years, but since that had not manifested, he contacted Kamala. He was familiar with her work, loved her first book, and knew that she taught a course on "How to Write a Book in 90 Days," so he trusted she'd be the perfect collaborator.

Dez drove into San Diego on Thanksgiving weekend to sign the book contract. After getting Michael's blessings and arranging for him to watch the baby, Kamala invited Dez to a ritual to consummate their relationship as co-authors.

Kamala and Dez created a sacred space with pillows and candles to start the ***SHAMAN Method of Sex Magic***. They began by discussing their intention of writing a practical guidebook that would make sexual healing and Sex Magic accessible to all those who are ready. They held space for each other's fears and limiting beliefs about the project. After voicing any physical boundaries and intimate needs regarding sexual union, they made love for the first time. Instead of coming together as teacher or student, healer and seeker, Kamala and Dez came together as empowered equals. They recognized the divinity in each other's reflection and danced together in the Buddha field.

That evening, they opened the channel to the collective consciousness. In this alchemical exchange, Dez transmitted his guides and allies to help Kamala write and offered his seed to his childhood dream of bringing heaven on earth. And in that moment, Kamala was impregnated with this book.

Aho Mitakuye Oyasin!

Afterword
Community Building

Since the first publishing of this book there have been a number of game-changing developments in the work and lives of Baba Dez and Kamala Devi. We offer the following updates as invitations for you to continue your learning, growing and teaching. We welcome you to join us in the following:

1) ISTA-International School of Temple Arts
2) SEX Magic-The Movie
3) Temple Arts Productions
4) TantraTheater.TV
5) Tantra-Palooza

1. ISTA-International School of Temple Arts

What started as the Baba Dez World Tour quickly evolved into ISTA, a non-profit educational and religious organization founded in 2007 which is co-operated by a consortium of leaders in Sacred Temple Arts disciplines such as Tantra, Taoism, Meditation, Yoga, Shamanism, and Sex Education.

The Mission: ISTA is committed to raising sexuality & consciousness education across the globe to grow community, provide conferences and trainings to practitioners and teachers, and to provide business tools and collaborations to support the re-emergence of Temples around the globe. We do this by working with life force energy, the beginning, middle and end of everything. We as humans connect Father Sky and Mother Earth through our bodies as conduits.

Join us for an International Conference Near you. www.SedonaTemple.com, www.schooloftemplearts.org

2. Sex Magic: Feature Length Documentary

Running time: 80 min

It's your average "Boy meets Girl, Boy loses Girl, Boy gets Girl back story." But, in this story, the Boy is BABA DEZ, a renowned polyamorous (multiple relationships), sacred sexual healer, and the Girl, MAYA, is a Priestess of the Temple Arts, with a history of sexual abuse. To get her back, Dez must embark on a heroic journey, one that pitches him into a labyrinth of philosophical challenges and contradictions. *Sex Magic* takes an irreverent look at very reverent people, where devotees and practitioners of the ancient art of Tantra travel down the risky emotional path and attempt to channel their sexual energy toward spiritual growth and manifestation of their desires.

A prominent sacred sexual healer, Baba Dez is a pillar of the Sacred Sexuality practitioner community. His work is doing sexual healing with clients to help them overcome past abuse issues, or just to enrich their sexual and spiritual lives. He also organizes Sex and Consciousness Conferences around the world. His life's goal is no less than to save the planet by "doing the work." Of his many apprentices, Dez has chosen Maya (meaning illusion in Hunduism), a beautiful aspiring Tantrica to be his queen. Maya is the perfect feminine reflection of himself, albeit much younger and far less experienced.

Together they host international conferences, inevitably rendezvousing with a myriad of Dez's lovers, both former and current. But pursuing a life of pleasure turns out to be not so pleasurable for Maya, evoking long-buried issues of jealousy and abandonment. Repulsed by the continual parade of Dez's lovers, Maya can take no more and she leaves him. She explains the reason she left was that he had been with too many women. When asked, Dez reluctantly admits he's been with 1 to 2 thousand women.

In addition to the devastation of the loss of his queen, a rumor circulates that he's inappropriately using his lingam (penis) in healing work with his clients. This is perpetuated from a dakini he mentored, who also accuses him of inappropriately coming on to her, saying he has an insatiable need. Dez explains it's dangerous for a man to do this work, suggesting it's the "wounded feminine lashing out." He turns inward, to a path of celibacy, although he continues to move his energy through his self-pleasuring ritual (non-ejaculatory masturbating).

But celibacy doesn't last long. Dez goes to Hawaii with two lovers; one a raw food chef, the other an accomplished writer and sacred sexual healer. Together, they're writing a book about *Sex Magic*; the process of creating a god connection through lovemaking to manifest one's dreams and desires. Married and with a young child of her own, Dez's co-writer claims that by making love with Dez, she's able to "download" all his wisdom given to him by his teachers. And for Dez, she "holds space" for Maya's return. In a fun-filled week's vacation they visit a secret Yoni (vagina) Cave where ancient Hawaiians performed fertility rituals, pick fresh fruits & vegetables to the delight of the raw food chef, work on the book, and frolic in the sun & surf. That is until Maya calls.

While some may see an existential crisis in the clash between a man's belief system and his reality, Dez stays resolutely confident that *Sex Magic* works and will manifest the return of his beloved Maya.

3. Temple Arts Productions

Temple Arts Productions is a virtual university with instant access to streaming online videos from many masters in Sacred Sexuality, Tantra, and Sex Magic. This site features educational videos from past conferences and teacher training programs. Offerings include the great pioneers such as Charles Muir, Caroline Muir, David Cates, Betty Martin, Betty Dodson, Triambika, Shawn Roop, Reid Mihalki and dozens more! These instructional videos are geared towards educating Teachers of the Temple Arts. The info-packed Conference presentations and the extensive training videos are invaluable. These teachings and content are highly specialized and are virtually unavailable anywhere else.

Register now and/or become an affiliate and discover cash rewards in 2010. www.templeartsproductions.com/

4. Tantra Theater

Kamala Devi is the founder and director of a collective of teachers, healers, and performance artists that are not afraid to wrestle with issues of sexuality and spirituality on stage.

MISSION STATEMENT: SD Tantra Theater Troupe combines ritual and performance to transmute sexual guilt, shame and fear into art, healing and liberation. We celebrate that every aspect of life's drama is sacred.

VISION: The San Diego Tantra Theater training provides a safe, challenging, non-judgmental space for spiritual seekers to experience their full expression. During a 90-day course we collaborate on creating performances that promote a greater understanding of sacred sexual issues in conscious communities within and beyond San Diego. Our personal, vulnerable and sometimes controversial presentations inspire learning, open discussion and spiritual awakening. The troupe provokes continual re-examination of self in relationship to all things sacred and spiritual. During performance, both artists and audience have an opportunity to realize the creative power within their sex center. Using comedy, drama, and dance, we aim to educate, entertain and enlighten.

Enjoy hours of hot streaming video clips from past performances. Just click on a button that says "Now Playing." We hope to transmit the spiritual inspiration for your own tantric awakening. Tantra Theater embodies the experiential nature of Tantra and aims to transform its audience.

www.TantraTheater.TV

Gratitude

 OUR FAMILY: A big warm hug goes out to Kamala's beloved Michael McClure. Dez's wonderful parents Ted and Margaret Nichols, for a lifetime of love and support; his three older brothers Ted, Phil, Brad and his three younger sisters Maggie, Janet, Sandy; and a huge, extended Austrian-Hungarian family. Kamala's parents Spencer and Laurie for being on purpose in the world. Rosa and Randy for living one day at a time. Linda McClure and Bob Goggin for Devin-sitting. Frank McClure for line-drying laundry. Miguel for many hours of mentoring. And Kamala's dear grandparents, Larry and Terry, for modeling a loving marriage that lasted over seventy years!

 OUR SUPPORT TEAM: Juniper Campbell, a dream manager for keeping so many projects organized and on track. Anyaa McAndrew, Ariel White, Chris Luth, Cindy Lee, Cynthia Hernandez Sanchez, Das Furtado, Debra Hanson, Eric Liebman, Jess Yadley, Jonathan Schell, Kypris Aster Drake, Lawrence Lanoff, Liz Hahn, Mariette Pan, Natasha Troussova, Rhiyana Holiday, Robin Nichols, Sam Frey, Shawn Roop, Steven Jay, Viraja Ma, The Erotic Way Tele-course, Sisters in Truth, The San Diego Tantra Connection, and all the courageous souls who are working to heal the sexual wounds of the planet.

 TEACHERS & ALLIES: Anna Marti, Cain and Revital Carroll, Charles and Caroline Muir, David Cates, Françoise Ginsberg, Glen Benton, Gloria Reeder, Heidi Benson, Julien Canuso, Laurel Yonika, Paul Novacek, Rayna (Hoopnotica) McInturf, REiD Mihalko, River and Diamond Jameson, Russell Archibald, Sarasawti Ting, Shakahn and Jaguar Kukulcan, Sri Param Eswaran, Vasumitra Zeerok, William VanVechten, and Master zYoah.

 GUIDES & GURUS: Abuelita Ester, Baba Ji, Daren Singer, Osho, Robert Frey and Lakshmi. And we offer our gratitude to the collective wisdom of our ancestors that have brought us to this NOW, so we didn't have to repeat all of their learning experiences.

 CONTENT READERS: Shawn Roop and Todd Whitaker
COPY EDITORS: Rachel Moore and Robyn Talbott
MASTER EDITOR: Robin Nichols
BACK COVER PHOTO: Tara Eby
COVER ART: Andrew Gonzales
GRAPHIC DESIGN: Miguel

Appendix
Sacred Sexual Healing Exercises

Exercise #1: Sensate Focusing

BENEFITS: Increases personal and interpersonal awareness. Enhances communication and reduces performance anxiety and sexual pressure. Helps shift the focus during lovemaking from goal orientation to the experience of being in the moment. Creates trust and safety in a relationship. Individuals are empowered to take more responsibility for their own pleasure rather than assume responsibility for someone else's enjoyment.

PREPARATION: The couple agrees to ban intercourse and explicit touching of breasts, nipples, and genitals for the purpose of this exercise. Decide who will be receiving and who will be giving. Practice with or without clothing as long as both persons are warm and relaxed. We recommend you schedule your sessions in advance, at least twice per week for 20-60 minutes per person.

METHOD: In the first stage of Sensate Focusing, the receiver lies back with eyes closed and receives slow, light non-sexual touch. Whether touching or being touched, both people bring their awareness to the subtle textures, temperatures, and sensations of touch. The person doing the touching focuses on what feels good, not on trying to please the other. Sexual arousal may occur naturally, but do not have sex. Practice in complete silence so that both people can stay focused on the physical sensation of touch. (If the receiving partner is ever uncomfortable, he or she should clarify what is wanted or assert boundaries, if needed.) This session is usually timed. Some therapists suggest participants lay on their front for 15 minutes and on their back for 15 minutes. This stage can be repeated as many times as it takes for both people to be completely relaxed before proceeding to the next phase.

The second stage of Sensate Focusing may include the breasts, yoni and lingam, but intercourse and orgasm are still prohibited. The person doing the touching is to begin with light, feathery touch on the whole body before moving slowly, deliberately to the genitals and breasts.

This is when we can begin a nonverbal communication technique called "Hand Riding." The receiver places one hand on top of the hand of the person doing the touching and gently indicates what is wanted, e.g., more or less pressure, a faster or slower pace, or to move to a different body part. The primary intention is to add direction. The person doing the touching focuses on her exploration, not on trying to pleasure the person being touched.

In the third stage of Sensate Focusing, the couple may begin to touch each other mutually. Intercourse is still off limits, no matter how sexually aroused the couple may become.

In the subsequent stages of Sensate Focusing, couples continue with mutual touching, within agreed on parameters such as woman-on-top position without penetration, or penis on clit, vulva and breasts, but not inside. The tip of the penis may only be inserted into the vaginal opening if the penis is soft.

ADDITIONAL NOTES: During all stages of Sensate Focusing, the focus is on sensations and the exercise may be stopped or slowed down if either partner becomes anxious or orgasm-focused. Do your best to experience the moment and not judge performance. When anyone is worried about doing it right, then it's not being done right. Relax, loosen up and have more fun. If either person becomes tense or anxious during this exercise, it's time to slow down or stop to breathe. No need to hurry.

Exercise #2: Natural Breath

BENEFITS: Relaxes the nervous system, reduces stress and tension, and calms the mind. Massages and tones the internal organs, especially the digestive organs. This method of breathing is efficient, requiring less effort for the heart and lungs to oxygenate the body.

PREPARATION: Start by lying on the floor, facing up, with a pillow under your knees. If more comfortable, you may elevate your legs on a chair or the couch. Allow yourself between 5-30 minutes to practice without interruption.

METHOD: Close your eyes and begin in stillness. Become aware of your natural breath. Simply observe the breath; do not try to change it. Be aware of each and every in-breath and out-breath. Begin to say mentally, "I am aware of my inhale; I am aware of my exhale." Continue in this way in your own time. Let yourself relax into the continual, smooth ebb and flow of your breath.

Come closer and closer to your breath. Notice how your breath is flowing. Is it fast or slow? Shallow or deep? Even or irregular? Are you sometimes gasping for breath? Notice the temperature of your breath. Observe with the attitude of a detached witness.

Feel your breath flowing in and out at the back of your throat. Bring your awareness down to your chest and feel your breath flowing in the trachea and bronchial tubes. Next, feel your breath flowing into lungs. Be aware of your lungs expanding and relaxing.

Shift your attention to your rib cage and observe the expansion and relaxation of this area. Bring your awareness down to your belly. Feel your abdomen move upward on inhalation and downward on exhalation.

Finally, become aware of the whole breathing process from your nostrils to the bottom of your belly. Take as long as you like. When you feel complete, bring your awareness back to your physical surroundings. When you are ready, open your eyes.

VARIATIONS:

1. Bring one relaxed hand onto your belly. As you inhale, feel your belly rise and fill with air like a balloon. As you exhale, feel the breath emptying. Inhale, breath fills your belly and lifts your hands; exhale, your belly falls, leaving a soft, gentle hollow in the abdomen.

2. Once you feel comfortable with the above technique, you may want to incorporate words that can enhance the exercise. For example, mentally say "relaxing" while inhaling and "releasing" while exhaling. The intention is to invite healing on the inhalation and release all that no longer serves you on the exhalation.

Exercise #3: Complete Breath

BENEFITS: Increases lung capacity, increases oxygen supply to the blood, raises hemoglobin levels, improves metabolism, slows the heart rate, lowers blood pressure and has calming effect on central nervous system.

PREPARATION: This practice is also known as Three-Part, Dirgha or Full Belly Breath. We will explore the three regions of the breathing process: the belly, the chest and the collarbone area. This is the prerequisite to most deeper yogic breathing practices. Allow yourself between 5-30 minutes to practice on a daily basis.

METHOD: Start by sitting in a comfortable cross-legged position. Imagine a balloon in your lower belly. Through your mouth or nose, blow out all your air and deflate the balloon by contracting your navel towards your spine.

Inhale deeply through your nose, drawing your breath into the balloon and expanding it. Exhale completely.

Inhale deeply, gradually filling the balloon. When the balloon in your abdomen is full, continue inhaling into your lungs, expanding your rib cage, expanding the spaces between your ribs.

Exhale all the air from your lungs and ribs, and imagine emptying air from the balloon in your abdomen.

Inhale deeply, filling the balloon, filling your lungs, filling your upper chest and throat, raising your collarbones, until you are completely filled with breath. If comfortable, retain your breath for a few seconds, keeping your eyes and face relaxed.

Exhale slowly, releasing air from your upper chest, shoulders, collarbones, ribcage, and then from the balloon in your belly. Contract your navel towards your spine, squeezing out all the air.

Continue this practice, increasing the duration of your inhale, retention and exhale. The ratio should be 1:1:1. For example, inhale for four seconds, retain for four seconds, and exhale for four seconds. Do not use a clock to time yourself— allow your body to be your clock.

VARIATIONS: Some yoga teachers like to expand the practice to nine parts: the front, back and sides of the belly, the heart and the collarbone areas.

Exercise #4: Alternate Nostril Breathing

BENEFITS: Alleviates headaches, migraines, anxiety, boredom, and fatigue. Balances the right and left hemispheres of the brain. Balances the masculine and feminine energies. Creates an immediate sense of well-being and contentment. This practice is also known as Channel Purification Breath, Nadi Shodhana (sweet breath), and Sukha Pranayama (comfortable or happy breath).

PREPARATION: Sit in a comfortable cross-legged position with your spine straight and tall. Rest your left hand comfortably on your left knee in Jnana Mudra (tips of thumb and forefinger touching). Arrange your right hand into Vishnu Mudra. (Make a fist and release your thumb, ring finger and pinky. Hold your first and middle fingers curled towards the base of your thumb. Keep your ring finger and pinky together.

Some people find it useful to cross their ring and pinky fingers.) If you are unable to do Vishnu Mudra, simply use your right thumb and right ring finger for this practice.

METHOD: Place your right thumb on your right nostril. Exhale completely. Gently press your right nostril closed with your right thumb. Inhale gently through your open left nostril. Close your left nostril with your right ring finger, release your thumb, and exhale through your right nostril. Inhale through your right nostril. Close your right nostril with your thumb, exhale through your left nostril. This completes one round of Alternate Nostril Breathing. Continue with this pattern, breathing rhythmically. Breathe slowly and smoothly, inhaling fully, exhaling completely. The pattern is Exhale Inhale Switch Exhale Inhale Switch.

VARIATION: Analoma Viloma is a more advanced breathing practice with a 4:8:4 ratio. Inhale through your left nostril for a count of four, exhale through your left nostril for a count of eight, and retain your breath for a count of four. Repeat on your right side.

ADDITIONAL NOTES: Most people do not breathe equally through both nostrils. After doing this practice, you may notice a different nostril becomes dominate on the average of every 2-3 hours. Studies utilizing EEG technology have shown that inhaling through the right nostril stimulates the left hemisphere, which regulates the nervous system.

Exercise #5: Boundary Setting

BENEFITS: Clear and strong boundaries allow people to honor themselves and to respect and honor others. Completing this exercise will produce confidence and clarity, save time, increase energy and raise your emotional reserves. This work develops self-respect and upgrades the quality of your connections. People with clear boundaries no longer attract needy people and are not drained by their relationships.

METHOD: Read through the following list of examples. Then create your own boundaries by making a list of 10 things that people can no longer do or say to you or around you. Consider all areas of your life: professional, personal, sexual, family, and social. Be thorough. Everybody's boundaries are different. We suggest you start by looking at the arguments, challenges, and frustrations that you have had recently and ask yourself, "Where did my boundaries get crossed?"

EXAMPLES OF PROFESSIONAL BOUNDARIES:
* ❀ I don't answer the phone before 10am or after 6pm.
* ❀ I only work 4 days per week.
* ❀ I place a Do Not Disturb sign outside my door when I'm working.
* ❀ I ask clients to turn off their phones when we are in a meeting.
* ❀ I ask all clients to pay in advance.
* ❀ All clients must call to re-schedule within 24 hours if they are to receive a credit or refund.

EXAMPLES OF PERSONAL BOUNDARIES:
* ❀ I ask my guests to take their shoes off when they enter my temple.
* ❀ Friends and family cannot raise their voice at me in anger.
* ❀ People cannot talk to me about problems, negativity, or victim stories for over 5 minutes unless we've pre-arranged the time and space to do so.
* ❀ People cannot call me names, or make derogatory humor or negative statements towards me or those I love.
* ❀ I don't tolerate gossip about myself or others.
* ❀ People cannot blame, shame, guilt, or in other words, not take responsibility for their own communication.

EXAMPLES OF SEXUAL BOUNDARIES:
- ❀ I never sleep with anyone unless...
- ❀ I don't allow people to touch my genitals without verbal consent.
- ❀ I don't allow anyone to kiss me if they are sick.
- ❀ I don't engage in oral sex until I've seen someone's genitals in the light.
- ❀ I ask my lover(s) to wash their hands before touching my genitals.
- ❀ I always use a condom for penetration with new lovers.

EXAMPLES OF OTHER PEOPLES BOUNDARIES:
- ❀ I ask if it's a good time to talk when I phone someone.
- ❀ I don't offer my services unless people have asked and paid for it.
- ❀ I don't hold people to my own personal standards.
- ❀ I don't take it personally when someone is upset.
- ❀ I don't yell between rooms.

ADDITIONAL NOTES: You may have noticed that boundaries can occur in words, actions, and space. Most boundaries have to do with the manner in which we are spoken to, the physical space we share with others and the requests that are made of us by lovers, clients, family and friends.

Exercise #6: Rainbow Relaxation

BENEFITS: Deepens awareness of self and body, raises and heals the overall vibration, relaxes and purifies the subtle body. Awakens the Kundalini, heals imbalances and develops ability to focus and concentrate.

METHOD: Lie down and relax. Breathe deeply and clear your mind.

1. Bring your awareness to the base of your spine. Located in the perineum between the anus and the genitals is the first chakra. Visualize the color red. Think security...

grounded…fire…heat. Imagine this area heating up and allow the color red to spread throughout your pelvis.

2. Next, bring your attention to your genital region. This is the sex chakra, which governs the creative force within our body. Imagine an orange or golden glow. Think sexy … life-force…arousal…creation…inspiration.

3. Allow this energy to rise like warm lava flowing towards your navel. A couple fingers-width below your navel is the center of your power chakra, which is the color yellow, like sunshine. This center regulates our overall vitality and transmits inner wisdom. Imagine healthy digestion…the comfort of a nourishing meal … the sense of confidence and knowing that comes when you have a gut feeling.

4. Allow this power to radiate out from the center like sun shining through clouds up towards your ribs and heart. Imagine your heart, lungs, ribs and the space around your chest opening and flowing with the green of growing things. This is our center for love and compassion. Your heart center radiates down through your shoulders, arms, and wrists to your healing hands.

5. As it radiates back up through your shoulders and towards your neck, the color changes from green to blue. Your throat chakra is the color of cool blue water. This is the communication and expression center which governs our voice. Imagine your vocal cords and all of your words cleansed by the cool blue color, so that you speak only truth. Perhaps you even hear the sound of your true expression emanating from your throat. Imagine this energy buzzing and resonating upward towards your face.

6. Gather all of your attention between your eyebrows. The third eye point is a concentrated point in the middle of your mind. It is the color indigo. Your focus is like a single-pointed purple lightbulb within your mind. This chakra provides our insight, intuition and psychic powers. Imagine the way that lightning flashes and turns the sky purple. Similarly,

your mind is electrified and your cranium is filled with the gift of concentration.

7. This clairvoyant capacity naturally takes you above your crown to the final chakra. The crown chakra is violet or white and is shaped like a thousand-petal lotus flower unfolding above your head. This chakra opens into our super-conscious, or higher self. Violet is the last color on the spectrum and symbolizes all colors at once. Imagine your entire body lit up and surrounded by a bright halo of love and light.

VARIATIONS: Once you have mastered chakra visualization, you may add movement, breath and sound to each chakra. You may also practice moving through the chakras in descending order. Advanced practitioners may bring this exercise into partner play. It may be practiced during lovemaking, while sitting in Yab-Yum, or while gazing into each other's eyes. When practiced with a partner, the chakras will interact, communicate and resonate, creating a subtle but sacred geometry opening between the two bodies.

Exercise #14: Chakra Affirmations

BENEFITS: The potential value of this practice is so vast, it is impossible to itemize all the benefits. Minimally, you may experience a deeper relationship with your body, greater confidence in sex and a richer connection to Spirit. But that is not all, stay open to the magic of synchronicity all around you!

METHOD: Before falling asleep each night, deepen your breath, read through the following list of sacred sexual healing affirmations and notice which ones resonate, positively or negatively. Take particular notice of which ones make your tummy contract. Read those over and over until you feel more relaxed. Close your eyes and breathe deeply after each affirmation. Breathe the affirmations into your chakras. We suggest you continue this practice for twenty-one consecutive days or as long as it takes for each chakra to open and your body to accept the affirmation as truth.

FIRST CHAKRA: THE ROOT
1. My fear dissolves as I circulate sexual energy.
2. I am connected to Mother Earth when I make love.
3. My sexual energy keeps me young and vital.
4. As I open my body to more sexual abundance, I invite abundance in all areas of my life.
5. I am transmuting fear, guilt and shame into pleasure.
6. I feel the juicy Kundalini energy rising up my spine each time I make love.
7. I choose myself and enjoy a daily masturbation meditation.
8. I feel secure and confident in my sexual choices.
9. I am enjoying full sexual health and abundance.
10. I release my sexual past and welcome new erotic possibilities.

SECOND CHAKRA: SEX CENTER
1. I give myself permission to experience my full sexual expression.
2. I exercise healthy and appropriate sexual energy.
3. I am a radiant sexual being.
4. I have a soft pink healthy yoni (or a powerful wand of light).
5. I extend healthy sexual boundaries and honor those of others.
6. I easily circulate my orgasms from my genitals to my whole body.
7. I deserve to receive sexual pleasure.
8. I embrace and celebrate my genitals.
9. My sexuality stimulates my creative brilliance.
10. I am sexy, creative and free.

THIRD CHAKRA: POWER CENTER

1. My sex drive is healthy and strong.
2. I listen to my body wisdom when it comes to sex.
3. I am a powerful, potent lover.
4. I share and expand vital energy each time I make love.
5. I am empowered in my sexual choices.
6. I release all cords that bind me.
7. I have an abundance of sexual energy.
8. I am unique and powerful in my sexual expression.
9. I welcome change in my love life.
10. Sex helps me tap into and feel deep emotion.

FOURTH CHAKRA: THE HEART

1. I keep my heart open while making love.
2. I experience compassion and connection during sex.
3. I release all past heartaches and open to receive more love.
4. I deepen my connection to my beloved each time we make love.
5. I expand my orgasmic energy by drawing it up to the heart.
6. Making love raises my love levels.
7. I accept and receive love through my lovemaking.
8. Love flows into my life naturally.
9. I am a magnet to loving relationships.
10. Love is here now.

FIFTH CHAKRA: THE THROAT

1. I effortlessly communicate my sexual boundaries.
2. I am empowered and expressive when it comes to what I want in bed.
3. I am fully expressed in bed.
4. Talking dirty is fun and healthy.
5. I share my fantasies with ease and grace.
6. I am eloquent in the language of love.

7. I give myself permission to moan and make noise when I am in my pleasure.
8. Talking truthfully about sex comes easily to me.
9. I am a creative channel for erotic poetry, stories and song.
10. Moving sexual energy cultivates vulnerability, authenticity and truth.

SIXTH CHAKRA: THE THIRD EYE

1. My mind is at peace around issues of sex.
2. I easily circulate sexual energy to my third eye.
3. Sex stimulates my seeing and knowing.
4. Sex activates my inner vision.
5. I have a strong sense of sexual intuition.
6. I release all delusion or lies around sex.
7. I naturally tap into my inner vision during orgasm.
8. I easily infuse my intentions with sexual energy.
9. I am the conscious creator of my own love life.
10. I manifest my dreams with sex magic.

SEVENTH CHAKRA: THE CROWN

1. My sexuality is integrated with my whole self.
2. I am a spiritual being having a sexual experience.
3. I dedicate my sex to the enlightenment of all beings.
4. Sex helps me dissolve the illusion of separation.
5. My sexual energy is rocket fuel toward my fully-embodied enlightenment.
6. I commune with my higher power through sex.
7. Sex is my spiritual practice.
8. I offer my body to the pleasure and play of the divine.
9. I bring more and more conscious awareness into my sexual practice.
10. Sex is a form of worship and prayer.

VARIATIONS:

1.Select your favorite affirmation to use for each chakra, and then practice a full-spectrum meditation where you speak or chant one affirmation at each chakra.

2. Identify which chakra needs the most work and select several affirmations to chant or vibrate into that area. We suggest you continue this practice for as long as it takes for your chakra to open and your body to accept the affirmation as truth.

3. Use your intuition; make up your own Chakra Affirmation Practice. Have fun!

Glossary

Tantric Terms

Over the past few decades of studying the ancient sacred sexual healing arts, we have become familiar with and rather fond of the following words, sounds, forms and meanings. We do not read, write or speak many of the languages referenced here. We acknowledge that spelling, usage and definitions vary widely in various schools and circles. This is a work in progress and is offered here as a resource for our readers.

AHO! A native American Lakota expression, often used after someone has spoken in sacred circle. It roughly translates to "Amen" or "It has been heard." People also say it in conversation when they agree with what has been said. Accompanied by "Mitakuye Oyasin" is a prayer that translates to "We are all related." It is a prayer for every living being on earth, human and non-human.

AJNA. The sixth chakra, situated between the eyebrows. It is sometimes called the Third Eye. Two wing-like petals or subtle channels emanate from it.

ANAHATA. The fourth chakra, found in the cardiac region. It is sometimes called the heart lotus. Twelve mystic ducts or petals emanate from it.

ANANDA. Sanskrit for bliss, joy and spiritual ecstasy.

AMRITA. Divine nectar or elixir of immortality. Refers to the female ejaculate that flows from the urethra of some women during orgasm. Amrita is considered to be a powerfully healing substance.

ARCHETYPE. The original pattern or role models in collective consciousness.

ASANA. Yoga posture. Used to prepare the body-mind for greater spiritual experiences, and to help the body contain the Kundalini awakening.

AURA. The subtle field of energy in and around the physical body.

A-U-M. The three sounds that compose the root mantra, Om. The sound-values of Om and their symbolic interpretation are described in the Upanishads: "A" as the waking consciousness, "U" as the dream-consciousness and "M" as the consciousness during deep sleep. Om, as a whole, represents the all-encompassing cosmic consciousness.

AYURVEDA. Science of life. Ayurveda is the traditional system of medicine in India, which dates back thousands of years. The Sanskrit root ayu means "life," and veda means "pure knowledge."

BABA. A term of affection and respect for a saint or holy man. Literal translation is father or grandfather. It is most often used to address a monk, spiritual seeker or teacher.

BANDHAS. Internal muscular and energetic locks. Moola Bandha, which is also known as the PC pump, or Kegel muscles, can greatly increase sexual pleasure and aid in ejaculatory control.

BARDO. Purgatory between death and rebirth.

BHAIRAVI. A Tantric sect. The original Tantrics to perform group sexual rituals of many asanas known as Chakra-Puja or Circle Worship.

BHAKTI-YOGA. Yoga of service and devotion for one's chosen deity. The practice often involves kirtan and chanting.

BIJA MANTRA. Seed or syllable mantras that contain energy. Tantric texts say the universe evolved out of the fifty original bija mantras, which correspond to the fifty letters of the Sanskrit alphabet. Used for awakening, purifying and activating the chakras.

BINDU. Focal point of meditation. In ancient Tantric ritual yantras, the focal point was made with a drop of menstrual blood or a dot of semen.

BODHISATTVA. One whose essence is enlightenment. Bodhi is the Sanskrit word for "enlightenment" and sattva means "essence." A divine being who remains on the human plane to help others.

BRAHMA. The Creator of the Cosmos and priest of the Gods in the Hindu sacred triad: Brahma – Creator, Vishnu – Upholder, and Shiva – Destroyer. In Tantric cosmology, Brahma is the creator of the world and is the embodiment of all creativity.

BUDDHI. Knowledge of the cosmic unity.

CHAKRA. A Sanskrit word meaning wheel or circle. Refers to the seven centers or points of spiritual power that reside in or compose the human astral/subtle body. Energetic centers in the body, located along the spine, which are involved in interaction between body and consciousness.

CHAKRA-PUJA. A circle ritual practiced collectively by a circle of Tantric initiates. The rite traditionally involves five sacrifices.

CHI (QI). Chi is the Chinese word for the subtle energy in the body that moves along pathways called meridians. A clear flow of energy through the meridians is the key to radiant health, eroticism and intimacy.

DAKA/DAKINI. Sanskrit for sky-dancer. The Daka or Dakini is a man or woman who has been trained in the sacred sexual healing arts. In Buddhism, they are intermediaries between practitioners and the transcendental. This being embodies the divine lover to teach, inspire, and support others into their full expression. An adept Daka or Dakini can channel or embody Shiva and Shakti, the archetypes of the divine masculine and feminine.

DEVI. Goddess or female participant in Tantric ritual.

DHARANA. Acute concentration. Focusing attention on a single point and holding it there. The sixth limb of raja yoga.

DHARMA. From Buddhism; represents universal law. It is commonly used to refer to one's spiritual calling or divine duty.

DHYANA. Sanskrit word for meditation, referring to the process of quieting the mind to free it from preconceptions, illusions and attachments. The seventh limb of raja yoga.

DIVINE FEMININE. The creative life-giving force. The essence of the feminine in all her various aspects. Shakti is the female or the dynamic aspect of the Ultimate Reality, the energy that permeates all creation. In the context of sacred sexual healing this word is interchangeable with the emotional body.

DIVINE MANIFESTATION. Where we get out of the human ego and become conduits for divine will.

DOULA. A pregnancy and birthing coach. A non-medical assistant who provides physical, emotional and spiritual support during the prenatal, birthing and/or postpartum period.

DURGA. Mother Goddess, protector. "She who is difficult to go against." Durga represents the triumphant aspect of Shakti, the cosmic energy of destruction, particularly the removal of the ego, which stands in the way of spiritual growth and ultimate liberation.

EMBODIMENT. Bridges the world of spirit (or thought) with the world of form (or matter), where the mind and body are only separate because culture has separated them. Embodiment also refers to studying an abstract concept by observing immediate sense perception.

ETHERIC DOUBLE. Beyond one's physical existence there is a parallel "etheric double" that constitutes one's subtle body. The subtle sheaths are related to the gross body at several psychic points.

GANESHA. The elephant-headed God, son of Shiva. Ganesha is the remover of all obstacles, physical, emotional and psychic. He is invoked at the start of any new undertaking.

G-SPOT. The G-spot is short for Grafenberg-spot or, in Tantric circles, Goddess-spot. It is also known as the sacred spot and is located just behind the front wall of the yoni, right behind the pubic bone toward the belly. It swells when stimulated, and creates heightened energy response in the female.

GURU. Dispeller of darkness or teacher. A guide on the spiritual path.

HATHA. Force. Represents the union of the sun (ha) and moon (tha). Hatha yoga is the ancient Indian system of physical postures and breathing exercises that balances the opposing masculine and feminine forces in the body.

HEALER. A person trained in the art of restoring energetic balance and wholeness.

HEALTHY MASCULINE. The inner masculine who witnesses without judgment, creates safety and holds space for the feminine.

HOLDING SPACE. The willingness to be present with another person. To be physically, emotionally, mentally and spiritually available for someone else's process. It also implies listening without judgment. This is a quality of the divine masculine.

HOLOGRAPHIC. All the information contained in a volume of space can be represented by a theory that lives in the boundary of that region.

HOLOGRAM. A fragment of the whole, which contains all the essential elements of that whole. For example, a drop of the river contains all the essential properties of the whole river. A hologram is a symbol that acknowledges that all things in the universe are infinitely interconnected.

IDA. Energy channel terminating in the left nostril. Opposite in polarity from the pingala.

JAPA. The process in which a devotee repeats the name of the God or mantra that go along with the in and out flow of breath. It can be said aloud or just be a movement of the lips or the mind.

JITANDRIYA. Orgasm.

JIVANMUKTA. Human form.

KALI. Dark one. Feminine aspect of time, a transcendental symbol of human abilities. The aspect of Divine Mother that fights evil and destroys the ego and spurs transformation. Daughter of Durga, often characterized by a ferocious appearance.

KAMA. Desire. Lust and longing used as a means to liberation or transcendence.

KAMA SUTRA. The classical Indian treatise on the Art of Love. It is the earliest of the surviving Hindu love manuals, written around the second century A.D. by a sage called Vatsyayana. Other later texts, such as the Ananga Ranga and Koka Shastra, drew their inspiration from the Kama Sutra. Kama means love, and sutra means scripture, aphorism or writings.

KANDA. Located in the area of the perineum.

KARANA. Sanskrit word meaning the twelve instruments or organs: five organs of action (vocal cords, hands, feet, rectum and sex organ); five organs of perception (touch, taste, smell, sight and hearing); and the mind and the intellect. Also refers to a puja ritual of union.

KARMA. The accumulated effect of deeds and actions in this life, past and future lives.

KAULA. Left-handed sect of Tantra usually associated with literal translation and use of the Tantric Scriptures. Rituals may include physical sexual union.

KOSHA. Electromagnetic field the body generates. The human body is considered to have between three and nine such envelopes.

KRISHNA. One of the many incarnations of Vishnu, whose teaching is featured in the Bhagavad Gita. Often depicted playing his flute, he embodies divine joy, love, playfulness and male eroticism. Krishna's death inaugurated the Kali Yuga, which is still in full swing today.

KRIYA. Yogic cleansing rites for internal purification or energetic purification that manifests in the body as illness, temperature change, shivers, shakes or spontaneous sounds.

KUNDALINI. "She who is coiled." Refers to the powerful creative sexual energy that resides like a sleeping serpent near the base of the spine. When this dormant energy is gently awakened it rises up the spine and expands consciousness. A full Kundalini awakening can bring the seeker to enlightenment.

LAKSHMI. Good fortune. The Goddess of abundance, wealth and beauty. The female counterpart of the God Vishnu.

LAYA YOGA. Also known as Kundalini Yoga. The path of meditation and subtle energy work. A form of yoga intended to awaken and channel Kundalini energy. Laya Yoga can be understood as the higher, meditative phase of Hatha Yoga. Laya Yoga and Kundalini Yoga together are subsumed under Tantra Yoga.

LINGAM. Sanskrit for the male sexual organ, meaning wand of light. The phallic symbol of masculinity, associated with Shiva.

LOTUS. Represents the varying intensities of the energies working in the different chakras. In Tantric art, the lotus is a symbol of purity, self-transcendence and expanding consciousness. Because of its smooth and oily surface, the lotus is not sullied by the mud and water in which it grows. It is also a Tantric term for the yoni.

MAHAMUDRA. The great seal. A term in Vajrayana Buddhism for the realization of the true nature of mind. Refers to a Tantra yoga position in which the practitioner sits with the left heel pressed against the perineum. The nine orifices of the body are closed for the control of the breath. In some Tantric schools Mahamudra means Tantric union. In Gnostic practices Mahamudra refers to realizing the inner woman. The mind's emptiness in a non-dual, androgynous realization.

MAITHUNA. Sanskrit word for the ritual of sexual union. The ceremonial union of Shiva with Shakti. A Tantric rite aimed at raising the Kundalini through physical love.

MALA. A necklace with 108 beads used to perform mantra meditation.

MANDALAS. Circles, symbolic of cosmic forces, used as a support for concentration.

MANIPURA. Third chakra located in the solar plexus. Center of power, identity and knowledge.

MANTRA. A sacredly empowered pattern of rhythm and syllables. Used to quiet the mind and balance the inner body. Mantra is a spiritual formula, a combination of sacred syllables transmitted from age to age in a religious tradition that forms a nucleus of spiritual power.

MAYA. The seductive Goddess of illusion. She manifests as a veil between mind and truth. She is the delusion of separation.

MILLION DOLLAR POINT. Hollow point in the perineum that when pressed firmly will block the outward flow and facilitate the upward flow of the seminal fluids. It is said that when this technique is used properly, the man will "feel like a million dollars."

MERU. Shiva's mountain, which is a metaphor for the human body.

MOKSHA. Ultimate spiritual liberation from the cycle of birth and death.

MUDRA. Physical position that produces psychic responses. Ritual of manual gestures or physical positions used to help liberate the mind from bondage.

MUKHAMAITHUNA. Sanskrit term for 69 or mutual oral sex. The male and female bodies come together to form a yantra and worship the lingam and yoni.

MULADHARA. First chakra. Its emanation on the surface of the body is in the area of the perineum and lower genitals, which grounds and connects the individual to Mother Earth.

NADIS. Energy channels in the body. Most authorities say there are 72,000 of them. They are similar to nerve passages in the body.

NAMASTE. A traditional salutation that means the divine light in me bows to the same divine light within you. The gesture (mudra) of Lambaste is made by bringing together both palms of the hands before the heart.

OM. The primal sound or vibration that constantly emanates from the entire universe. It is the sound of creation and destruction, representing the beginning and the end. See AUM.

PADMA. Lotus flower. Also the symbol of a yoni.

PC MUSCLES. Pubococcygeal muscle group. Both women and men have PC muscles, which run from the pubic bone to the tailbone in a figure eight around the genitals. They play a vital role in both male and female sexual response. These strong muscles help to increase blood flow in the pelvic region, heighten sexual sensation, intensify orgasm and help to achieve orgasm and ejaculation.

PINGALA. A subtle channel in the spinal column, which terminates in the right nostril. It has a positive polarity. It spirals around the sushumna channel and terminates in the right nostril.

PRANA. Life force energy. Also refers to the "vital air" or power of the breath.

PREMA. The beloved. Pure love devoid of egoism.

PURUSHA. The ideal or cosmic man. The individual soul; the embodied form of God as the individual soul. Equivalent to the Cabbalistic "Adam."

PRAKRITI. The primal matter of which the universe consists.

PRANAYAMA. Literally translates to "control of the breath." Refers to breathing exercises that are used in meditation and yoga.

PARADIGM. A conceptual model or format upon which ideas are based.

PRIESTESS. A female leader or teacher of ancient sacred healing arts.

RASA. Joy of life. Pleasure in the pure sense of feeling.

RED TANTRA. The aspect of Tantra that relates to the mastery of passion, desire and sexual skills.

RISHI. Mystical seer or wise sage.

RUDRA. Another name for Lord Shiva. Also refers to a Tantric breathing practice that involves visualization and retention.

SACRED SEXUAL UNION. The divine union of the yoni and the lingam. It can be physical or imagined.

SACRED SPACE. A place of tranquility created through intention, respect and focus. It is created by cultivating an environment that is filled with energies that support, uplift, comfort and transform our inner and outer awareness, and benefit our highest good.

SACRED SPOT. An energetic pole for sexual fulfillment. In a woman it is the energetic access to the second chakra located at the G-spot just inside the roof or top wall of the yoni. In a man it is located at or below the prostate gland at the root chakra.

SACRED SPOT MASSAGE. An internal yoni massage intended to heal past wounds and awaken and release orgasmic energy.

SADHANA. The disciplined, regular practice of meditation techniques, spiritual discipline and or devotional practices. The Sanskrit term literally translates to "groove."

SAHAJOLI. Seminal energy.

SAHASRARA. Seventh chakra located at the crown. Represented by thousand-petal lotus flower that connects us to the cosmic absolute.

SAKTIPAT. Transmission of Kundalini awakening by a guru to a disciple.

SADHU. One who has renounced the world for the divine path. Holy beggar. Ascetic.

SANNYASIN. Hindu renunciates or ascetics who in the traditional caste system live in the streets or temples and who have dedicated their lives to spiritual pursuits. In the '70s Osho reappropriated the word for his followers. Neo-sannyasins are committed "to live life in its totality," with an emphasis on love, laughter, creativity and a celebration of the senses.

SAMADHI. God realization. Enlightenment. The final goal of yoga.

SAMKALPA. Resolution or intention to achieve the desired goal. A vow to perform a particular spiritual practice for a specific length of time, at a specific time of day, in a specific place.

SARASWATI. "She who flows." The Goddess of arts and learning and patroness of the Sixty-four Arts. Saraswati is the feminine energy counterpart of Brahma. She is typically portrayed holding a lute or vina.

SAT-CHIT-ANANDA. Literal translation: truth + consciousness + bliss = realization.

SAVASANA. Traditionally, this is the final relaxation pose in yoga and translates to "corpse pose." In Tantra it is a sexual asana in which the male lies corpse-like and the female completes the sexual act without movement from the male.

SEX MAGIC. The practice of using arousal to focus the will for the purpose of creation. Any ritual wherein sexual energy is infused with conscious intention in order to manifest desire into physical reality.

SHAMAN. A priest, priestess or healer who walks in both the physical and the unseen world of Gods, demons and ancestral spirits.

SHAKTI. The feminine and active principle that is the cosmic force of creation. She is the leading transcendental symbol of Tantra and Tantric rituals. Derived from the Sanskrit root shak, meaning "potency" or "the potential to produce."

SHAKTA TANTRA OR SHAKTISM. Hindu Goddess worship. This is the doctrine or worship of the active aspect of God, or the Divine Mother. Shaktism is sourced back to Paleolithic times and is very alive in small Indian villages today.

SHADOW WORK. The practice of claiming the hidden aspects of the self. This Jungian process is based upon the reflections that are provided by people, things and situations that manifest around us. We untangle our dreams, signs and projections in order to see that which we cannot see clearly on our own.

SHANTI. Sanskrit term for inner peace. Often repeated three times after a prayer to evoke inner, outer and world peace.

SHEKINAH. From the Hebrew Kabbalah, meaning the Holy
Spirit that exists within the genitalia.

SHIVA (Siva). In Tantra, Shiva is the masculine principle
representing pure consciousness manifesting in the creative
union with Shakti. Also known as the deity responsible for
death and destruction.

SIXTY-FOUR ARTS. In ancient Tantra, the art of sexual
love was the noblest of the sixty-four arts and relied
on the other arts for its support. Included in this list are
musicianship, culinary arts, dancing, flower arranging and
swordsmanship, among others.

SUSHUMNA. The principle energy channel that runs up
the spinal column. The electromagnetic field that is the
"highway" for the Kundalini energy.

SUTRAS. Threads, themes or teachings. In India, the major
points of an entire philosophical system may be expressed
in a series of sutras, or aphorisms, meaning a condensed
and cryptic statement that usually can be understood only
through commentary.

SVADISTHANA. Second chakra located at the genitals. It
relates to sexuality and creativity.

TANTRA. Sanskrit word that literally means "warp on a
loom," referring to the threads that make up the fabric of
the universe. An esoteric spiritual discipline involving
integration of the opposites. In Hindu scriptures, Tantra was
marked by mysticism and used in the worship of Shakti.
The Buddhist Tantra school uses visualization, mantras and
breathing practices to acquire supernatural powers. Tantra
practices transcend the sensual experiences of the body.

TANTRIKA. A male or female practitioner of Tantra.

TARA. A popular Buddhist Goddess who is adored for protecting us from evil and for her support in overcoming obstacles. Her name is derived from the verb tara, meaning to cross, for she enables the devotee to "cross the ocean of existence." Tara is the symbol of tranquility and cosmic peace.

TATRAK. Concentrating on a single point or object such as a ghee lamp without blinking or moving the eyes.

VAJRA. A Tibetan term for the male sexual organ meaning "thunderbolt" or "scepter of power."

VAJROLI-MUDRA. The adept is expected to draw in the female seed or energy through the erect penis into this body during the sexual union, a process called sahaholi. Emission of the semen is not to occur. If semen is released, both male and female energies are to be drawn back into the body prior to withdrawing the male member from the vagina. This last process is called amaroli.

VEDAS. Ancient texts consisting of 100,000 verses in four divisions: the Rig-Veda from about 2000 BC, considered the oldest literature of the world; the Yajur-Veda; the Sama-Veda; and the Atharva-Veda. Written in Vedic, an early Sanskrit dialect. The Vedic period is dated circa 2500 500 BC.

VISHNU. Lord of preservation.

VISHUDDHA. Fifth chakra located at the throat, which governs communication, song and full expression.

WITNESSING AND BEING WITNESSED. Seeing, hearing, feeling and being seen, heard and felt. Oftentimes this experience can help ground or authenticate something or someone. This process can be very transformative and cathartic; it is an important part of loving and being loved.

WHITE TANTRA. Relates to the yogic or spiritual aspects of Tantric practice and consists of exercises or postures (asanas) combined with special breathing (pranayama), hand or finger gestures (mudras), internal muscular exercises (bhandas), chanting (mantra) and meditation. The skills and benefits of White Tantra practices increase one's ability to master Red (sexual) Tantra.

YAB-YUM. Translates to mother-father pose or seated-astride position. An asana in which a woman sits astride and facing her partner, heart-to-heart. In this position, all of the chakras are aligned. The Tantric image of Yab-Yum represents the male uniting in perfect balance with the female, creating an image expressing the sacredness of sexuality.

YANTRA. Geometric representation of divine order, used to deepen contemplation. Sacred geometry of interlocking triangles and circles used as a focus for healing meditation. The Sanskrit word yantra derives from the root yam meaning "to sustain" or "hold." In spiritual practice a yantra is used as a focus point for visual meditation.

YELLOW EMPEROR. Huang-Ti (2697-2598 BCE), who figures prominently in the medical and sexological teachings of Taoism. The oldest books on love known as the ***Handbooks of Sex*** were written by this legendary Chinese emperor nearly 5,000 years ago. He is said to have ascended to heaven, "having perfected himself through practicing the Sexual Secrets."

YIN-YANG. The Taoist representation of the way the feminine and masculine energies come together in divine union to form the universe. The circular symbol consists of two equal portions, each containing an element of the other. Symbolically, it represents the interplay of two paradoxical energies that both harmonize and battle. Two mutually correlated opposites, such as heaven and earth.

YOGA. To yoke or join together, referring to union and communion. The goal is to merge the individual self with the universal self. It is a holistic way of relating to the body that involves an increasing awareness on all levels: the physical, mental, emotional and spiritual.

YOGINI. Female practitioner of yoga.

YONI. Female sexual organ, womb and source of life. It is a Vedic term meaning "the source of all life." It is loosely translated as "sacred space" or "sacred temple." It includes the vulva, labium, vagina, clitoris and sacred spot. It is physical in women and ethereal in men.

YUGA. Time period, age or eon. There are said to be four yugas: Satya, Treta, Dvapara and Kali. We are currently living in the Kali Yuga.

Resources
Recommended Readings

SACRED SEXUALITY:

Amara, Sexual Agreements (2006)

Charles & Caroline Muir, Tantra: The Art of Conscious Loving (1989)

Daniel Odier, Desire: The Tantric Path to Awakening (2001)

Dr. Deborah Taj. Anapol, Polyamory: The New Love Without Limits (1997)

Georg Feuerstein, Tantra: Path of Ecstasy (1998)

John Mumford, Chakra & Kundalini Workbook: Psycho-Spiritual Techniques for Health, Rejuvenation, Psychic Powers & Spiritual Realization (1994)

Kenneth Ray Stubbs, Women of the Light: The New Sacred Prostitute (1994)

Mantak Chia, Healing Love Through the Tao: Cultivating Female Sexual Energy (2005)

Mantak Chia & Douglas Abrams Avara, The Multi-Orgasmic Man: Sexual Secrets Every Man Should Know (1996); Chi Self-Massage: The Taoist Way of Rejuvenation (2006)

Mantak & Maneewan Chia, Healing Love Through the Tao: Cultivating Female Sexual Energy (1986)

Mantak Chia & Michael Winn, Taoist Secrets of Love:
    Cultivating Male Sexual Energy (1984)

Margo Anand, The Art of Sexual Ecstasy (1989); The Art of
    Sexual Magic (1996)

Mieke Wik & Stephan Wik, Beyond Tantra: Healing Through
    Taoist Sacred Sex (2005)

Nik Douglas & Penny Slinger, Sexual Secrets (1979)

Osho, Tantra Energy and Relaxation: Discourse on Tilopa's
    Song of Mahamudra (1975); From Sex to Super-
    Consciousness (1979)

Sir John Woodroffe aka Arthur Avalon, Mahanirvana Tantra:
    Tantra of the Great Liberation (1913); Sakti and Sakta:
    Essays and Addresses (1965); Principles of Tantra (1968);
    The Serpent Power (1972)

Sunyata Saraswati and Bodhi Avinasha, The Jewel in the Lotus
    (1987)

SEX MAGIC:

Donald Michael Kraig, Modern Sex Magick: Secrets of Erotic
    Spirituality (2002)

Frater U.D., Secrets of Sex Magic: A Practical Handbook for
    Men and Women (1995)

Secrets Of Western Sex Magic (2001)

Napoleon Hill, Think and Grow Rich (1937)

SHAMANISIM:
Carlos Castaneda, The Teachings of Don Juan (1968); A
    Separate Reality (1971); Journey to Ixtlan (1972); Tales
    of Power (1975); The Second Ring of Power (1977); The
    Eagle's Gift (1981); The Fire from Within (1984); The
    Power of Silence (1987); The Art of Dreaming (1993);
    Magical Passes (1998); The Active Side of Infinity (1999);
    The Wheel Of Time (2000); Dorothy Bryant, The Kin of
    Ata Are Waiting for You (1976)

Max Freedom Long, Secret Science at Work: The Huna
    Method as a Way of Life (1953)

Michael J. Harner, The Way of the Shaman (1990)

Mircea Eliade Shamanism: Archaic Techniques of Ecstasy
    (1964) Sandra Ingerman, Soul Retrieval: Mending the
    Fragmented Self Through Shamanic Practice (1991)

Terrence McKenna, The Archaic Revival (1992)

SEXUALITY:
Barbara Keesling, Sexual Healing: The Complete Guide to
    Overcoming Common Sexual Problems (2006)

Betty Dodson, Liberating Masturbation: A Meditation on Self
    love (1974); Sex for One: The Joy of Selfloving(1996);
    Orgasm for Two: The Joy of Partnersex (2002)

Beverly Whipple, John D. Perry, & Alice Kahn Ladas, The
    G Spot: And Other Discoveries About Human Sexuality
    (1982)

Dossie Easton & Catherine A. Liszt, The Ethical Slut: A Guide
    to Infinite Sexual Possibilities (1997)

Eve Ensler, The Vagina Monologues (1996) Play

Godfrey Silas & Leila Swan, Liquid Love: The G-Spot Explosion (2006) DVD

Janet Irvine, Talk About Sex: The Battles Over Sex Education in the United States (2004)

Jo-Anne Baker & Rosie King, Self Sexual Healing: Finding Pleasure Within (2001)

Joseph Kramer, Evolutionary Masturbations (2004); Fire on the Mountain: Male Genital Massage (2007); Primal Man Nude Massage (2007) DVD.

Lynne D. Finney, Reach for the Rainbow: Advanced Healing for Survivors of Sex (1992)

Marshall Herskovitz, Dangerous Beauty (1998; film)

Nick Karras, Petals (2003)

Peter A. Levine, Sexual Healing: Transforming the Sacred Wound (2003)

Rachel Venning & Claire Cavana, Sex Toys 101: A Playfully Uninhibited Guide (2003)

Wendy Maltz & Carol Arian, Sexual Healing Journey: A Guide for Survivors of Sexual Abuse (1992)

Zaihong Shen and Gillian Emerson-Roberts, Sexual Healing Through Yin & Yang (2000)

SPIRITUAL/SELF HELP:

Barbara DeAngelis, Secrets About Men Every Woman Should Know (1990)

Beth Hedva, Betrayal, Trust, and Forgiveness: A Guide to Emotional Healing and Self Renewal (2001)

Ceanne DeRohan, Right Use of Will (1985); Original Cause I (1986); Original Cause II (1987); Earth Spell (1989); Heart Song (1992); Land of Pan (1995); Imprinting (1997); Indigo (1999)

Don Miguel Ruiz, The Four Agreements (2001); The Mastery of Love (2002)

Eckart Tolle, Power of Now (2005); A New Earth (2007)

John Sanford, The Invisible Partners (1979)

Julia Cameron, The Artist's Way: A Spiritual Path to Higher Creativity (1992)

Kelly Bryson, Don't Be Nice, Be Real (2002)

Lawrence Lanoff, The Drunken Monkey Speaks: A Course in Freedom (2007)

Robert A. Heinlein, Stranger in a Strange Land (1987)

Wayne Dyer, The Power of Intention: Learning to Co-Create Your World Your Way (2004)

ZENDOW PRESS

Order Additional Copies

To order additional copies of *Sacred Sexual Healing* securely online, please visit KamalaDevi.com. This book is available at special quantity discount for bulk purchases, retail sales, fundraising, and educational needs.

Additional Materials

More by Baba Dez Nichols:
❀ Sex Magic aka The Work (Documentary)
❀ Blame it on the Moon, original music (CD)
Check out the Sedona School of Temple Arts!

More by Kamala Devi:
❀ Don't Drink the Punch: An Adventure in Tantra
❀ Wrestling with Jealousy by Kamala Devi and Reid Mihalko
❀ Beyond Monogamy: Liberate Your Love Life!
❀ Earning you BLACKBELT in Relationship (DVD)

Public Appearances

Authors Baba Dez Nichols and Kamala Devi are available for public appearances and for private healing sessions. To inquire about our availability and services please visit our websites or send us an e-mail.

Contact Us

www.babadez.com   www.KamalaDevi.com
www.SedonaTemple.com   www.TantraTheater.tv
Dez@BabaDez.com   KaliDas@KamalaDevi.com

Printed in Great Britain
by Amazon